Ashéninka Stories of Change

SIL International
Publications in Sociolinguistics

Publication 4

Publications in Sociolinguistics is a serial publication of SIL International. The series is a venue for works covering a broad range of topics in sociolinguistics. While most volumes are authored by members of SIL, suitable works by others will also form part of the series.

Series Editor

M. Paul Lewis

Associate Editor

Gloria Kindell

Volume Editor

Marilyn A. Mayers

Production Staff

Bonnie Brown, Managing Editor
Margaret González, Compositor
Hazel Shorey, Graphic Artist

Ashéninka Stories of Change

Ronald James Anderson

SIL International
Dallas, TX

Copies of this and other publications of SIL International may be obtained from

International Academic Bookstore
SIL International
7500 W. Camp Wisdom Road
Dallas, TX 75236-5699

Voice: 972-708-7404
Fax: 972-708-7363
Email: academic_books@sil.org
Internet: http://www.sil.org

Contents

List of Tables

List of Figures

List of Maps

Acknowledgments

I could not have completed this study without the inspiration, help, and support of many others. Several Ashéninka individuals consented to be interviewed and observed, sharing the story of their life. Many of these provided me with hospitality and guided me between locations.

Stanford professors on my reading and examining committees helped give focus and direction to this study. My principal advisor, Shirley Brice Heath, showed much patience as she guided me through the beginning stages of research to the preparation of the final copy. Professors Heath, Charles Ferguson, Ray McDermott, and Melanie Sperling gave several specific recommendations to make the study more interesting and useful for others.

Family and friends also aided in the research and manuscript preparation. Janice Anderson read drafts of several chapters and converted indigenously-drawn illustrations to computer files. David Payne, Judy Payne, and Mary Ruth Wise shared with me many of their insights into Ashéninka language and culture. My children, parents, sisters, in-laws, fellow students at Stanford, and colleagues of SIL International helped me to keep my life balanced and provided the support needed for me to finish.

Thank you to all.

1

Introduction

I learned to spin when my mother said, "You must learn to spin because it is very important to be clothed. It would be a disgrace if you became an adult and did not know how to weave and could not supply clothing for your husband." MER[1]

When I learned to weave, I watched my mother make baskets and I imitated her, but making a much smaller one. My mother would say, "Very good, that is how you do it, just like I do. Watch how I do it and you do likewise." JOS

My mother guided me by taking my hand and helping me pull the cotton....I used a spindle that was smaller than my mother's. I began to spin cotton when five years old because I had nothing else to do, like go to school. LOL

When a boy is ready to marry, he is ashamed if he does not know how to hunt. If he is not a good hunter, his wife will leave him right away. A man must feed his family. If he does not, he is worthless. MRC

My son said, "Father, how is it that you are so good at shooting birds?" I told him my ivenki magic plant was my secret. I said that if he wanted, I would teach him to use it. I taught him, and then

---

[1]These are my English translations of excerpts of interviews conducted in the Spanish and Ashéninka languages. Interviewees are distinguished by a three-letter code. A detailed discussion of the interview, recording, and transcription process is found in the appendix.

*he had good aim. I taught my sons everything that my grandfa-
thers taught me, so these things will not disappear.* APR

*I wanted to be like my brother-in-law. Whenever he went to the
river, he brought back fish. Whenever he went hunting, he brought
back game. I wanted to be like him, but I could not because I was
in school and had to give up on my desire.* ABC

*I want to teach my sons many things. I don't want them to forget
how to build a house or how to plant a garden. Our work has gotten bigger. Once, we just had to teach how to plant a garden and
hunt, but now we also have to teach math.* SAM

These are voices of adult Ashéninkas;[2] they are members of an ethnic
group which numbers about 20,000 and is scattered over a large area of
the Amazon jungle of east-central Peru. They speak here of socialization—ways they and their children learned and were taught and wish to
continue to be able to learn.

The problem

The Ashéninkas confront change from two perspectives—the individual
and the sociohistorical. All Ashéninkas recall through their stories the
four centuries of change since their earliest contacts with Spanish speakers. Today's parents and children feel the greatly quickened pace of
change that has come recently with new roads, new crops, schools, and
national upheavals. The socialization of today's children reflects both
sources of change—the remembered and often idealized ways of earlier
tales and years, and the constant necessity of adapting to processes of
learning and teaching of the contemporary era. This study examines
Ashéninka socialization through data drawn from audio tapes of

---

[2]"Campa" was the most common term used to refer to the Ashéninka. Though the local
European and mestizo population often used the term "Chuncho", until recently
government agents, missionaries, and researchers preferred "Campa". From the Ashéninka
perspective, Campa is preferred over Chuncho. Before linguistic and cultural differences
were recognized, "Campa" referred to the Nomatsiguenga and the Caquinte also. "Campa"
is used in this study to refer to closely related Arawakan groups other than the Ashéninkas
or the Asháninka.

   The word "Campa" is probably of Spanish origin, but the Campa refer to themselves as
Asháninka or *Ashéninka*, which means 'our relatives'. Ashéninka and Asháninka are
regionally preferred terms—no one uses both to refer to his/her in-group. For the purposes
of this study, I use the term Ashéninka to refer to the language of the people who live in the
regions of the Gran Pajonal, and the Alto Perené, Pichis, and Ucayali rivers; as well as to
the culture and society.

open-ended interviews recorded in 1987 and 1988, fieldnotes of observations of Ashéninka life written over fourteen years between 1974 and 1988, and a collection of more than 500 traditional stories.[3]

Through their oral history, i.e., traditional stories, and their accounts of what they do today, Ashéninka adults tell how they recall the experiences, processes, and stories that were keys to their socialization. Both traditional stories and contemporary accounts bear evidence that Ashéninka elders feel the lure of the national culture and government-sponsored schooling that challenge traditional ways.

Franciscan missionaries went to the Ashéninka in the seventeenth century and were shortly driven away. The Ashéninka remained isolated from the market economy but found ways to have a continuing supply of metal tools until the end of the nineteenth century, when they began to harvest latex during the rubber boom. Though expert at using the products of the jungle environment to provide their food, shelter, and clothing, in the 1960s the Ashéninka began to enter the national economy on a grand scale to earn money to buy modern manufactured goods. They traditionally lived in small, isolated family groups without leaders to unite them, but since the 1960s they have lived in villages of 60 to 300 people with schools and elected leaders. Year by year, shifts in national politics, regional activities of guerrilla groups, and access to a cash economy push and pull Ashéninka culture and socialization practices between young and old.

The specific issue of study here is the breadth of Ashéninka socialization as they recall their ways of learning in the past and now in the present and acknowledge that "now" seems a very rapidly paced period of drastic social change. Ashéninka society can be characterized as technologically primitive, but it is, in many surface ways, rapidly catching up to the rest of Peruvian society. Surface changes include metal pans substituting for clay pots, house dresses and pants replacing home-spun *cushma* 'robes', and the abandonment of facial tattoos. But deeper values of human relations, such as accommodation to the spirit world and fears of the unknown, remain from earlier years, driven deeper by the sense of deficiency which the Ashéninka feel. Adults adjust in their own ways and in their views of how children learn and what their role is in this process.

Many theories of socialization focus on the role of parents as the agents of socialization, e.g., adults as teachers and children as learners. Other theories focus on the role of societal forces and rituals. This study demonstrates that though these theories account for many aspects of Ashéninka

---

[3]Twenty-four stories translated into English appear throughout this study to illustrate and confirm some of the points discussed; 109 stories written in the Ashéninka and Spanish languages are published elsewhere in three volumes (Anderson 1985, 1986a, 1986b).

socialization, their culture illustrates the need for focusing on two other factors: (1) a move away from the usual model of socialization characterized as transmission of skills, customs, and beliefs from transmitting agents to receiving subjects and (2) an examination of the process of adaptation to the agency, contexts, and content of socialization under circumstances of rapid social change.

Perspectives on socialization

The individualism and sociologism philosophies

Researchers recognize the Ashéninka as a cultural group separate from surrounding groups. More than 20,000 individuals share basic Ashéninka cultural knowledge, though they are spread over a large area. Many values and practices appear to be the same today as they were three hundred years ago when Franciscan missionaries first described the Ashéninka. This continuity of patterns of behavior and beliefs rests on the retention of certain ways of teaching and learning as a member of Ashéninka society. A closer look at this process, as remembered and practiced, points out many problems with dichotomous theories of socialization.

Two opposing philosophies—individualism and sociologism—usually characterize the relationship of the individual to society. Basic individualistic philosophy bears these characteristics:

> (1) autonomous individuals are the causal forces that create society; (2) the individual therefore has a kind of ontological priority over "society"; (3) socialization renders the individual fit for society through rational conversion and coercion; (4) through their actions people create society; and (5) individuals, or more precisely, the conditions for action, constitute the corrected sphere for analysis (i.e., motives are the source of history). (Wentworth 1980:2)

The focus here is on the agency of individuals in constructing society, each person deciding that various practices and beliefs are useful. Adults coerce children to accept cultural practices and beliefs that appear to be rational, at least as they are constructed and presented by the older generation. Individualistic philosophy gives no special consideration to what happens to socialization during rapid social change, when individuals must create and adopt new philosophies or technologies as they are introduced and acknowledge that social or ecological changes make old ways inefficient.

The sociologistic philosophy contrasts with the individualistic philosophy:

> (1) the causal flow is from society to the individual; (2) society has ontological priority over the person; (3) the societal cause becomes embodied in the personality during socialization; (4) individuals are products of society, that is, historical social structures; and (5) society is the correct object of analysis (i.e., the structure of society governs the actions of individuals and therefore the course of history). (Wentworth 1980:2)

This philosophy places agency with the cultural system as it determines the actions of individuals. Conformity to the culture is not a rational choice but is necessary for an individual to be an accepted member of society.

Some Ashéninka practices appear to conform to the individualistic philosophy and others to the sociologistic philosophy. Ashéninka society has experienced dramatic changes related to the goals of physical survival and economic self-maintenance. One change was a dramatic intensification of contact at the beginning of the twentieth century with Spanish speakers who brought disease and economic competition. These changes motivated individuals to seek out modern medicine to cure sickness and to change their land-use patterns and work schedules to increase their agricultural productivity. On the other hand, some Ashéninka practices appear to conform more to the sociologistic philosophy. Ashéninka beliefs, norms, and ideologies have a strong influence on the formation of an individual's character and the continuation of culturally symbolic practices. The Ashéninka continue to value honesty and patience, though others have used these values to cheat them; they continue to find power in magical plants, though they are taught in school that magic is not rational; and they continue to punish those accused of witchcraft, despite the disapproval of Peruvian government authorities.

The polar opposition of the philosophies of individualism and sociologism fits poorly in the complex situations of socialization around the world—especially in Third World or developing nations, and internally colonized groups, such as the Ashéninka. Many Ashéninka practices have elements of both the individualistic and sociologistic philosophies of socialization. During hunting, for example, individual choice of weapon is changing from the bow and arrow to the shotgun as experienced hunters start teaching novices to use a shotgun that offers both greater ease and effectiveness despite the high cost. On the other hand, magic remains a primary component of the hunting activity, even when using a shotgun;

hunters continue to follow hunting dietary taboos, believe in forest spirits, and rub special plants on their weapons for luck.

Activity theory and socialization

Socialization typically involves adults teaching their own children. In such circumstances a parent brings a bias to the task, raising their "children to confront the world as they understand it on the basis of their own experiences" (Cole and Griffin 1987:10). However, in many societies, parents are not the only socializing agents. Related caregivers such as grandparents or older siblings may be the primary agents of socialization, presenting parts of the culture to the child or reinforcing the socialization efforts of others. Moreover, much socialization occurs informally, even out of the awareness of both elders and children.

Soviet activity theory provides a useful perspective on informal teaching and learning based on the writings of Soviet psychologist Lev Vygotsky. Any function in a child's cultural development appears on two planes—the social plane and the psychological plane. First, it appears between adults and children acting together interpsychologically and then within the individual child intrapsychologically. Vygotsky's study of the social component of cognition led to the concept of a zone of proximal development, defined as the difference between a child's "actual developmental level as determined by independent problem solving and the level of potential development as determined through problem solving under adult guidance or in collaboration with more capable peers" (Vygotsky 1978:86).

Vygotsky's theories admit to a cultural system that immerses children in a learning, demonstrating, interactive social group. Included in such a system are adults and older children as sometime teachers, but also children becoming group members through their active out-of-awareness learning. Through "activity that confronts and lends structure to the entry of nonmembers into an already existing world" (Wentworth 1980:85), the culture presents and represents itself to the novice, providing the social plane of the interpsychological relationship between adult and child. Adults make and label and display aspects of the culture to the child. As the child matures and learns more of the culture, adult-child instruction decreases and independent learning by the child increases. But "a new world so entered does not exert an irresistible hold on the novice. Perspectival differences, outside influences, creative skepticism and limits to the socialization process itself may act to limit or reverse entry" (Wentworth 1980:85). Though any novice is presented a strong case for conformity to the existing world of adults, individualism can alter the specifics of a person's entry into the culture.

Such alteration is evident among the Ashéninka. Though parents instruct children in the activities and values of Ashéninka culture, a child or adolescent might reject learning a traditional skill like weaving or a traditional value like humility. When asked about a child's rejection of instruction, a parent typically replies, "I taught her, but she didn't learn. Ask her yourself."

Guided learning and socialization

Guided learning is formal or informal instruction in which an adult is typically the teacher and a child the learner. Teaching and learning outside the context of school is called by many names, including mediated learning, guided participation, apprenticeship, and proleptic instruction. The explanations of these terms draw heavily from the concepts of activity theory.

Brown and Farrara (1985) call "mediated learning" the inter-generational presentation of the adults' world in which an experienced adult frames, selects, focuses, and feeds back an experience in such a way as to create learning events appropriate for the child. As the child progresses in learning, the adult systematically shapes joint experiences so the child is drawn into taking more responsibility for the learning.

Rogoff (1990) uses the term "guided participation" to emphasize the child's extensive collaboration in the teaching and learning process.

> Guided participation involves children and their caregivers and companions in the collaborative processes of (1) building bridges from children's present understanding and skills to reach new understanding and skills, and (2) arranging and structuring children's participation in activities, with dynamic shifts over development in children's responsibilities. Children use social resources for guidance—both support and challenge—in assuming increasingly skilled roles in the activities of their community. (Rogoff 1990:8)

Like Brown and Farrara, Rogoff finds adult structuring of learning events to be crucial to successful learning of parts of the adult world. As learning progresses, the child takes more responsibility for learning and fills increasingly skilled roles.

Successful instruction depends on the ability of expert and novice to communicate effectively. Initially, the adult must assess the level of competence of the child.

> Caregivers arrange the occurrence of children's activities and facilitate learning by regulating the difficulty of the tasks and by modeling mature performance during joint participation in activities. While caregivers may rarely regard themselves as explicitly teaching infants or young children, they routinely adjust their interaction and structure children's environments and activities in ways consistent with providing support for their learning. (Rogoff 1990:17)

Later, the child learns to view problems from the same perspective as the adult.

> Underlying the processes of guided participation is *intersubjectivity*: a sharing of focus and purpose between children and their more skilled partners and their challenging and exploring peers. From guided participation involving shared understanding and problem solving, children appropriate an increasingly advanced understanding of and skill in managing the intellectual problems of their community. (Rogoff 1990:8)

Sustained guided participation eventuates in apprenticeship; the novice comes to evaluate and solve problems in the same manner as the expert.

Wertsch and Stone (1979) call expert to apprentice teaching and learning "proleptic instruction". Rogoff and Gardner expand this idea.

> In this process a novice carries out simple aspects of the task as directed by the expert. By actually performing the task under expert guidance, the novice participates in creating the relevant contextual knowledge for the task and acquires some of the expert's understanding of the problem and its solution. Proleptic teaching contrasts both with explanation, where the adult talks about a task rather than guiding the child through the task, and with demonstration, where the teacher carries out the task rather than involving the child in action. Proleptic instruction integrates explanation and demonstration with an emphasis on the learner's participation in the instructional activity. (1984:101–102)

Ashéninkas learn most traditional skills through such instruction. Boys typically work beside an expert when learning to make arrows—the novice imitates the movements of the expert. If a feather is not cut properly or glued to the shaft at the correct angle, the expert shows his "secrets" for doing these activities correctly.

When collaborative activity is the process of socialization, the individualistic and sociologistic perspectives each loses adequate explanatory power. Rogoff recognizes the contribution of both the individual and society in socialization, but she considers them inseparable from human actions.

> Individuals' efforts and sociocultural arrangements and involvement are inseparable, mutually embedded focuses of interest. Rather than examining context as an influence on human behavior, I regard context as inseparable from human actions in cognitive events or activities. I regard all human activity as embedded in context; there are neither context-free situations nor decontextualized skills. (Rogoff 1990:27)

This perspective discourages us from looking for a single "cause", context, or relationship for a learning occasion and encourages us instead to acknowledge the multiple components of activities that situate learning throughout the life of individuals in their changing social groups.

The need to go beyond dichotomies

Researchers often divide the world into dichotomous categories, constructing multiple frameworks and models. Examples are the dichotomy of teacher and learner and the opposing philosophies of socialization. Heath warns that in contrast to such views held by experts, across the world's cultures, "members [themselves] hold relatively few of these dichotomous views of teaching/teacher and learning/learner" (Heath 1989:345).

A discussion of Ashéninka socialization demonstrates the limitations of any dichotomous or strongly categorizing view of universal socialization patterns. In discussions of change, even though surface activities like the learning of hunting methods may change with the times, such activities also include the learning of deeper beliefs in magic, spirits, and justice, which may be resistant to change. To study a skill like hunting, it is necessary to look at it from many perspectives and recognize the breadth of knowledge learned. When an Ashéninka boy learns to hunt from his father, he not only learns the skills of hunting, but he also learns to "be like" and "act like" an Ashéninka hunter. Lave and Wenger tell of the apprentice who learns to become part of the community-of-practice:

> who is involved, what they do, what everyday life is like, how masters talk, walk, work, and generally conduct their

lives, how people who are not part of the community-
of-practice interact with it, what other learners are doing,
and what learners need to learn to become full practitioners.
It includes an increasing understanding of how, when, and
about what, oldtimers collaborate, collude and collide, and
what they enjoy, dislike, respect, and admire. In particular, it
offers exemplars (which are grounds and motivation for
learning activity), including masters, finished products, and
more advanced apprentices in the process of becoming full
practitioners. (1990:22–23)

Studies of socialization often ignore or downplay the role of spiritual
life in socialization, though it is often an integral part of the community-
of-practice. Researchers focus their study on what can easily be observed
and measured; yet numerous attitudes and beliefs, as well as ritual events,
lie within a group's spiritual realm of life. Ashéninka cosmology plays a
critical role in adults' conceptions of reality and views of both the natural
and supernatural.

The supernatural realm of which any given set of religious
beliefs purports to be an accurate description, is never simply a separate realm from that of nature. Both realms are
always understood to be complementary divisions of the to-
tality of reality, of all that exists, such that the observable
part—nature—is explained in terms of the operation of the
hidden part—supernature. The two realms may indeed be
comprehended as interpenetrating, their distinctive properties shading off into one another. Considerations of this kind
suggest that the distinction between nature and supernature
be made along the following lines: "nature" consists of all
that is, or can be, directly observed; "supernature" consists
of all that cannot be thus observed and can only be in-
ferred—the "hidden reality" of which we speak. The
supernatural, then, would include all beings, forces and
properties not directly observed but reputed to exist, including non-observable properties attributed to natural objects.
(Weiss 1975:527–528)

The spiritual life of the Ashéninka permeates their daily activities. They
believe that spirits are common, magic is needed daily, and that justice
prevails through nonhuman agents. Much of the spirit life can be observed or reported, but much of it is unconscious, albeit an integral part of
people's work and interactions.

In any given culture, ideas about nature and ideas about the supernatural are all of one piece: in combination they form the culture's set of beliefs about all of reality, and we cannot hope to understand one without the other. This holds true whether (as in the Campa case) no sharp distinction is made between the two sets of ideas or (as in the Western cultures) the two are divided neatly. (Weiss 1975:529)

Adults socialize their children into this spiritual life, as well as into a mundane life.

Thus, Campa culture fosters a striving toward knowledge and power on the part of males. Those who acquire such "supernatural" power in turn exert a steadying influence within Campa society and culture, their very existence and power continually reaffirming the verity of the Campa view of the cosmos and what constitutes ultimate reality. (Elick 1970:236)[4]

Men seek power through the role of shaman, but both men and women work at developing a spiritual awareness that makes them full participants in Ashéninka society. The spirit life is an integral part of the individual, culture, and life as it is known to the Ashéninka: "their culture is not merely another, a preferred, way of life, it is life, the life ordained in eternity by the ancient ones" (Elick 1970:236).

The Ashéninka are loyal to traditional ways and reluctantly change beliefs and practices, even in the face of major changes. Ashéninkas are socialized to be self-sufficient, to be socially acceptable, and to share a spiritual understanding that completes the identity of the individual as a group member.

Organization of the study

This study looks at the breadth and complexity of Ashéninka socialization through the cultural, individual, social, and spiritual spheres of life. It is organized to illustrate remembered perceptions of older socialization practices and current ways of learning and teaching the young in a period of rapid and drastic change.

---

[4]John Elick was a Seventh-Day Adventist missionary to the Ashéninka for several years before completing his doctoral studies at UCLA. He was a popular figure in the area because he was fluent in the Ashéninka language and knew Ashéninka culture well.

Socialization includes the presentation of an already existing world to novices. The Ashéninka world includes its ecology, history, and cultural norms, all crucial in establishing motives for socialization. Chapter two tells of the cultural world of the Ashéninka through historical texts written by visitors to the Ashéninka since the seventeenth century. The history of contact divides into six periods: the pre-colonial, colonial, rebellion and isolation, exploitation, Seventh-Day Adventist missions, and contemporary. The group progressively adopted new technology and has become increasingly dependent on the outside economy. Recent changes are linked to increased use of the Spanish language, changes in the Ashéninka system of authority, and the acceptance of schooling for Ashéninka children.

Chapter three tells of the cultural world of the Ashéninka through traditional stories. One interviewee says: "The story has to give a lesson. All of these stories have their moral." Oral history contributes to the formation of values that help shape Ashéninka identity and teach the cultural values of honesty, humility, patience, and respect. These stories also help to form the conscience of the individual, specify the ideals of social interaction, and reinforce spiritual beliefs.

The individual must be motivated to become socialized into the Ashéninka world. Many Ashéninka adults tell what motivated them to learn from their parents and later to become self-learners. One learns to spin because a parent says such learning is necessary: "It would be a disgrace if you became an adult and did not know how to weave and could not supply clothing for your husband." Another learns to hunt as a boy because he must prepare to marry and avoid being ashamed because he is "not a good hunter... A man must feed his family. If not, he is worthless."

Chapter four lays out the following individual motivations for learning traditional skills and values: (1) anticipation of future physical need, (2) social acceptance, and (3) identity formation. Changes in the motivation for learning, related to changes in the cultural world of the Ashéninka, are outlined here. These changes include the adoption of new technologies that leave some traditional skills unpracticed and not respected by the young.

Chapter five explores the social interaction of learning traditional technical skills such as hunting, arrow making, spinning cotton, weaving, and cooking. In these interactions, adults or "more capable peers" use various strategies to instruct and organize learning. Change is affecting these interactions as adults' time commitment to the outside economy and children's commitment to school leave fewer opportunities for adults and children to interact in traditional ways.

Chapter six describes the Ashéninka spiritual life that is important in the socialization of children and adolescents. The main focus of study is the *ivenki* magic plant and ways that the Ashéninkas' beliefs in spirits influence socialization.

Chapter seven ties together Ashéninka practices with theories of socialization. Though the contexts and activities of socialization are discussed separately in chapters two to six, learning is more accurately characterized as situated in a complex blend of history, beliefs, motives, practices, and persons. A more comprehensive description of socialization is presented than in the previously mentioned theories, a view that cognition in everyday practice is "distributed—stretched over, not divided among—mind, body, activity, and culturally organized settings" (Lave 1988:1). Finally, the persistent character of socialization is described in the different contexts of traditional Ashéninka society, changing Ashéninka society and schooling.

2

Voices of Historical and Cultural Change

The man who kidnapped me got paid. The one who brought me over the ridge also traded me for something. That is how it was. Later, after passing Shimani, a Quechua paid for me with pots, cloth, machetes, knives, and other things. DOM

People said the god Pachacama, also called Navireri, would return. He is also called Juan Santos Atahuallpa and would return to the jungle so it would develop and prosper. Not only Ashéninkas came [to see the Seventh-Day Adventist missionary Frederick Stahl], but also Machiguengas. About 500 people came from all over, from Apurímac, Madre de Dios, and Ucayali. They came here to the Perené. Piros, Shipibos, everyone came to see him who came to Metraro. He seemed to be the return of Atahuallpa, Navireri. They think Metraro is a sacred place, where they fought in the past. That is why they thought he had returned. CAR

We lacked money. For my part, I couldn't give my daughters enough money to buy their clothes. One asked me for money, and I said it would be better for her to leave and find work for a short time to make money. CAM

15

He didn't teach me to hunt because civilization had come. He said, "I am not going to teach you because with civilization, we will not use arrows or shotguns because there will not be any animals to hunt or even the jungle to hunt in." GER

These vignettes bring together the Ashéninkas' collective memories of the past and the sense of individuals that have played a role in responding to these events of abrupt and often absolute change: outside goods, missionary dictates, a cash economy, and new demands for learning that cast off the old ways. The world of the Ashéninka includes their ecological setting, values, technology, and historical knowledge, as well as current technology, specifically metal tools. DOM tells above how she was kidnapped as a child and sold for manufactured goods. She was kidnapped during a time of exploitation of the Ashéninka that led to mass conversion to the Seventh-Day Adventist faith, as told by CAR. The missionary Frederick Stahl, who came to the Ashéninka in 1921, promised divine punishment for evil people and healed the sick (Stahl 1932). These events caused Ashéninkas to recall stories from their oral history. The first centered on the god Navireri who ordered the local ecology in ancient days; the second told of the exploits of the rebel Juan Santos Atahuallpa who expelled the Spanish two centuries earlier.

Through their oral history, the Ashéninka recapture their periods of contact with other peoples: pre-colonial, Catholic missions, rebellion and isolation, economic exploitation, Seventh-Day Adventist missions, and the contemporary era. Each of these periods is characterized by its institutions, power structure, settlement patterns, and technology. All of these arbitrary divisions of history bear some degree of influence today and the shifts during transitional times between them are noticeable. Though the Ashéninka were widely dispersed throughout most of these periods and many events directly affected only a few Ashéninkas, cumulative and irreversible changes occurred that were diffused throughout Ashéninka territory and led to the present situation. The present situation is a mix of valued traditional skills and new technologies. Individual goals spring from the changes, social relationships are constrained by them, and spiritual beliefs are challenged by them.

The pre-colonial period: Ashéninka self-sufficiency

Little is known of pre-colonial Ashéninka history but evidence exists of trade with other groups, such as the Quechua who speak a different language and have different customs. Though the Ashéninka were self-sufficient in most

Map 2.1 The Ashéninka and Asháninka area

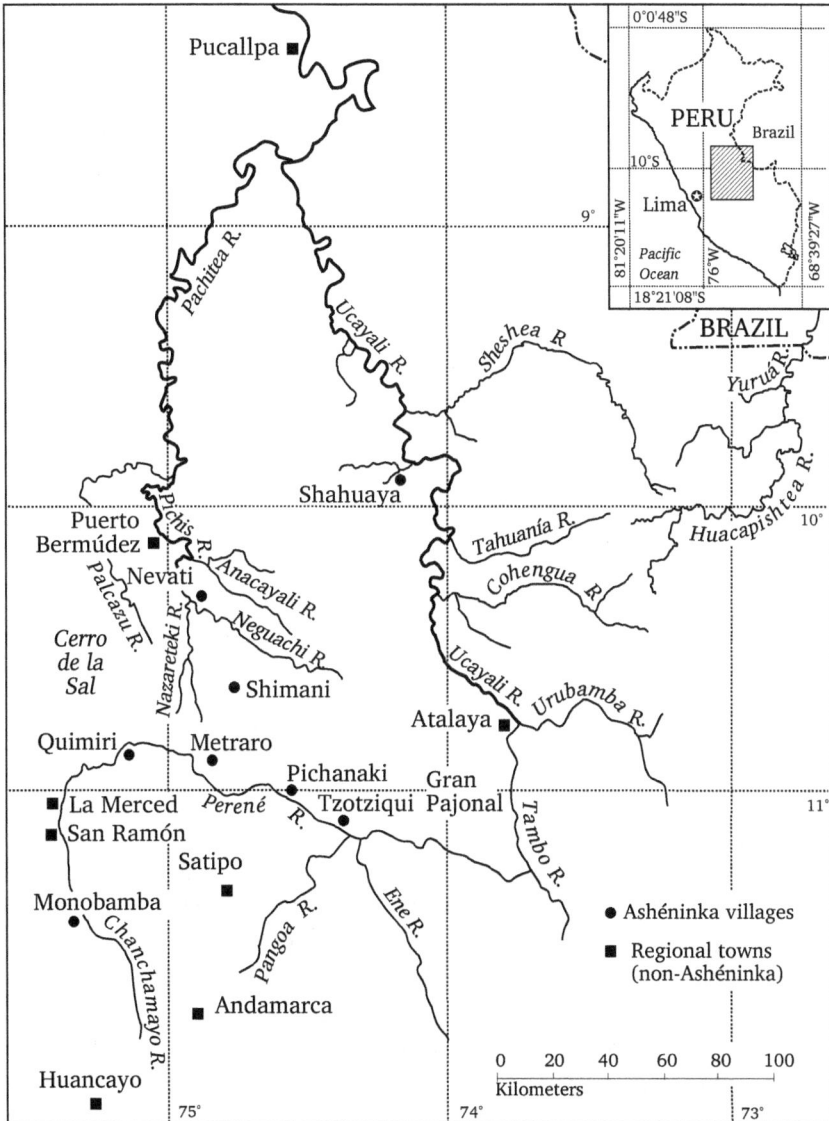

of their material needs, they had established trade with the highland Quechua before the early missionaries arrived (Craig 1972). Elick (1970) found many stone axes in the Ashéninka area made of andesite and other kinds of hard stone from the Andean area, evidence that these had arrived through trade. Also, the Spanish explorers of the seventeenth century saw Ashéninkas and members of other ethnic groups come steadily to the salt deposits on the boundary between the Andean and Ashéninka areas, a likely place for trade with the highland Quechua (Ortiz 1978).[5] The Ashéninka probably traded jungle products like animal skins, bird feathers, medicinal plants, and coca leaves for stone axes. Coca was an important part of Inca culture at the time of the conquest and is still chewed by many Quechuas. Today's Ashéninka also chew coca, growing their own supply in a climate and terrain ideal for its cultivation. Ashéninkas could manufacture their own stone tools but the harder stone from the highlands was an improvement over local materials.

Stone tools have not been used by the Ashéninka for many generations, but many individuals have some lying around the house as souvenirs. Ashéninkas of pre-colonial times used only stone and wooden tools—a laborious technology, as told in the following story.

When we worked with stone axes

Long ago, our grandfathers did not have machetes or metal axes.

A man who knew the work of an ax and machete took a rock and heated it. He made an ax and a machete out of stone. These were his tools for working his garden. To chop down trees, our ancestors hit them with a dull rock, unlike the way we use machetes today. To make their garden, our ancestors labored hard when cutting down trees with their old stone axes, occasionally throwing water on them. That is how they chopped down trees. They suffered making their gardens. They often planted manioc in the forest where a tree had fallen.

One of our grandfathers thought to get a rock and heat it to make an ax and a machete. They could make gardens, but they did not have files to sharpen the tools. That is how they

---

[5]The men probably took more salt than they needed and traded it to other Campas. Even today, traditional Ashéninka women weave all the clothing needed for themselves and their family, weaving excess clothing for trade and sale. An interviewee tells me that today a shoulder bag is worth the equivalent of a machete and a full robe *cushma* is worth the equivalent of an ax.

cut down trees, by hitting a tree and throwing water on it. That is how they prepared a garden. (Translated from *Ashéninka jantavaitantaro mapi* by Alberto Pablo Ravírez (Anderson 1986b).)

Figure 2.1 When we worked with stone axes[6]

No record exists of Inca domination of the Ashéninka, a proposition supported by the paucity of Quechua loan words in the Ashéninka language. Few words are shared; most are words introduced after the conquest.[7] With little outside contact, the Ashéninka world changed slowly. Early missionaries to the Campa and Machiguenga found many cultural similarities from village to village throughout an extensive area.

The somewhat stable society of the Ashéninka was irreversibly changed with the arrival of Franciscan missionaries. The Franciscans hoped to transform the cultural, individual, social, and spiritual aspects of Ashéninka life, but the most permanent and widespread cultural change was the adoption of metal tools.

---

[6]The drawings appearing in this study were drawn by Ashéninka artists interpreting each of the cited stories. The artists were Alberto Quispe Valles, Otoniel Ramos Rodríguez, and Darío Shuñaqui Gregorio.

[7]Some words borrowed from Quechua or from Spanish through Quechua are the following (Payne 1980): *otsitzi* 'dog', *mishi* 'cat', *atyaapa* 'chicken', *viracocha* 'Caucasian', and *coriqui* 'money'. All these were introduced to the Ashéninka after the conquest.

The colonial period: Franciscan missionaries introduce metal tools

The Ashéninka of the upper Perené valley were already in contact with colonial traders when the Franciscan missionaries arrived.[8] By 1570, the Viceroy Toledo wrote of frequent visits by jungle Indians to Lima and said also that up to 100 Indians in the Monobamba area (near the present town of San Ramón) professed Christianity. In 1585, the Jesuit priest, Juan Font, made the first survey expedition to Campa territory in the Apurimac River valley, a tributary of the Ene River.

Franciscan missionaries entered Ashéninka territory in 1635, founding the mission at Quimiri, near the present town of La Merced. By 1742, about twenty-seven missions were functioning in the Campa area. The Ashéninka generally welcomed the missionaries, who gave them gifts of metal tools. Goods and services given by the Ashéninka were repaid by the missionaries with knives, axes, and machetes. Tibesar tells of the importance of iron tools in the expansion of the mission effort.

> Frequent visits were made by the missionaries to the isolated groups with gifts of iron tools which were distributed in accordance with the social prestige of each Indian; trails were opened to unite the scattered groups and lastly several of the small groups would be persuaded by gifts of iron tools to settle near the home of some influential Indian, whose goodwill had already been secured by generous gifts, where larger fields would be cultivated to care for the denser population. (Tibesar 1952:25–26)

The Campa saw the missionaries as a better source of tools for which they were already trading with others. Metal tools revolutionized Campa agricultural practice. Ashéninka fields are now much larger than when only stone and wooden tools were available. Today's larger fields make it possible to brew more manioc beer, to manufacture dried manioc farina used for food on long trips, and to sell excess produce to mestizos.

A change in technology led to a change in power structures. Possession of tools and other trade goods gave individuals a new social advantage. Craig tells how metal tools created a need that went beyond the goal of easing the work load.

---

[8]Much of the historical data in this section and the next are taken from the following sources: Benavides 1986, Biedma and Tibesar 1981, Bodley 1970, Craig 1972, Elick 1970, Fernández 1986, Heath and Laprade 1982, Izaguirre 1923–1929, Lehnertz 1972, Ortiz 1978, Tibesar 1952, Steward and Metraux 1963, and Varese 1968.

> The accumulation of these items together with cloth goods
> and shotguns has since become a status symbol requiring
> much travel, social interaction, and complex barter—factors
> which tend to lessen the traditional tendency toward misan-
> thropic isolationism. (Craig 1972:20)

The Franciscans had intentions to transform Ashéninka culture in ways
that went beyond the introduction of metal tools. They wanted eventually
to integrate the Ashéninka into a wider society and welcome them into
the Catholic faith. The missionaries knew that the quickest way to gain
converts was to use the native languages. Many priests spoke the indigenous languages fluently, wrote lexicons, and translated parts of the Bible
and catechisms. About 1722, Friar Juan de la Marca was said to have
learned Ashéninka perfectly. He wrote Ashéninka grammars, dictionar-
ies, and some writings on doctrine.

The missions taught new crafts, agricultural technologies, and religious
doctrine. Children and adults studied separately, children learning the
catechism and adults learning doctrine and manual skills like metalwork-
ing and carpentry. The priests introduced many new plants from Spain
and the coastal area of Peru, plus cattle, sheep, pigs, and chickens. When
an adult showed more competence than others at a craft, he often was
made an instructor.

The Franciscans also introduced new patterns of socio-political organization more elaborate than those of traditional Ashéninka culture.
Changes were attempted in Ashéninka social relations and religious ori-
entation during the colonial period but these were short-lived. Only the
cultural changes brought by the introduction of metal tools endured.

Rebellion and isolation

Though the Franciscan missions had optimistic beginnings, all were destroyed less than a hundred years after their founding. The missions were
periodically attacked by bands of Ashéninkas beginning in 1674, when
the Ashéninka chief, Mangore, tried to start a general uprising that eventually faded. In 1723 the chief, Fernando Torote, was said to lead 3,000
others in baptism, but a year later he renounced his faith to take another
wife. He led uprisings against the missions for many years, as did his son,
Ignacio Torote.

Some Ashéninkas did not want to abandon old customs, some were
afraid of illness which spread quickly, and others were irritated by the
limits put on their freedom by the mission. Some Ashéninkas near the

Pichana tributary of the Perené valley had a lucrative business in the salt trade that was threatened by the priests, causing resentment on the part of the people. Biedma, who was a Franciscan priest to the Ashéninka at the time, proposed that shamans used all these reasons to incite resistance to the missions. Some joined in the violence but many others were not persuaded by these "frustrated rivals".

In 1742, the great uprising of Juan Santos Atahuallpa Apu Inca destroyed all the missions in the Campa area. Juan Santos was not an Ashéninka, but was part Spanish and part Quechua from the Andean region. He claimed to be a direct descendant of the Inca kings and planned to drive the Spanish from Peru. He and his band of followers went to the jungle to recruit Ashéninka and other jungle groups for their army that would expel the Spanish from Peru. Some researchers speculate that Juan Santos was followed by the jungle groups because of a general dissatisfaction with the missions and his charismatic nature and messianic rhetoric. The Ashéninka may have been ready to abandon the missions anyway, because a series of epidemics killed up to two-thirds of those living close to the missions. Whatever the reason, the Franciscans were killed or driven out and contact with Spanish speakers ceased until about 1850, leaving the Ashéninka in isolation for over 100 years.

The Franciscan missions had the potential to affect the Ashéninka greatly. Prolonged contact could have meant their physical extinction through disease or the establishment of a feudal system, as was the case in the Andean region. Ashéninka life would then have revolved around missions and feudal lords, who provided metal tools and other manufactured goods. As it turned out, technological innovations of metal tools, domesticated animals, imported trees, and some traditional stories[9] are all that remain of the colonial period. All other attempted changes were nullified and the culture reverted to conditions similar to those of pre-colonial contact.

The rebel campaign of 1742 advanced to the highland town of Andamarca, where it was defeated. The rebels arrived, but the cold weather was too much for the jungle people, forcing their return to the lowlands. The Spanish did not pursue them, preferring a policy of containment and defensive action only. The movement died.

---

[9]The most common and obvious of the borrowed stories are the *Juan del Oso* (John, Son of the Bear) stories. These are recognized by almost all Ashéninka adults. They are reset in the jungle, but maintain some foreign elements such as matches for fire and money. The stories are widespread throughout the Andes region and popular as far away as Colorado and New Mexico in the United States (Rael 1977), possibly being a popular story in Spain at the time the Franciscan missionaries came to the New World.

Commonly called the *Campas Bravos* 'Fierce Campas', the Ashéninka and other Campa groups had a reputation for being among the most dangerous of indigenous groups. Spanish contact with the less accessible Machiguenga continued during this time, but they were commonly referred to as the "peaceful Campas".

Within a generation, the Ashéninka forgot most of the skills taught by the Franciscans. They continued to forge machetes and axes for a short time in Quimiri (near the present town of La Merced), and raised some domesticated animals, but on a smaller scale than before. No evidence exists of Ashéninka reading, writing, or Christian worship during this time of rebellion and isolation. The Ashéninka continued to live and socialize their children as they had in the pre-colonial period. The culture changed little, with one major exception: they continued to use metal tools, which were widely traded throughout the Ashéninka area. In 1782, metal tools were a focal point of attention for the jungle groups and women were very busy making clothing and sheets from cotton so their men could trade them for metal tools.

Chronicled contact with the Ashéninka did not resume until 1847 with the construction of a fort at San Ramón in the Chanchamayo valley, upstream from La Merced. The Ashéninka met the reopening of contact with occasional violence to outside settlers. More distant areas of the Ashéninka remained isolated as late as 1870, and the Gran Pajonal area remained virtually unknown until more than fifty years later.

Economic exploitation: The Peruvian Corporation and the rubber boom

The market economy began to enter the Ashéninka area in the late 1800s. After the founding of the fort in San Ramón, colonists quickly took the best land from the Ashéninka and other groups in the Chanchamayo valley. Peruvian and European colonists had a low opinion of the Ashéninka, as expressed by Sinclair:

> Poor Chuncho! The time seems to be approaching when, in vulgar parlance, you must take a back seat; but it must be acknowledged you have had a long lease of those magnificent lands, and done very little with them. Whatever may be the value of the unearned increment, you have no claim for permanent improvements. The world, indeed, has been made neither better nor richer by your existence, and now the space you occupy—or rather wander in—to so little purpose, is required, and the wealth of vegetation too long allowed to

run to waste, must be turned to some useful account. The world was probably very young when you first found your way into this warm valley, but you have failed to "dress it and keep it," and the fiat has gone forth. You must make way for others. Albeit, this is not a case of dispossessing. In no sense can those vagrant tribes be called possessors of the soil. Creatures in a state of such abjectness, who do not evince the slightest desire to improve their own condition, could not, under any circumstances, be expected to ever render the pampas of the Amazon fit for civilised man. (Sinclair 1895:39)

In 1891, the Peruvian government granted 500,000 hectares of the Perené valley to the British-run Peruvian Corporation to help pay Peru's foreign debt to England, France, and the Netherlands.[10] The Peruvian Corporation gave the Ashéninkas who lived in the valley the choice of either moving off the land or staying to work the coffee plantations under difficult living conditions. Supervisor harshness, malaria, and the impossibility of getting out of debt made many want to flee their prison-like conditions. Other workers were brought to the valley from the Andean region and the Ashéninka soon became a minority.

The rubber boom spread up the Ucayali, Pachitea, and Pichis rivers, beginning a period of frequent contact with Spanish speakers in those valleys. The Ashéninka population spread between the east bank of the upper Ucayali River and the border with Brazil because of working in the rubber industry. In the Cohengua, Sheshea, and Yuruá river areas at the end of the twentieth century, all older adults have grandparents from the Tambo, Pajonal, or Pichis regions.

Peruvian rubber production began about 1870 and peaked in 1912. The Ashéninka and other groups were victims of violent raids that took men to harvest rubber, women for concubines, and children to be sold as servants. Labor contractors often paid and armed local chiefs to go to remote areas to capture Ashéninka women and children to work on the plantations and in the houses along the Ucayali River or as domestic servants in urban areas.

Incidents such as these come alive in the memories of today's Ashéninka. One woman tells the story of how she was kidnapped from her home on the Negro River in the Pachitea valley and sold.[11]

---

[10]Historical facts and figures in this section are derived from the following: Barclay 1985, Chirif 1981, Bodley 1972a, Bodley 1972b, Hvalkof 1986, Ortiz 1978, Torre 1978, and Varese 1968.

[11]Interview data is coded as (T.YEAR.TAPE.INTERVIEWEE). Speakers are coded as R for researcher, F for primary female interviewee, F2 for secondary female interviewee, M for primary male interviewee, and M2 for secondary male interviewee.

R: Can you tell me your story? How did you end up being a maid?

F: Long ago, when we lived in an isolated place; I was with my sister when a woman came and said, "What are you doing here?" I said, "Nothing." She then asked where my father was, and I said that he was fishing for *carachamas*.

R: That was near Puerto Bermúdez?

F: No, it was here at the Negro River, by the Llullapichis.

R: What were you doing there, getting gold?

F2[youngest daughter]: There were some ore deposits there.

F: Yes, there were metals there and my father made tools. Someone who sold women came to the house.

M [husband]: It was a Cashibo.

R: A man or a woman?

F: A man.

M: A warrior.

F: Yes, a warrior.

R: He was a Cashibo?

F: Yes. He said to me, "Where is your mother?" I said that she was fishing for *carachamas*. It was early, like eight in the morning. He said to me, "Let's go." I said, "No," and called my mother but he took my arm as I was screaming. My sister was gone, looking for something, so I was all by myself making manioc beer. He told me I had to go with him or he would harm me, so I went, screaming. We went to Puerto Yesupe [on the Pichis River]. Then he made me go to Aotiqui [on the Perené River], near Shimani. I was there for about a week.

R: You were with the one who took you?

F: No, with another. One kidnaps them in isolated areas and a Campa takes them over the ridge. They trade children for guns, ammunition, and pots. That is why they took women.

R: How old are you now?

F: Fifty years old. [I estimate about fifty-five]

R: Really?

F2: Approximately, because she doesn't know for sure.

R: How old is your youngest child?

F2: Twenty years old.

R: How old is your oldest child?

F2: She is about thirty-five years old.

R: So you were fifteen years old when your eldest child was born?

F: That is when they brought me here.

R: Did they sell you for something?

F: Yes, they sold me.

R: Who got paid, your father?

F: No, my father wasn't there. The man who kidnapped me got paid. The one who brought me over the ridge also traded me for something. That is how it was. Later, after passing Shimani, a Quechua paid for me with pots, cloth, machetes, knives, and other things. I didn't speak Spanish, so I didn't know what they said. I couldn't understand anything. They brought me over the ridge on mules when they had the trail. I was really tired. I saw my first car and asked a boy what it was. He told me it was called a car. That boy was also bought by them. (T.87.22.DOM)

This woman was forced to leave her home and family to live with mestizos in the strange environment of an Andean city where she worked as a maid until she escaped to the Perené region.

The patron system between the jungle ethnic groups and entrepreneurs began in this period. In this system, a businessman claimed a group of people and became their only source of manufactured goods. The Ashéninka received weapons, clothing, salt, and tools from their patrons in exchange for work, but with little hope of getting out of debt. Contact pressure steadily increased during this period, with frequent displacement, slave-raids, and much debt-peonage. Numerous instances of Ashéninka hostility toward the colonists and patrons are recorded. By 1913, the economic consciousness of many Ashéninkas was heightened. They often worked beside colonists from the Andean region who explained to the Ashéninka how they were being cheated by the patrons and the Peruvian Corporation. The Ashéninka could respond in one of three ways: cut the economic relationships and lose the technological advances they had become accustomed to, kill the patrons and their supporters to make an example of them, or learn to play the market economy game through modern education. No Ashéninkas chose the first option. Some chose the second option, resulting in the 1913–1914 revolt in the Pichis valley, the last major Ashéninka uprising. The third option, education, was about to be provided by Protestant missionaries.

Seventh-Day Adventist missions: Villages, education, and an adaptive ideology

Protestant missionaries brought modern education to the Ashéninka after liberalization of laws governing missionaries in Peru which resulted from the constitution's declaration in 1920 that the nation was Roman Catholic and the State would protect Catholicism. This was the first constitution that did not mention the exclusivity of Catholicism as the religion of the Peruvian State. In response to this slight liberalization, Protestant missionaries to the indigenous groups began to arrive in the 1920s. Like the early Catholic missionaries, they found their ministries more effective when they used the local languages, so many Protestant missionaries learned the languages. Their knowledge was often imperfect, and they depended heavily on indigenous evangelists to proclaim the Christian beliefs in the local languages. Though barely literate, these indigenous evangelists were very effective.

The most effective Protestant missionary to the Ashéninka and Asháninka was an American Seventh-Day Adventist named Frederick Stahl, who started his mission work in the Puno region of Peru. In 1921, he went to the Perené valley with a group of young Peruvian Seventh-Day Adventist lay preachers (Bodley 1972a). The worldwide Seventh-Day Adventist movement was still young, and the missionaries strongly emphasized the imminent return of Jesus Christ to the earth and the end of the world.

Many elderly Ashéninkas and Asháninkas remember their parents hearing the news of a white man declaring the world would soon end. They also remember their parents and many others leaving their homes to test this claim.

R: How did your father become a Seventh-Day Adventist?

M: His parents were in Puerto Ocopa and my grandfather was a headman. He had many wives. The priest told him that he had to marry just one wife. My grandfather didn't want to, so he went back into the jungle to live as he was accustomed. He was a shaman. Then he heard of something special in Metraro, which was well-known because many passed by there to get salt from the Cerro de la Sal. Even from the Gran Pajonal they went to get salt. They heard that in Metraro was a person who was tall, white, and had blue eyes. "He is God," they said. They had never seen God, so they said, "Let's go see if it is God." They wanted to see him in person. Everyone went because they were curious to see this strange person whom some said came from the sky. This was Fernando Stahl. Curious people came from everywhere. A woman interpreted his words. He said God is in the sky and though we don't know when, he is coming back. We needed to prepare for his return. Others said, "Let's see." Malaria was there and someone said, "God, cure this sickness." Stahl said, "Why not?" so the people brought their children to be cured. My father suffered from malaria, so my grandfather brought his son. The interpreter spoke to Stahl in Spanish. He gave my father a pill. They wondered what it was but he ate it. Days and weeks passed and he got better. My father said, "God cured me."

Stahl said he wasn't God, that it was just a medicine. My grandfather said that they should stay in that place. He said, "Here is a God who cures sickness." They stayed in Metraro. Since Metraro belonged to the Peruvian Corporation, they all had to leave. They moved downstream to Tzotziqui. Since the land there was also part of the Peruvian Corporation, everyone had to work in the fields. They got tired of that, so most of them moved to the Pichis valley. That was in 1948. My father was sent to find the best location in the Pichis valley. (T.87.08.MAR)

R: Why did your parents go to the mission in the first place?

M: People said the god Pachacama, also called Navireri (also called Juan Santos Atahuallpa), would return to the jungle so it would develop and prosper. Not only Ashéninkas came, but also Machiguengas. About 500 people came from all over: from Apurimac, Madre de Dios, and Ucayali. They came here to the Perené. Piros, Shipibos, everyone who came to Metraro came to see him. He seemed to be the return of Atahuallpa, Navireri. They think Metraro is a sacred place, where they fought in the past. That is why they thought he had returned. The first missionary was Fernando Stahl. Everyone came and everyone died there from measles. (T.87.14.CAR)

Stahl chose a very strategic location to begin his ministry. He began in Metraro,[12] a site east of the Cerro de la Sal that most jungle peoples passed on their journey to the salt deposits. Stahl's message was given credence when he cured many sick adults and children who suffered from malaria. Many thought Stahl's small miracle pills were a foreshadowing of even better things to come; hundreds decided to stay and learn about Stahl's religion through bilingual interpreters. He preached that the Word of God forbade killing, drinking, eating unclean meats, work on the Sabbath, and other specific activities (Bodley 1972a). Within a few years, a core group of believers remained who were fully committed to Seventh-Day Adventism, despite the outbreak of a measles epidemic that killed thousands of Ashéninkas, including dozens in Metraro.

In a study of Protestantism in Peru, Kessler characterizes Stahl and his work.

> The remarkable success of the work around Lake Titicaca is to a considerable extent due to the personalities of its missionary pioneers Frederick and Ana Stahl. Frederick was a well trained nurse, and his care of the sick was the basis on which the work started. Ana Stahl was a teacher and her help

***

[12]Juan Santos had also taken advantage of this site on the salt trail when he made his base camp there during the uprising of the eighteenth century.

> proved decisive in building up the educational work. The Stahls were energetic pioneers who realized the importance of the social application of the Gospel and presented their message in a way that was relevant to the needs of their hearers. Most important of all, in their spiritual attitude they were well ahead of most of the Adventists of the time. There was no sectarianism in Stahl. (Kessler 1967:230)

After the disasters of the exploitation period and the diseases that came with outsiders, Adventism seemed to restore order to an increasingly chaotic world (Barclay 1985).

Stahl and his co-workers not only taught Christianity, but they also became allies with the Ashéninka in their disputes with the Peruvian Corporation. Relations between the missionaries and the Peruvian Corporation worsened to the point that the missionaries and their followers were forced to move off Peruvian Corporation land. The mission divided and established two villages that later founded other villages.

A few years later, Stahl and some of his followers went to the Ucayali region, again siding with the jungle groups against the exploitation by the patrons (Bodley 1970). The missionaries and their converts ran away from the patrons and their debts, hiding on streams off the main river and founding new villages. In both the Ucayali and Perené regions, and later in the Pichis region, the missionaries tried to make the Ashéninka independent of the Peruvian Corporation and the patrons, while still trying to preserve for them some participation in the market economy. The mission eventually received moderate-sized grants of land from the Peruvian government and organized the villagers to produce agricultural products for sale, giving some Ashéninkas an alternate source of income and freeing them from perpetual indebtedness. However, until the end of the twentieth century, many men from these villages contracted themselves to seasonal work for a patron, preferring payment in advance, despite the consequences.

Schooling began as a response to economic exploitation. Often, Ashéninkas worked for the Peruvian Corporation beside mestizos who knew how to manage their accounts. Some of these mestizos helped Ashéninka men speak Spanish and understand money. The Ashéninka found these skills useful and wanted their children to learn them. Missionaries started schools at the request of the Ashéninka, hoping to empower the Ashéninka against economic exploitation. The schools taught arithmetic, reading, writing, and religious doctrine. Group work projects to earn money for the school and raise vegetables were also part of the curriculum.

The Seventh-Day Adventist missionaries did not plan to translate the Bible into the Ashéninka language; they relied on bilingual interpreters to teach the fundamentals of the faith, so mother tongue reading and writing were not taught in the school. All reading and writing lessons were in Spanish. Few adults went to school, though most adults attended twice-daily devotional services.

The first schools were not an overnight success. The Ashéninka were told from many sources that an education for their children would help them in the economic aspects of their lives, but for many, the cost of living in a village was too high. The Ashéninka traditionally lived as isolated nuclear families or in small groups of adult brothers and sisters, but the missions and the schools encouraged all people—family and strangers—to live in villages, which disrupted traditional settlement patterns.

A fear of sorcery was a barrier to forming a village or sending children to school. The Ashéninka believe that young-to-adolescent children can be witches who cause great harm by burying refuse taken from a victim, so Ashéninka children are taught to avoid children who are not close family. A child contaminated by another is believed to become a witch—a risk that many parents were not willing to take.

Another barrier to forming a village was the fear of sickness. Ashéninkas attribute measles, whooping cough, polio, and flu to contagion, not sorcery. Living in a village became taboo for many who said, "If you live in a village, you will get sick." The common sense of this was reinforced every time someone in the village became ill. Some villages are still abandoned, almost overnight, when sickness appears. Though being in a village was considered dangerous to one's well-being, many saw the benefits of membership in the religious community and the economic empowerment of schooling as worth the risk.

Schooling for the Ashéninka was an economic burden for the families of the students. The Seventh-Day Adventist mission was poor and could barely finance the living costs of the American missionaries. Peruvian lay preachers, the churches, and the schools were financed by those being served; parents and students were expected to build and maintain a schoolhouse, buy study materials, and pay a modest salary to the teacher. The school was typically supported by a communal field that was worked by parents and students on special work days, with the profit from the sale of cattle or crops going directly to the school.

Initially, teachers were Seventh-Day Adventists from the Andean region who learned Ashéninka, but by the early 1950s, some Ashéninka young men taught in the schools. In these schools, the Ashéninka language was spoken only when necessary for accurate communication; everyone was expected to learn to speak, read, and write in Spanish.

In the Pichis valley, family leaders came to the Seventh-Day Adventist mission station of Nevati to ask that schools be started for their children. The American missionary in Nevati chose fifteen young Ashéninka men whom he sent to these villages to teach school and preach. Some villages became disenchanted because of the school's economic requirements and the strict Seventh-Day Adventist code of behavior. These villages still wanted schools, so they requested them from the Peruvian government, which established the first Pichis valley government school for Ashéninkas in 1959. By this time, district officials looked favorably on Ashéninka requests for schools because the expansion of private Seventh-Day Adventist schools produced tension with the nearby mestizo town of Puerto Bermúdez, especially with the Catholic priest.

By 1963, another four government schools for Ashéninkas were established and the number of schools steadily increased to ninety schools in the Pichis, Perené, and Ucayali regions in 1990. The Ashéninka were still responsible to pay for study supplies and to build and maintain a thatch-roofed schoolhouse, but the government paid the salary of the mestizo teachers, and the pressure to adopt the Seventh-Day Adventist code of behavior lessened. Other mission groups founded schools in the Ashéninka area, but their significance is small in comparison with that of the Seventh-Day Adventists.

Though the events of the exploitation and Seventh-Day Adventist periods were significant, they directly affected few Ashéninkas. Only in the contemporary period did these events, and others to be discussed, bring changes that affected almost everyone.

The contemporary period

The Ashéninka who wanted to participate in the market economy sent their children to school to remove some disadvantage of dealing with mestizos. As the number of schools increased, other changes happened that increased the need for skills taught in the schools.

Fernando Belaunde Terry, President of Peru 1964–1968 and 1980–1985, spoke of the Perené and Pichis valleys as the future economic salvation of Peru and started road-building projects in the two valleys. The mere proposal of these roads started a land rush by mestizo colonists, most taking land traditionally cultivated by the Ashéninka. Many Ashéninkas disliked the mestizo colonists and moved away. During this time of social upset, Ashéninkas who once worked as teachers or lay preachers for the Seventh-Day Adventist mission became the political leaders. The first attempt to organize the Ashéninka politically was in 1959 in the Perené region, where the assembled delegates agreed to ask for land reserves with boundaries that would be respected by the colonists (Casanto 1986). Throughout the 1960s, villages sent delegations to Lima to protest colonist infringement of Ashéninka lands.

Independent of these troubles, a military coup deposed Belaunde in 1968 and installed the left-of-center general Juan Velasco Alvarado as president of Peru. The new government carried out a comprehensive agrarian reform program, and a series of decreed laws gave indigenous peoples many new land and political rights.

Soon, groups of young anthropologists and sociologists from the government went to the Perené and Pichis regions to raise Ashéninka consciousness about their new civil and land rights. These anthropologists seem to have preferred to work with the more bicultural, bilingual, educated Ashéninkas trained in the mission schools. These government-sponsored activists from Lima formed an alliance with the Ashéninka against both the colonists and regional politicians. They organized village councils composed of a chairman, vice-chairman, treasurer, secretary, works supervisor, lands organizer, lieutenant governor, and other minor positions. Villagers called periodic community meetings and sent delegates to regional meetings where they discussed mutual problems and petitioned local and federal government agencies for changes (Casanto 1986). Recognizing the colonist threat to their well-being, the Ashéninka enthusiastically accepted these political innovations. Few villages, however, were completely successful. Many groups could not incorporate into villages for lack of anyone who spoke Spanish or could read. Many villages could fill only one or two of the village government positions with literates. Today, any man who is in good standing and is literate can be elected to a village position.

The 1979 constitution of Peru gave the indigenous minorities a legitimacy never before seen in Peru. With regard to indigenous populations, chapter four of the Constitution of 1979 was titled "Education, Science, and Culture". Regarding language issues, Article 23 stated, "The State guarantees the parents the right to take part in the education process of their children. The parents have the right to decide the kind and place of education." Article 34 said, "The State will preserve and stimulate the manifestation of the indigenous cultures." Article 35 said, "The State promotes the study and knowledge of the indigenous languages. It guarantees the right of the Quechua, Aymara, and jungle groups to receive primary education in their language" [my translations].

Map 2.2 Ashéninka and Ashánika regional dialects

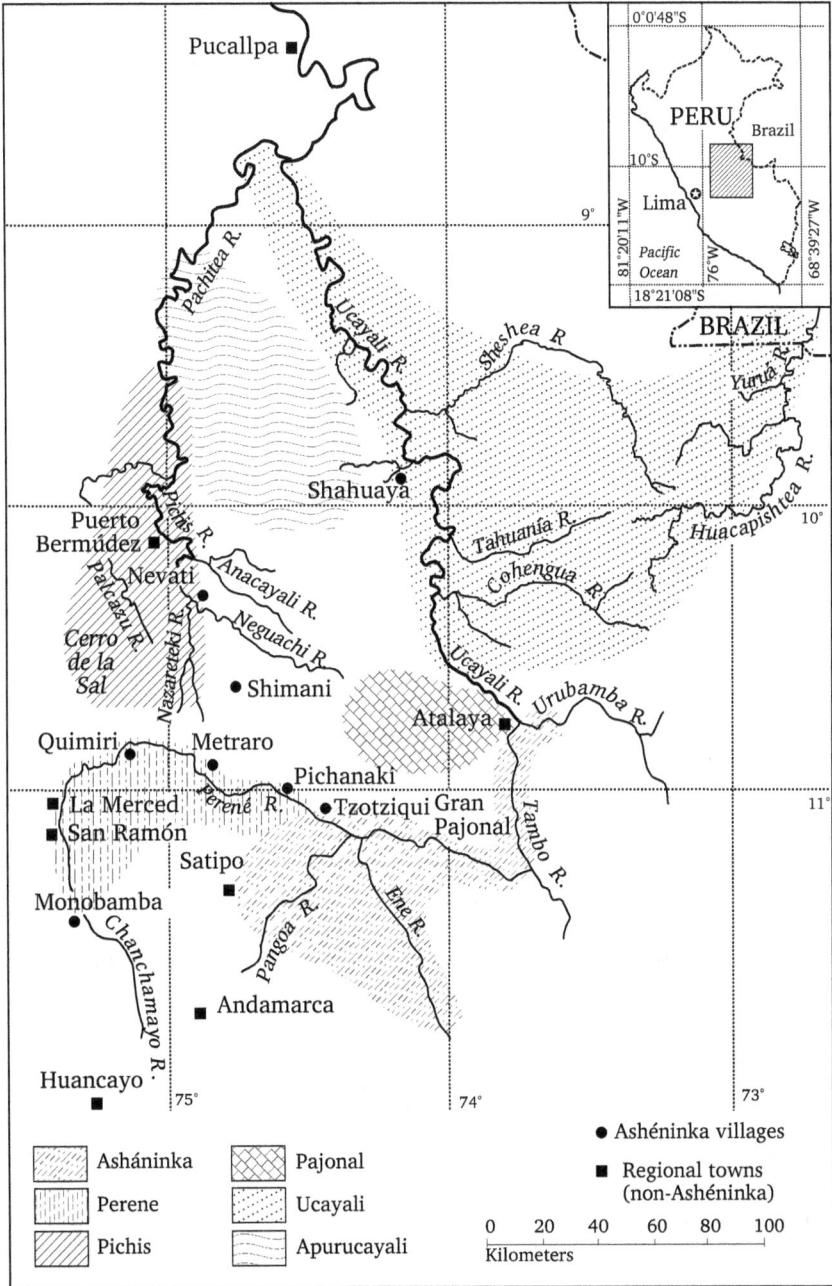

Indigenous people were given jobs as bilingual school teachers and bilingual paramedics before 1979 in other areas of Peru, but the legislation that permitted such appointments was not strong enough to be enforced in the Ashéninka area until after the passage of the Constitution of 1979. Gradually since 1980, Ashéninkas with a high school education and training in pedagogy have begun to replace mestizo teachers in village schools. Also, Ashéninka paramedics have been trained, hired, and assigned to many village clinics and even to district medical centers, where they treat Ashéninkas and mestizos.

These changes in employment opportunities have altered the attitude of many to education. Since 1979, Ashéninkas have begun to want education for their children, not only to participate in the market economy or to protect village interests threatened by the colonists, but also to qualify for government jobs reserved earlier only for mestizos. The Ashéninka's desire for education changed from that of a first generation wanting the ability to figure accounts with patrons, to the next generation wanting to protect their interests through participation in democracy, to the current generation aspiring to professions that require post-primary education.

These changes of increased contact, universal schooling, and instrumental use of Spanish have changed the nature of the Ashéninka's "world". The cultural world projected by their mestizo neighbors competes with traditional Ashéninka culture.

Traditional Ashéninka life

Traditional Ashéninka society divided labor between men and women. Men typically cut trees and underbrush for the garden, planted manioc, hunted, fished with a hook or arrow, built houses, and made tools for these activities. Women cultivated and harvested the garden, prepared food, brewed manioc beer, fished for minnows with baskets, cared for children, spun cotton, and wove clothing and baskets. Women did work that kept them close to the house while men often worked far from the settlement.

Traditional Ashéninkas married when the woman was thirteen to sixteen years old and the man sixteen to eighteen years old. Prior to marriage, girls became expert spinners of cotton and boys expert hunters and strong workers. Marriage partners worked as a team to become self-sufficient.

From infancy, children learned that men's and women's roles were different. Small children learned adult labor in their play: girls imitated women's activities, such as cooking with small pots, and boys imitated men's ways, such as shooting toy arrows at fruit. Mothers cared for both boys and girls from birth to about eight years old, giving them small jobs, such as carrying food or firewood from the garden. At about nine years of age, boys began to accompany their father into the forest, while girls continued to accompany their mother in the garden or home.

Individuals are now less constrained by their ecology and the need to conform to these traditional roles. Today, they must decide how much they want to work for others, how long to stay in school, whether or not they want a service profession, or if they want a political office. The social world of the Ashéninka has changed as parents spend more time at work and children more time in school with their peers. The spiritual world of the Ashéninka is forced to be more covert than in the past because of the stigma attached to some traditional beliefs.

The present situation

Language shift to Spanish

The establishment of schools in most Ashéninka villages caused many Ashéninkas to change the way they raise their children. Before 1982, all instruction in the schools was in Spanish, and teachers often retained a child in the first grade until he or she learned enough Spanish to participate orally in class. To aid the child in learning Spanish, many Ashéninka parents speak only Spanish to their small children. For many children, the only occasion they have for speaking Ashéninka is when they speak to their playmates or grandparents. I have met many adults who say they were raised in this manner and claim they now cannot speak Ashéninka, though they can understand it. Other Ashéninkas speak Ashéninka to their children, leaving the school and their playmates to teach Spanish. These children grow up speaking both languages, switching language according to the context. Language use is shifting to Spanish; Ashéninka is no longer spoken exclusively in all contexts.

Spanish is the preferred written language. A general village meeting may be conducted in Ashéninka, but the minutes of the meeting and any documents produced are written in Spanish. Though the neighboring Asháninka, Shipibo, and Yanesha prefer to write personal letters in their ancestral languages, the Ashéninka who speak Ashéninka have always written letters in Spanish. The other groups are different because most villages in their regions had bilingual schools since the 1950s or 1960s. The bilingual schools taught writing first in the local language, and later in Spanish.

Spanish is the preferred language in Christian churches. The Seventh-Day Adventist missionaries began by preaching and reading the scriptures in Spanish and having someone translate. Children at the mission schools were taught to read, write, and speak Spanish. The older believers and new converts who speak little Spanish pray in Ashéninka, but younger people and most church leaders pray in Spanish. All the hymns are in Spanish, though a chorus or two are sung in Ashéninka. As of 1990 members of SIL International had begun to translate parts of the New Testament in the Ashéninka language, but the published portions are used for individual, informal study more than for formal church services. The situation is different in the surrounding language groups. The Ashaninka, Yanesha, Shipibo, Nomatsiguenga, Machiguenga, and Piro have had the complete New Testament and hymnals in their language for several years and use them almost exclusively in their church services.

Spanish is used in most economic activities. Buyers of Ashéninka products and those who sell goods to the Ashéninka typically speak only Spanish. Families go to town on a buying trip expecting to speak Spanish, even within the family, so that either their ethnicity will not be obvious or they want to be polite to those around them. Some Ashéninkas are ashamed of the stigma attached to "Indians" who cannot speak Spanish. The following interviews show how some are embarrassed when mestizos or other language groups discover their ethnicity.

F: When I was fifteen or sixteen years old, I went to Huancayo and my father visited me. I had friends where I worked. My father spoke to me in Ashéninka and my friend said, "Ah, you are really an Ashéninka." I had never felt lower in my life. Later, I felt like I didn't ever want to speak my language. But later, I thought maybe I was better than her. When I returned here, I thought maybe being a native was better than being a mestizo, so I felt better again. Since then, I never felt like not speaking Ashéninka. I wanted to see this friend who called me a Chuncho [derogatory term]. She said, "Look at this Chuncha, how she talks."

R: Someone actually said this to you?

F: Yes, in Huancayo.

M: That is what they call us, but not so much any more.

R: Did they start to gossip about you or anything?

F: A little. I returned there and they insulted me again, so I insulted them back, saying, "You Quechuas don't know how to live right. You all live filthily. The Chunchos are better." So I paid them back.

F2: Sometimes it hurts. (T.87.17.AMA)

F: I remember when I studied in Pampa Silva. One day, my father spoke to me in Ashéninka in front of my friends.

R: How old were you?

F: I was thirteen in the first year of high school. He talked to me in Ashéninka and my friends laughed. I was ashamed. I wondered why my companions were laughing at my father. My father always came to visit me. One day, I asked my friends why they laughed at my father. "No," they said, "we are laughing because we don't understand what he is saying to you." I felt ashamed that day. (T.87.17.LLA)

The mestizo colonists treat the Ashéninka as though they have lower prestige than themselves. The children of mestizo colonists often make derogatory remarks to Ashéninka children and intoxicated mestizo men often insult those who are obviously Ashéninka.

F: [to her sister] What he means is that you have seen that when we are in the park in La Merced, a woman will go by in her *cushma* and people call out to her, "Hey, Chuncha, etc." You have seen this.

R: I think that children would especially be affected by this kind of behavior.

F: When we are real small, we don't even know when they are insulting us. But when we are twelve or thirteen, then we realize they are insulting us.

F2: But why do they insult us?

F: I want to insult them back (everybody laughs).

F2: But sometimes I say, "Why are they talking to me like that when we are all Peruvians?" (T.87.17.AMA)

The colonists easily identify Ashéninkas who wear the traditional *cushma*, have facial tattoos, or speak Ashéninka or an accented Spanish. When an Ashéninka is "found out", he or she is often ridiculed or avoided. Ashéninkas often feel unwelcome in some restaurants and hotels, though this does not happen as often as it did twenty years ago.

To avoid the ridicule of others, Ashéninkas have gradually given up many physical markers of their identity. Only rarely do young men or women have tattoos or pierced lips, and most men have given up wearing the *cushma* in favor of a shirt, pants, and shoes. When in the company of Spanish speakers, many Ashéninkas try to avoid calling attention to themselves by not speaking Ashéninka; they speak Spanish or nothing.

A degrading stereotype of the Ashéninka by outsiders characterizes them as animal-like or uncivilized. Franciscan missionaries of the seventeenth century (Ortiz 1978) and twentieth century mestizo school teachers and patrons often classify Ashéninkas as either civilized or uncivilized. The Ashéninka and mestizo definitions of civilized differ. Many Ashéninkas want to project the image of being "civilized"; yet for the Ashéninka, being civilized has nothing to do with savageness, violence, or religion, but with the skill the individual has to "pass" in mestizo society. The typical civilized Ashéninka man can converse somewhat in Spanish, owns a shirt and pants, and sends his children to school. A man who wears a *cushma* and speaks Ashéninka at home is still civilized because he and his family can "pass" when needed. Gradations of being civilized exist, some people being more adept at fitting in with the mestizo culture than others. An informal threshold point exists at which a family passes from being rigidly traditional, or uncivilized, to being flexibly adaptive, or civilized.

Language is important in establishing and maintaining Ashéninka friendships. In interviews, Ashéninkas often state they are more trusting of and open with people who speak either Ashéninka or Asháninka. They feel contempt for young people who left the village and later returned, no longer wanting to speak their mother tongue and even refusing to eat manioc. Such refusal is seen as a rejection of heritage. Blood ties continue with the immediate family, but other relationships are informally severed. Young women reject Ashéninka identity more frequently than young men. The following is how some Ashéninkas explain this situation:

F: I have seen this in La Merced, but with girls that come from the Puerto Bermúdez area. They are the children of Ashéninkas but they deny speaking our language, even when they return to their village. They go for only three months and claim that they have completely forgotten our language. But in my case, I was gone for four or five years and I didn't forget any of my language. I arrived here and spoke perfectly. The others forget after just three months. Maybe it is their puffed-up pride or arrogance.

M [F's father]: They don't even want to eat manioc.

F: They want to eat a different kind of food.

M: This is true.

F: This is true.

M: Those from Bermúdez are like that but we here are not.

F: Here we are not. Almost all who return are like before.

R: Why do you think it is different in Bermúdez from here?

F: I don't know. Maybe for ignorance or they haven't been educated in school. This is somewhat my idea because someone who knows cannot deny what they really are by birth. It must be their pride that makes them think they are better than others. This is how I understand it.

R: F2, is this how you see it?

F2 [F's sister]: Yes. I have seen this. For example, here many girls have left but have returned normal. They teach us what they have learned but they are not selfish and stuck on themselves. In other places they are, like in [a downstream village]. They have three young women who are from [the Pichis region]. People came to take them to work as maids. When they returned after a few months, I visited my sister. She said that these three girls returned and were somehow different. They didn't want to eat manioc or fish any more. I wondered why. I didn't believe my sister and accused her of exaggerating. She told me it was true, saying they wouldn't even walk barefoot any more. They won't even go to the garden to dig manioc, saying too many flies are there.

M: That's right.

F2: For me, it would be good to talk to these girls. I wanted to talk to them but they said they were from Lima, that they weren't from there. I don't know why they denied knowing these things.

R: Isn't it true that some men leave to join the army. Do they act like this when they return?

F: I have a relative who was in the army, but he returned as if nothing changed. He speaks Ashéninka normally.

R: In Bermúdez, they say that it is the women more than the men that deny their language and culture. Why is it? Are the women more sensitive to criticism or something? Are relationships between women different from relationships between men? Is a man's life different from a woman's? Why the difference?

F2: I think that the men have more relationships between men. Women are more apart. For example, a woman cannot tell her problems to a man. There is more confiding between women. This is why the women have their friends.

R: Do the men share their problems with other men?

M: Only with someone with whom they confide.

R: Do men criticize other men for not speaking Ashéninka more than women criticize each other? How do you feel when a girl says that she no longer wants to eat manioc?

F2: The girls who are sixteen or seventeen years old often refuse to accept the advice or criticism from her mother or others. This is the arrogance they have.

R: But the men cannot do this?

F2: The men are different because the advice of their elders is obeyed. They are told that men must act like men. They have to obey all the advice of their elders. They say they will do such and such because they are men and must not be like women who don't want to eat manioc. That is how they talk among men. They pay more attention to the older people.

R: But the women do not?

F2: No, not after they go to the city.

R: Why do the women not respond like the men?

F: Because some of their mothers support the daughters. When the girl returns from working as a maid in the city, the mother says that her daughter now doesn't eat manioc because Lima has changed her. The mother supports her daughter. Others say that three months doesn't change anyone, but the mother will defend her daughter.

R: But the fathers do not support their sons if they don't want to eat manioc?

F: I haven't heard of this among men.

F2: Fathers insist that their sons eat manioc because it is our custom.

M: My niece went to Lima and, when she returned, didn't want to eat manioc or *carachama* fish. This is true. But the men, no. When they go to the army and return, they don't change. My nephew went to the army and he ate everything when he returned. He didn't deny his language. He greeted us as always. Only when he greeted us in front of his officers did he speak in Spanish. But the officers told him that since we were Ashéninkas, he should greet us in Ashéninka. (laughs) They wanted to hear how we spoke. But women are different. They don't want to talk or eat like we do. I don't understand why the women are like this.

R: Do you think it is the fault of the mother?

M: I don't know.

F2: My mother says that it is the mother's fault. (T.87.18.AMA)

These women typically marry outside the group, in contrast to the men, who are often given positions of leadership in the village government and have more use for the Ashéninka language.

Spanish is used in many social contexts. Ashéninkas are hospitable with their neighbors and invite them to parties. They are often invited, in turn, to a party at mestizo neighbors' homes. Soccer and volleyball competitions are common, with Spanish used as a common language. In the Perené region, Mestizo-Ashéninka intermarriage is common, and the family then speaks Spanish. Some villages are becoming increasingly mixed, with Spanish fast becoming the dominant language of the village.

Schools leave less time for traditional activities

About 80 percent of Ashéninka children between the ages of seven and twelve attend school. Almost as many girls as boys attend, and about the same number of each finishes elementary school. The number of boys who graduate from high school is only somewhat higher than that of girls. Parents send both their sons and daughters to school for its economic utility and because it removes the stigma of being "uncivilized". Those Ashéninkas who now consider themselves civilized call other Ashéninkas uncivilized who do not speak any Spanish and are nonliterate. To remove the label of uncivilized requires that one's children attend school and become somewhat bilingual.

Boys and girls enter Peruvian schools at the age of six, the same age that boys and girls begin to learn many traditional Ashéninka work skills and attitudes. Most children stay in primary school until the age of fourteen and some attend secondary school until the age of twenty. This long time with periods away from the constant companionship of their parents affects the child's choice of traditional skills and mastery of those skills.

The most obvious change is in the skill of spinning cotton thread and weaving. Traditionally, spinning thread was the default occupation of women. If a woman was not doing another activity that occupied her hands, she spun thread or wove clothing. She clothed herself, her family, and had extra clothing for her husband to trade. At the age of six or seven, a girl began to learn to spin cotton from her mother or grandmother. This activity is time-consuming and calls for much expert supervision. At the onset of puberty, the girl traditionally entered a small hut to spend an entire month doing nothing but eat, spin cotton, and sleep (Torre 1978). Schooling is quickly changing this practice. Fewer schoolgirls learn to spin thread, and their sojourn in the little hut is only a symbolic couple of days so she does not get behind in her studies. The inability to spin cotton and weave clothing makes them dependent on store-bought clothing that, in turn, demands increased agricultural production or wage-labor. This need for clothing causes some unmarried girls to seek work as maids in a city outside the Ashéninka area. One woman who worked as a maid gave the following explanation for seeking such work.

R: Why did your daughter leave for the first time?
M: We lacked money. For my part, I couldn't give my daughters enough money to buy their clothes. One asked me for money, and I said it would be better for her to leave and find work for a short time to make money.
R: F, was it like that?

F: I left to learn to cook, iron, etc. We don't have irons here. I didn't
    know how to iron when I left. I learned so I could later teach my sis-
    ter. Also, I needed money to buy clothes. My father didn't have
    enough money. I wanted to help my younger brothers and sisters,
    too. That is why I left to work. (T.87.18.CAM)

A similar situation has affected boys and hunting. Schoolboys have less
time to develop their hunting skills, and the influx of mestizos and increase in cultivated land has depleted the supply of game. Many men have
given up teaching their sons to hunt. A man raised in the Perené region
tells that his father felt that teaching him to hunt was not worth the effort,
though he himself wanted to master this most basic of traditional
Ashéninka skills.

R: Tell me about what your father said was the way people taught in
    the past.
M: My father told me how he was taught by his father, teaching di-
    rectly. When the little boys were very small, they were taught to
    make little arrows. They had magical plants that they applied to the
    boy so he would be a good hunter. My father was a great hunter, at
    least he told me so. My father has barely taught these things to me.
    I really don't know about the magical plants that help one to be-
    come a good hunter. He didn't teach me because civilization had
    come. He said, "I am not going to teach you because with civiliza-
    tion, we will not use arrows or shotguns because there will not be
    any animals to hunt or even the jungle to hunt in." (T.88.06.GER)

Older Ashéninkas say the younger people are not as strong, honorable,
or skillful at traditional occupations as they should be at their age. The
time taken by modern schooling is taking time away from practicing these
traditional skills, which has decreased the level of expertise.

The world of the Ashéninka has many common features that endured
through the historical periods and across geographic regions, but some
features vary regionally. Each region—Perené, Pichis, Ucayali, and
Pajonal—has predominant characteristics related both to the traditional
world and to their changing society.

Regional overview: Perené

The Ashéninka of the Perené valley live upstream from the mouth of the
Ipoqui River, along the Perené and Chanchamayo rivers to the village of
Pampa Michi. They chose to live away from the urban centers of La Merced

and San Ramón. I estimate that 6,000 Ashéninkas live in the region in villages of 60 to 500 people among approximately 80,000 colonists.

The Perené region is in the department of Junín and the province of Chanchamayo. A gravel road following the Chanchamayo and Perené rivers was completed in the mid-1970s, with branches of the road extending to almost every Ashéninka and mestizo village. Almost half the Ashéninkas live on the valley floor and the other half in the hills on either side. The altitude of the valley floor is about 350 meters above sea level, with some villages in the hills as high as 1,200 meters above sea level.

The land of the Perené and Chanchamayo valleys is almost fully utilized by the Ashéninka and the colonists. Little game remains in the forest, and fishing in the river is poor. The mestizo and Quechua colonists characterize the Ashéninka as lazy, who enjoy leisure and do not use their land to its fullest potential. Compared to the Ashéninka of other regions, however, the Ashéninkas of the Perené work very hard at agriculture.

Map 2.3 The Perené region

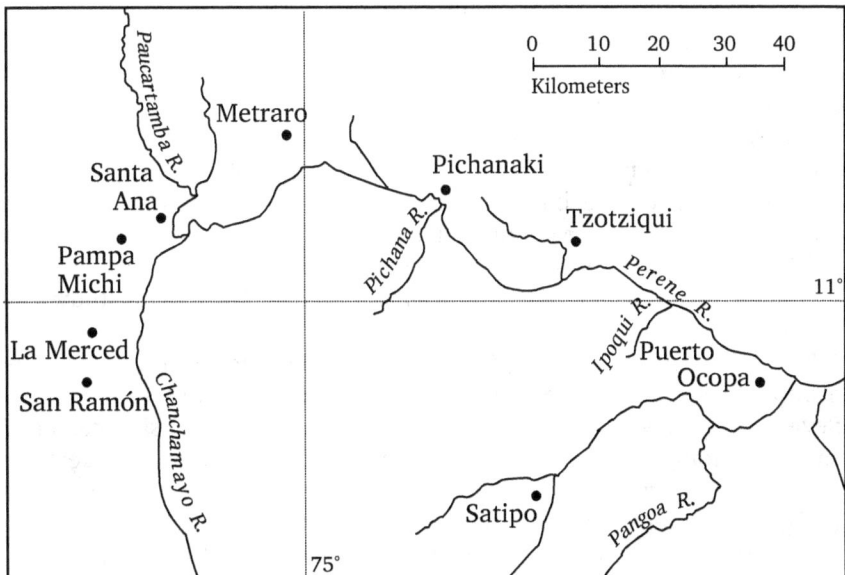

Since the 1970s, they have been restricted to particular plots of land for their crops. The slash-and-burn rotation style agriculture the Ashéninka are accustomed to is no longer possible, so intensive agriculture has become the rule. The Ashéninka of the valley floor grow papaya, avocado, and citrus for sale, and grow the ever-present manioc and plantains for their daily diet. The Ashéninka of the higher elevations grow coffee for sale, some selling to cooperatives and others selling to truckers who come to the village.

The Seventh-Day Adventist (SDA) missionaries began the first schools in the 1920s. Many people over the age of 60 can read. The Peruvian Ministry of Education began supporting schools in the 1960s, though the SDAs continue to operate three private schools. The Ashéninka of this region are by far the most educated; dozens have completed secondary school and a few have studied at the professional school and university level.

The SDA schools attracted both Ashéninkas and colonists. By the time Ashéninka villages gained title to their reserves, mestizo families had already claimed inclusion in communities. Government-supported schools in Ashéninka villages also attracted colonists. Initially, mestizo children walked from outside village boundaries to school, but soon village governments permitted mestizo families to build homes in the village proper. After many years of residency and acceptable conduct, some mestizo families became incorporated into Ashéninka villages.

The Ministry of Education eventually established schools in almost all mestizo and Ashéninka villages, but bilingual schooling is not an option because every village has some mestizo families. The few Ashéninka teachers in the region teach in Spanish. No secondary schools function in Ashéninka villages; those who study in secondary schools must travel to San Ramón, La Merced, Santa Ana, or Pichanaki. Those who study in a university must travel to Huancayo or Lima.

The Ashéninka of the Perené region are the most acculturated of all the groups. Villages have been organized longer, more have followed the Seventh-Day Adventist faith, intense contact with the outside has been sustained longer, and more intermarriage with mestizos or Quechuas takes place. A language shift to Spanish is occurring because of schooling in Spanish, intense contact, the desire to avoid stigma, and intermarriage. Mixed couples are a majority in some villages. Reasons for intermarriage are that the couple became sweethearts while students in the village school, or a mestizo man hopes to gain some economic advantage from his perspective, while the Ashéninka woman hopes to gain economic advantage from her perspective. These marriages are often criticized and typically have a short duration.

Men prefer to wear modern clothing but many women continue to wear the traditional *cushma*. Women rarely spin cotton and weave, preferring to buy colorful material from which to make their *cushmas*. Weaving is done only to make a "ceremonial" *cushma* for a husband or older son to wear at parties or political assemblies, but the custom is changing from weaving them to buying them from Ashéninkas of the Pichis or Pajonal regions. Women's baby-carrying hip slings have been replaced by the baby-carrying back *manta*, which is typically used by Quechua women.

Some traditional practices continue and others have declined. Ashéninkas and Quechua colonists continue to chew coca. Few Ashéninka young men become shamans because of mission influence and because mestizos confuse shamanism with witchcraft. The few shamans are now called "herbalists". Many Ashéninka adults still hold the basic values of respect for elders, humility, and not stealing, but these are eroding, which many think is caused by contact with mestizo children in the school.

Men now do more of what was traditionally thought to be women's work. Men have fewer trees to fell, game to hunt, fish to catch, and less reason to travel for days or weeks at a time. Men spend much time cultivating and harvesting their crops, some using donkeys to aid in their labor. Women spend much less time spinning cotton and weaving than in the past, with this time now used to cultivate and harvest the crops for sale.

The Ashéninka of the Perené region were the first group to be threatened with the loss of their lands. Being driven from their lands by the colonists and the Peruvian Corporation, they hoped that educated leaders would help them to stand their ground. The SDA mission educated many children, and by the 1950s, some became leaders who could represent their villages to government agencies.

In the late 1960s, government-sponsored activists went to the Perené region to organize the Ashéninka politically. Almost all villages began to elect officers who met with the officers from other villages in occasional general assemblies. Though family and personal rivalries made total participation impossible, some good came from these efforts: land titles were obtained, some government agencies became more responsive, and the political parties vied for the vote of the Ashéninka in local and national elections.

Regional overview: Pichis

Approximately 10,000 Ashéninkas live in the Pichis valley and its tributaries. This includes Ashéninkas who live in a few villages on or near the Pachitea River. The Ashéninka are still the majority in the Pichis valley, though a new road opened in the mid-1980s has started a wave of immigration. The region contains speakers of the Pichis and Apurucayali subdialects.

Most of the Pichis region is in the department of Pasco, province of Oxapampa. A few villages on the Pachitea River are in the department of Huánuco, province of Pachitea.

The Pichis valley is bounded to the west, south, and east by mountains with ridges from 1,200 to 2,000 meters above sea level. The valley itself is flat and wider than the Perené valley. Most Ashéninkas live on the valley floor and along tributaries that wind into the surrounding hills.

To the west of the Pichis live the Yanesha or Amuesha who dress similarly to the Ashéninka and have a similar contact history. Although Yanesha is an Arawakan language, Ashéninka and Yanesha are unintelligible to each other. To the south live the Ashéninka of the Perené region. These two groups have frequent contact with each other. A road now goes from La Merced, through Puerto Bermúdez, to Pucallpa.

To the east is a vast wilderness that separates the Pichis from the Pajonal and Ucayali regions. Little contact occurs between the Pichis and these two regions, though many migrated from one region to another. To the north is the Alto Ucayali plain, a vast, flat area that is home to the Cashibo and Shipibo.

The Ashéninka of the Pichis are less prosperous than those of the Perené. The Pichis valley is not as accessible to markets as is the Perené. Also, heavy rains in the rainy season limit the kinds of crops that can be grown. At the beginning of the twentieth century, rubber harvesting was the main activity, but today no particular crop or economic activity dominates. Some Ashéninkas raise cattle and others raise hogs, but none do so on a grand scale. Many contract out to cut trees for the cattle ranches of mestizo and European settlers. Most Ashéninkas grow extra rice, manioc, plantains, and beans to sell to wholesalers in the market of Puerto Bermúdez, the district capital. Some women make handwork for sale in La Merced, Lima, or Pucallpa. The men of the Apurucayali and Pachitea valleys cut trees for patrons in the lumber business.

These Ashéninka can survive in a subsistence economy because game and fish are abundant. They are less dependent on the national economy than those of the Perené region, but they want the prosperity they see in

Map 2.4 The Pichis region

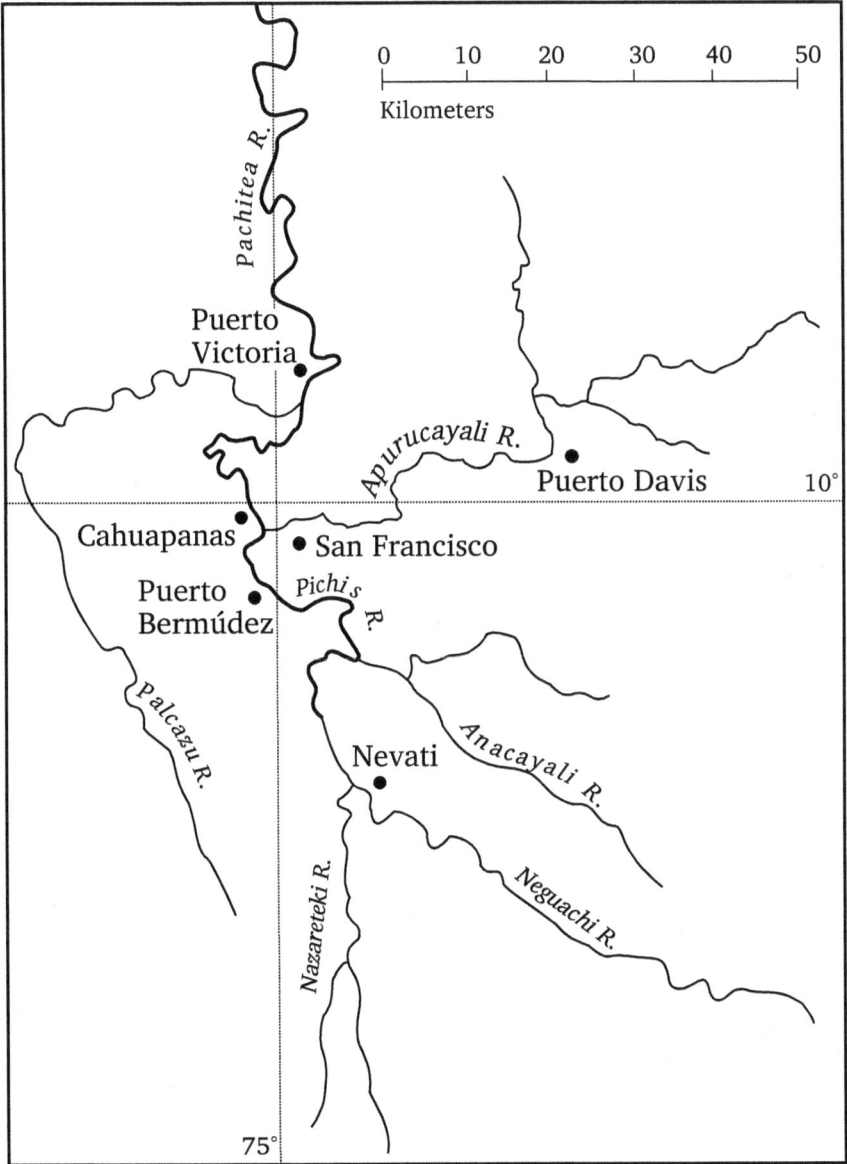

the Perené. The Ashéninka of the Pichis were enthusiastic supporters of the new road, every village lobbying to have the road pass close by. Now that the road is open, villages are making deals with lumber companies to have branch roads made to their village in exchange for the lumber in the path of the road. The Ashéninka have often organized into cooperatives to try to find a crop to sell for profit, but with little success.

The Peruvian government reserved large tracts of land for the Ashéninka in anticipation of road construction. Unlike the Ashéninka of the Perené, up to seven Pichis villages joined in groups to form large land reserves. The large tracts of land permit slash-and-burn and rotation agriculture, the traditional Ashéninka methods. Mestizo neighbors complain that the Ashéninka do not know how to use their land effectively and that it should be taken from them. Fortunately, the Peruvian government is committed to protecting Ashéninka lands.

The first schools were in Nevati, operated by the Seventh-Day Adventist mission, and in Cahuapanas, operated by the evangelical South American Mission. Both missions had branch schools near the original ones that began in the early 1950s. The Peruvian Ministry of Education began to establish government-sponsored schools in 1964, and gradually increased its coverage to every village in the region that could register twenty-five or more students six to fifteen years old.

The main mission schools had American and mestizo teachers. Branch schools had Ashéninka teachers who taught written Spanish, but who bridged the communication gap by using the Ashéninka language. Mestizos taught in all government schools until the early 1980s, when some bilingual Ashéninka teachers were hired. The villages supported the hiring of indigenous teachers but district education officials initially opposed it. Today, almost one-third of Ashéninka villages have a bilingual school with an Ashéninka teacher. Most of the others are requesting bilingual teachers because they feel that a teacher who speaks Ashéninka is more effective than someone who speaks only Spanish. Few schools in Ashéninka villages have mestizo students.

Most schools have one teacher for thirty students in grades one through six. A few larger villages have two or three teachers with as many as eighty students. The schools typically have a dirt floor and thatched roof, with furnishings made of native materials by parents. Parents must buy their children's books and supplies. Because of the general lack of funds, few students come to school with adequate supplies. Teachers lecture, and students copy in bound notebooks the lessons written on a chalkboard. Often, only the teacher has books. Most exams are oral. More than half the students are in the first and second grades, with the average student requiring two or three years to go from the first to second grade. Most adults are nonliterate. Those adults who are literate attended one of the mission schools or immigrated from the Perené.

Less intense contact, larger land reserves, and the later arrival of schools combined to lessen the degree of Ashéninka acculturation to Spanish society in the Pichis compared to the Perené. Less Spanish is spoken and fewer have stopped using traditional Ashéninka skills like weaving and hunting. Men typically wear pants and women wear *cushmas* made from store-bought material. Women weave small bags, baby-carrying slings, and *cushmas* for trade.

Though the Seventh-Day Adventist religion is strong in the region, most Ashéninkas follow traditional beliefs, especially relating to the use of magical plants, belief in sorcery, and consultation with a shaman (though few admit being shamans). Many feel pressure to leave old ways and acknowledge the stigma attached to those who do not speak Spanish or dress like a mestizo. Parents hope that school will give their children practical skills and help them "pass" in the outside world.

By the late 1970s, most villages were politically organized with an elected set of leaders. Not all the village leaders were literate or spoke Spanish, many relying on others to interpret for them. Since then, many of these leaders have been replaced by younger men who have some schooling.

The region-wide assemblies elect leaders and make their concerns known to government and private agencies. The leaders of the assemblies are all educated men from either Cahuapanas, Nevati, or the Perené region. These assemblies were once combined with the Perené and Amuesha assemblies, but each group gradually limited itself to its own area for logistical and communication reasons. Representatives from the Pichis general assemblies represent the region in Peru-wide assemblies of indigenous groups.

Regional overview: Ucayali

The Ashéninka live on the tributaries of the Upper Ucayali and the Yuruá rivers. To the west of the Ucayali, they live on the Aruya, Shahuaya, Chicosa, Unini, and Tabacoa tributaries. To the east of the Ucayali, they live on the Puntijao, Cohengua, Tahuanía, and Sheshea tributaries. I estimate the Ashéninka population of this watershed to be about 5,000 people. Approximately 300 Ashéninka live on a different watershed, i.e., the Yuruá and Embira rivers close to the border with Brazil.

The Ucayali Ashéninka region is in the department of Ucayali, province of Coronel Portillo. The long distances between most settlements has caused many minor dialect differences. Many Ashéninkas near the villages of Unini and Chicosa speak the Pajonal dialect more than the Ucayali dialect.

Fewer Ashéninkas in the Ucayali region live in villages than do those in the Perené or Pichis regions, preferring to live as single family units or near a headman. Villages and settlements are typically far apart, often separated by distances requiring many hours of travel by canoe. Mosquito infestation and poor soil for cash crops discourage mestizo settlement in the area. The only mestizos are a few ranchers and patrons in the lumber business. This most extensive of Ashéninka regions is shared with the ethnic groups who preceded the Ashéninka in the region: the Shipibo, Conibo, Amahuaca, and Yaminahua. These are of the Panoan language family and have many cultural differences, which inhibit their frequent contact with the Ashéninka.

The ancestors of the Ashéninka arrived during the rubber boom and decided to stay after the rubber bust to work lumber for patrons. Many family groups are moving to villages because of schooling opportunities for their children.

Most Ashéninkas of the region live comfortably in a subsistence economy. Protein is bountiful with much wild game and fish. The soil easily supports traditional Ashéninka agriculture with bountiful crops of manioc and plantains. Most Ashéninkas work for Ashéninka-speaking patrons, in exchange for manufactured goods like store-bought cloth, shotguns, ammunition, pots, axes, machetes, and radios. After receiving goods from a patron, men are bound to supply a quota of logs the patron will sell in Pucallpa. Men leave home in groups, sometimes with their families, to camp near a stand of trees, cutting cedar used for furniture or softer wood used for paper pulp or plywood. After working two or three months, the men return home.

In the 1930s, Frederick Stahl began the first schools in the villages of Shahuaya and Unini. Later, the South American Mission started a school in Chicosa. In the 1970s, the Seventh-Day Adventist mission added a school in Sheshea. These schools had little success compared to those of the Perené and Pichis valleys; all but the school in Unini are now supported by the Peruvian Ministry of Education.

Few adults in the Ucayali region are literate, with the exception being those in the villages of Shahuaya, Chicosa, and Unini. The Ministry of Education was slow to establish schools because the patrons opposed them. Also, it takes many days to travel to potential school sites and mestizo teachers refused to teach in such inaccessible areas. In the 1980s, the Ministry of Education established bilingual schools throughout the Ucayali region, hiring Ashéninka teachers from the Pichis region. Approximately

Map 2.5 The Ucayali region

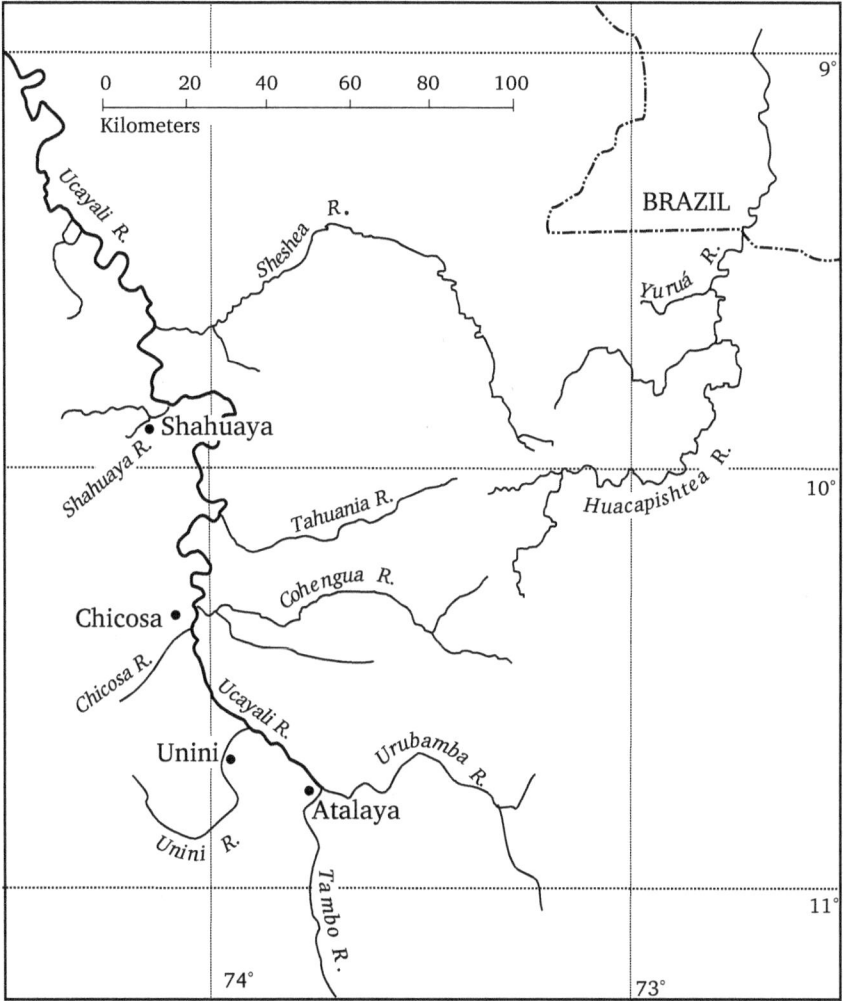

twelve bilingual schools are now in the Ucayali region, with the first students completing primary school in 1990.

Acculturation to Spanish ways varies from river to river and village to village. In Unini, Shahuaya, and Chicosa acculturation is similar to that in the Pichis region. Many profess evangelical Christianity, dress in pants and store-bought materials, and speak Spanish in the school. Those in isolated areas, whose only outside contact is with a patron, live a traditional lifestyle: little Spanish is understood, people marry at an early age, magical plants are used often, sorcery is feared, and most young men train to be shamans. Painted faces are common in the Ucayali region. The traditional values of humility, honesty, and respect for elders is very strong.

Political organization in the Ucayali region is minimal. Because of their early-established schools and proximity to the main river, the villages of Chicosa, Unini, and Shahuaya received land titles and have elected officers, but these do not meet in regional assemblies. The other villages do not see a need for land titles or a village government; they still follow the lead of the headman on internal matters and let the teacher represent the village to the outside.

Regional overview: Pajonal

The Ashéninka of the Pajonal live on a plateau at an average elevation of 1,000 meters above sea level. It is a rolling plateau with man-made grassy areas scattered throughout. Streams originating in the Pajonal flow into the Ucayali and Pichis rivers. About 5,000 Ashéninkas live in the Pajonal, scattered in many settlements around different headmen.

This plateau sits at the junction of the departments of Junín, Pasco, and Ucayali. The boundaries of these departments have shifted many times in the last fifty years. Though little of the Pajonal is in the department of Junín, the only regular air service comes from the town of Satipo in Junín, and the only marked trail to the outside passes Puerto Ocopa in Junín.

The mestizo village of Oventeni was founded in the 1920s, but the Ashéninka have been affected little by other mestizos or colonists. The Pajonal area is not accessible by boat, and trails to other regions are closed during the rainy season. It takes two to five days to walk to the Tambo, Pichis, or Ucayali regions, where men sometimes travel to fish or trade.

Most Ashéninkas of the Pajonal live in a subsistence economy. They sometimes work for a local patron by tending cattle, cutting forest for pasture, or harvesting coffee. The pay is very little compared to what Ashéninkas receive in other regions, since the mestizos of the Pajonal have tried to establish a feudal system in which they claim all the land and the Ashéninka work as peons. The Ashéninka of the Pajonal have few manufactured goods and almost no market for their products.

The mestizos of Oventeni opposed government establishment of schools for Ashéninkas in the Pajonal. The Seventh-Day Adventist mission attempted to found a school in the village of Pavoti in the 1960s, but it failed because poor soil and scarce protein make survival on the restricted Seventh-Day Adventist diet impossible. Oventeni has had a school since the 1950s but few Ashéninkas attended. Only in the 1980s were the first government-supported schools established for the Ashéninka. The Peruvian government now supports approximately fifteen small bilingual Ashéninka schools in the Pajonal region, most averaging about twenty students.

Map 2.6 The Pajonal region

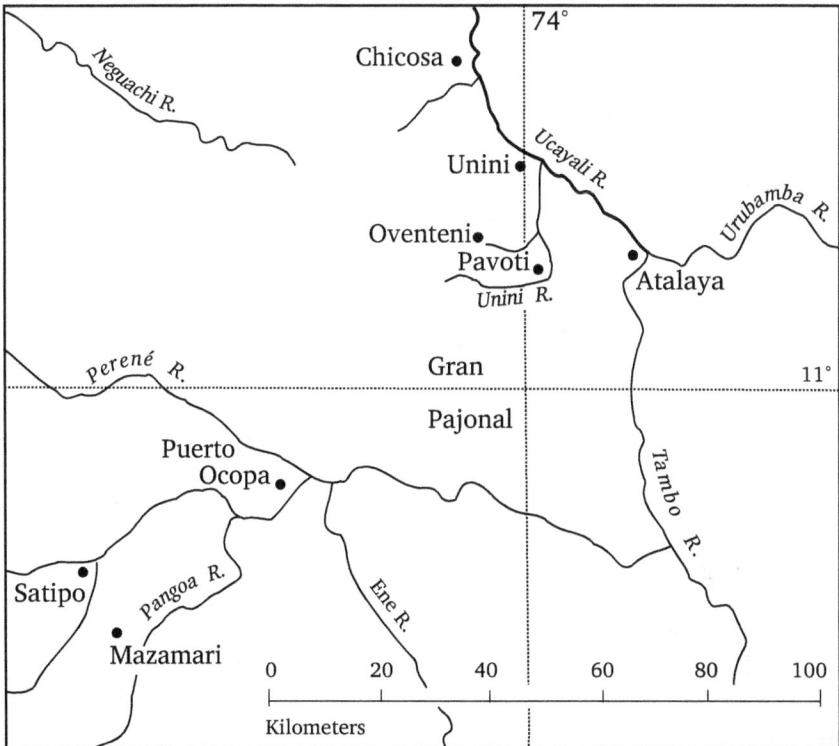

The Pajonal Ashéninkas are the most traditional. They have had the least outside contact, and did not even participate in the rubber boom at the beginning of the twentieth century. Though evangelical missionaries have put much effort into their work among the Ashéninka in recent years, shamanism and traditional beliefs are strong. The marriage custom of preference for a cross-cousin is still practiced more than in other areas, and traditional Ashéninka values are very evident.

The mestizos of Oventeni have long opposed Ashéninka political organization. In the 1960s, a leftist insurgency came to the Pajonal that tried to duplicate the Juan Santos Atahuallpa rebellion, but the mestizo combatants were soon defeated. The Ashéninka did not participate in the insurgency, preferring to keep to themselves. Recently, the attempt to introduce a feudal system in the Pajonal produced many injustices that forced the Ashéninka to organize to keep their lands. Most villages now have a village government and send delegates to general assemblies, though these organizations are still opposed by the mestizo population.

Conclusion

Throughout Ashéninka history, outsiders and innovations have left their mark on the Ashéninka. The Franciscan missionaries introduced metal tools and a few domesticated animals. The need for metal tools attracted many Ashéninkas to the market economy, and once they became a part of the market economy, the Ashéninka saw that the knowledge of writing, arithmetic, and Spanish were useful for interacting with their employers. Protestant missionaries soon arrived to establish schools. Schooling proved useful to the Ashéninka and the children of literate adults came to be routinely expected to be schooled, also.

The purpose of schooling quickly changed. Originally, schooling was seen as necessary to learn to manage individual accounts. Later, schools prepared bilingual leaders to represent the villages to government officials. Since the granting of indigenous rights by the Peruvian Constitution of 1979, schooling prepares Ashéninkas for professional jobs like paramedic and school teacher. This gave value to an even higher level of education and added a new dimension to the power structure by giving higher prestige to those with more education.

Socialization into the world of the Ashéninka involves becoming situated in the world in which one finds oneself. This pertains to the ecological surroundings of the rich and vast Ucayali, the poor soil conditions of the Pajonal, and the intense agriculture of the Perené. The world of the

Ashéninka also includes living with the reputation of being descended from warriors and having less of a tradition of schooling than do their mestizo neighbors.

The Ashéninka share much of a common world from region to region. They share some of the same traditional subsistence skills, language, values, and beliefs. Until recently, they shared a similar contact history and access to metal tools and other manufactured goods. Though contact is more intense in the Perené region than in the Ucayali, a large part of their worlds is alike.

The traditional oral history that frames the Ashéninka world is more real to the Ashéninka of today than the historical events since contact. Chapter three looks at the Ashéninka traditional stories that are told to Ashéninka children. The values promoted in these stories influence individual goals and social interaction in all aspects of Ashéninka life.

3

Voices of Oral History

The story has to give a lesson. All these stories have their moral.
That is why we believe that we shouldn't be disobedient or the owl
will come and take our eyes. We must go with our parents and
help them. ALE

They said that long ago, people who stole chickens had their
hands cut off. They said that if we stole things, people would cut
off our hands. Then what would we work with? We would have
nothing to eat. "You would die of hunger," they always said. Af-
ter they said this to us, we never touched the things that were not
ours. VIC

An important part of the Ashéninka world presented to children during
socialization is the content of many traditional stories that tell about
Ashéninka ideals. Storytelling is one way of transmitting information, values, and attitudes to young people without their knowing they are being
taught. A story can have a metaphoric application to real life or provide
models for behavior. The metaphor or model may or may not directly
state the moral, but as ALE says above, "All these stories have their
moral."

Many stories are similar to those of other ethnic groups, but the most
popular Ashéninka stories continue to be told because they are entertaining and appropriate for the Ashéninka context. The values, attitudes, and
humor present in the stories reflect Ashéninka values, attitudes, and humor. These are less susceptible to change than are Ashéninka economic

activities and Ashéninka adaptation to the ecological setting. Modern changes affect individual motivation, social interaction, and spiritual belief in pragmatic ways. The values and attitudes promoted in traditional stories, on the other hand, affect individual motivation, social interaction, and spiritual belief in idealistic ways.

One goal of socialization is to learn "acceptable conduct", which is taught explicitly by parents and is reinforced in traditional stories. Wentworth reminds us that the learning of acceptable conduct is a slow process, one that is not internalized for many years.

> The rigid young child has managed to decipher and then learn a discrete behavioral sequence or a correct form of behavior. The older child, on the other hand, has internalized the rules (design, blueprint) by which respectable conduct can be constructed. As a result, variations in discrete items become less disruptive to the child's appreciation of a situation. (Wentworth 1980:66)

Traditional stories incorporate subtle rules and roles, as well as cultural jokes, personal stories, and exaggerated group events.

> Socialization, therefore, is first a presentation (to the novice, through interaction and by others) of the rules whereby "respectable" behavior might be constructed. Secondarily, it is a presentation of techniques, maxims, trivia and all those other discrete items. (Wentworth 1980:68–69)

In the Asháninka region, Weiss, who collected his tales in the 1960s, found two types of Asháninka traditional stories.

> One type would include all myths serving to explain the present reality in terms of past occurrences that brought the present state of reality into existence. These myths can be called cosmogonic. The bulk of the Campa myths collected in the field and presented here are of this type. The other kind of myth is explanatory in an entirely different manner: myths of this type serve to explain, by illustration, how the cosmos operates. These myths may be called exemplary: they include the many apparently pointless stories making up the bulk of many collections of mythological materials. Few of the Campa myths are of this type. The exemplary myth, in effect, translates the subjunctive formulation, "If x were to occur, y would or might result," into the past indicative, "On one occasion, x occurred, and y resulted." (Weiss 1969:535–536)

In contrast to Weiss's work, done over thirty years ago, this study is based on more than five hundred stories of the "exemplary" variety—at least in parts of the story line, if not as a central theme. But Ashéninka traditional stories are known to vary greatly. John Elick, who did research in the Pichis region, comments on the variability of Ashéninka stories between regions.

> Campa mythology is rich and detailed. Though the details may vary considerably from one area to another the stories exhibit a structural similarity that effectively reminds the Campa listener that he is unique in the world, but is now abandoned amidst the hostile forces of evil that erupted into *Kipatsi* from the world below. (Elick 1970:202)

Despite the variability, Ashéninka stories reflect structural linkages and claims to a cultural uniqueness for the Ashéninka.

My collection of traditional stories and those referred to by the interviewees in this study are overwhelmingly of the "exemplary" variety. The fact that these were collected over the past two decades suggests that the Ashéninka have shifted to prefer stories that show cause and result in the past. The most common of these stories remind listeners that dangerous animals will punish misbehaviors, and that misfortune will come to those who show inappropriate anger, disobedience, pestering, thievery, stinginess, or disrespect. Adults say they tell these stories to children to help form the conscience of the child.

The storytelling event

Ashéninka storytelling is an informal event for both adults and children. Some stories are told among adults at a party or when visiting. Other stories are told to children. These are typically solicited by a child who asks a caregiver to tell a familiar story during a period of rest. These are usually told at night, while children are still awake, or during a rainstorm, when outdoor work is impossible.

R: Did anyone tell stories to you at night?

F: Yes, my mother told stories to me at night, especially about the jaguar that ate some people one night. She told stories almost every night while we were spinning cotton. (T.88.07.LOL)

M: My grandfather told many stories to me because I spent almost all my time with him. When we were walking, working, or at night, he told me many things. (T.88.02.RAM)

M: My mother told stories occasionally when there was nothing else to do and we were resting. She usually told them when we had visitors. My mother and the visitors told stories to each other while I stayed awake and listened to them. (T.88.23.ABC)

Interviewees tell of learning the stories by hearing them often and sometimes repeating them among children. They tell of correcting each other when a story detail is left out, but children are rarely quizzed about the content.

Adults link the theme of a story to specific contexts when they want to control the behavior of a child. When I asked, "What stories do you remember hearing from your parents or grandparents?" the first story that always came to mind was one about the jaguar, usually told in the context of trying to keep children quiet.

M: My grandfather told stories to me. He told them at night, telling us, "We must be quiet at night or a jaguar will come and eat us." I was naive in those days, so I always stayed close to my grandfather because he would be my defense. I stayed quiet. (T.88.02.RAM)

R: What did the children think of these stories?
F: The stories were usually told at night. They were about the jaguar, so we would be afraid and not play around, be respectful, and not make noise at night.
R: Do you tell these stories to your children?
F: I try to tell them to my children, though they are very small. I want them to be afraid of the jaguar because with this fear, they will be quiet in the afternoon, so I can rest and they will obey better. (T.88.04.EVE)

F: Some of these stories scared me, especially those about accidents. I tell these stories to my children to tell them, "If you don't obey this or that, the jaguar might eat you." This keeps the children from playing and making a lot of noise at night. My mother and older sisters would spin cotton and talk while the younger children slept quietly. (T.88.07.LOL)

Ashéninkas say that the jaguar is naturally attracted to noise, which gives some legitimacy to the link between being quiet and avoiding the jaguar. Parents use this excuse, however, to coerce their children to be quiet when there is no obvious danger from the jaguar. The utility of the story as a tool for child manipulation is eventually "caught" and internalized by older children. At a certain point, the jaguar stories help individual caregivers coerce children into appropriate behavior. The permanence and prominence of the jaguar stories is assured by their utility in the socialization process.

The jaguar stories and social control

The jaguar is the most feared of jungle animals. In dozens of jaguar stories, the jaguar is a buffoon that is easily fooled by lesser animals; in others, the jaguar is defeated by Ashéninka heroes; and in most stories, the jaguar punishes someone for improper behavior. The following story tells how having a bad attitude caused palm grubs to turn into a jaguar and kill a complaining woman.

Grubs that turned into a jaguar

Once, a man went looking for edible grubs. He took his wife and his two sisters with him. When they found the grubs, they put them in the wife's basket.

One sister looked into the basket of her sister-in-law and complained, "My sister-in-law won't give me any grubs."

Her sister-in-law answered, "Sister-in-law, we all live in the same house, cook, and eat together."

The man's sister wanted to fill her basket with grubs, too. The man said to his sisters, "Let's go."

Figure 3.1 Grubs that turned into a jaguar

"Okay, since you have yours." The woman was angry with her brother and would not go home with him. The man and his wife went back to their house without them. The wife cooked the grubs and they ate them.

As the two sisters returned home, one complained about her brother, saying, "He wouldn't give me any grubs. He's stingy."

As they went along the trail, she felt the basket on her shoulders become very heavy, *metzitzitzi*. When she looked back, she saw a jaguar. Her anger caused the grubs to turn into a jaguar. The jaguar attacked the woman and ate her, *pok*. Then it ate the other sister too, *pok*.

The brother waited all night for his sisters to return. At dawn, he went to look for them. He arrived where the jaguar had eaten the women. He saw their blood, and knew they had been eaten by a jaguar.

That is what we have heard about the people who were eaten by the grubs that changed into a jaguar. (Translated from *Mavo ipeyanacari cashecari* by Alberto Pablo Ravírez (Anderson 1985).)

The woman's bad attitude in this story resulted from anger toward her brother expressed in complaining. The jaguar not only ate the guilty person, but her innocent companion also.

A bad attitude toward certain animals can bring negative outcomes also. In the following story, a frivolous attitude toward a species of worm resulted in a near tragedy.

The woodworm changes into a jaguar

A man always made fun of the woodworm. That is why one day, the worm changed into a jaguar. The jaguar came to the house of the man at night and carried away his three-month-old baby. The father did not notice that the jaguar had taken his child, though the baby lay between the mother and father.

Later, the jaguar vomited the baby next to the trail, the baby still being alive. The mother heard the jaguar scream. She arose quickly, *tonkorek*, looked for her baby, but did not find him. She said to her husband, "Get up! Enough sleep! Where's my son?"

The husband got up and lit his lamp. He was frightened when he heard his son crying by the trail.

His wife went toward the sound, carrying a burning ember, moving it from side to side, *menki, menki,* looking for the child. She found her son with his diaper very wet. She carried him home. There she warmed water and washed off the jaguar's vomit. The mother cried, saying, "Fortunately, the jaguar didn't eat my son."

From that time on, the mother took special care of the boy. He grew up, married, and had children.

That is the story of the woodworm that changed into a jaguar. (Translated from *Queshito ipeya cashecari* by Alberto Pablo Ravírez (Anderson 1986b).)

Figure 3.2 The woodworm changes into a jaguar

Such stories are told with sufficient detail that a child has difficulty determining if the story is totally fictional.

Shamans and jaguars are closely linked in Ashéninka culture because shamans are believed to have the power to convert themselves at will into a jaguar. Being a shaman used to be an attractive occupation because a man could protect himself and help others, while holding the prestige of one that has curative powers. Ashéninka mothers used to encourage their daughters to marry shamans and sometimes offered two daughters in marriage to a powerful shaman. The following story tells of a young man who falsely claimed to be a shaman so he could impress three potential wives, but he was punished by a real shaman-jaguar for his deception.

The liar

A man wanted to be a great shaman, so he grew a lot of tobacco. This man wanted to change into a jaguar like the best shamans. He often painted his mouth with tobacco paste, so people would think he were a shaman.

One day at a party, the man who pretended to be a shaman yelled, "Danger!"

He painted a stick of balsa wood, *sakiri, sakiri,* to resemble the tail of a jaguar. The man attached the stick as if it were his tail. He went to his pineapple garden where the trail was always cleared, took off his *cushma,* hung it on a tree, and roared like a jaguar, *jaaam, jaaam.* To be more like a jaguar, he took sticks and scratched the ground, *manthari, manthari.*

A real shaman came and said, "Where is the owner of the house?"

"He left, saying there was danger."

The shaman called for silence, and since he knew about these things, he said, "No, he is lying."

Then the liar returned and said, "Did you hear the danger."

"Yes, we heard it."

The party continued into the night. The liar said, "Don't celebrate any more because there is a big danger."

Since the real shaman knew of his deception, he said, "No, I don't see anything. I've looked everywhere."

The liar responded, "Something bad is going to happen tonight."

Everyone stayed together. The liar secretly painted his mouth with tobacco paste. He went to his garden and tried to scare the others by roaring, *jaaam, chaaa, chaaa,* as if he were a jaguar.

Then the real shaman came, but the liar didn't know he was a shaman. The liar said, "Friend, tonight something bad is going to happen."

The shaman, who was accustomed to drinking tobacco juice said, "How do you know what's going to happen?"

Then the liar took his balsa wood stick and went into his pineapple garden. He put his *cushma* beneath a log. While the women were partying, the liar growled, *jaaam, jaaam.* At the same time, the real shaman climbed a tree, *takik,* from where he watched. He saw the liar with his fake tail, scratching the ground. The liar appeared very brave. The shaman, however, turned himself into a real jaguar and roared, *jaaam*. Then he sprang on the liar, *pok*. The liar screamed, "Ooo, ooo, ooo! Jaguar! Jaguar!" The jaguar scratched the shoulder of the man, *manthari, manthari*. The liar ran to his house. He was naked, with scratches all over his body. He was so scared that he did not remember that he was naked. The real shaman laughed and said, "Friend, why do you say you are a shaman?"

The real shaman went home. The liar sat there, meditating. Three sisters were there who wanted to marry him because they thought he was a great shaman. They said to him, "Where did the jaguar scratch you?"

"Here."

"Why?"

"I was disoriented, so he attacked me."

One sister said to the others, "Sisters, we have to marry him. When we get sick, he can cure us."

Figure 3.3 The liar

The women began to tease and flirt with the liar because they wanted to marry him. One of them said, "Are you accustomed to drinking tobacco juice?"

"Sure, I always drink it."

"Can you drink all that is in your bamboo tube?"

"Sure, I can."

"Do it now, so we can admire you."

Since the liar wanted to show off, he drank all the tobacco at once, *kori, kori, kori.* He drank it all, though he never before had any. The girls began to laugh because they had caused him to drink it all. The youngest sister said, "Sisters, look, he's going to vomit."

The liar felt dizzy and began to sing: *Ayahuasca, ayahuasca, ayahuasca.* He was singing because he was about to die. He was staggering. The girls giggled, *iii, iii, iii.* The man vomited, *mook, mook, mook,* convulsed, and died.

That is how the liar died when three sisters made him drink tobacco. (Translated from *Ashéninca thaivari* by Alberto Pablo Ravírez (Anderson 1985).)

The man in this story made the error of falsely claiming to be a shaman and doing something dangerous to show off to potential wives. These attitudes and behaviors have predictable results in Ashéninka stories: the deceptive person is always found out and the person who foolishly does dangerous things always dies.

Ashéninka children are taught to keep their distance from old men who might be shamans and to show respect for older people, never laughing at them or making jokes about them. The following story tells about a shaman who turned into a jaguar after a woman teased him.

The jaguar and the two women

A jaguar appeared as a man to two women when the husband of one of them had gone hunting. He had previously arranged to have his wife's sister stay with her while he was gone.

Near evening, they saw an old man leaning on a staff, coming up the trail. He greeted the women, saying, "Hello, granddaughters!"

They replied, "Hello, grandfather. Rest here."

The old man (who was really a jaguar) said, "Thank you."

The sister who was a teaser asked, "Grandfather, where are you going?"

He replied, "I'm going upstream to see my squash garden."

The woman laughed at the old man. She kept laughing and said, "Grandfather, the garden where you plant squash is upstream?"

Her sister scolded her, but she paid no attention. The old man left in the evening. The wife watched where he went. When he was in the shadows, she saw him crouch down and turn into a huge jaguar. She said to her sister, "Did you see that? Why were you teasing that old man? He isn't human like us; he's a jaguar. He will surely return tonight to eat us."

The woman quickly built a ladder and climbed to the top of the house to stay all night. She called, "Sister, come up here. Climb the ladder!"

But her sister replied, "No, my grandfather told me to wait for him."

She sat below on the floor. In the middle of the night, the wife heard something come running, *tek, tek, tek.* She looked below, and saw a jaguar by her sister. From the roof, the woman heard the jaguar eating her sister.

When full, the jaguar went next to a large buttress of a tree and fell asleep.

Figure 3.4 The jaguar and the two women

When the husband arrived, the woman immediately told him what had happened. She said, "My sister was eaten by the jaguar that is resting by the buttress of that tree."

When the husband heard this, he quickly hit the jaguar with an ax until it died.

That is the story of the two women. One was eaten because she teased an old man. (Translated from *Cashecari ipeyari atziri* by Alberto Pablo Ravírez (Anderson 1986b).)

The woman who teased the old man did not heed the scolding of her sister to leave the man alone. Again, the jaguar is portrayed as an instrument of punishment to those of bad behavior. This story has multiple applications. It not only warns against being disrespectful of old people and not ignoring the advice of others, but it also warns children to avoid strangers.

Stories portray events that could happen to anyone. In the following interview, a young woman makes reference to a story similar to the one above.

F: We would be playing in the moonlight and someone would say to be careful, because the jaguar might come as a man like in the stories. So we look to see if a person is coming, thinking we will run away. (T.88.07.LOL)

Other stories are similar to those of the jaguar, telling of snakes, owls, and warriors harming people for their incorrect behaviors. The following interviews tell of children's fears of agents of punishment.

R: Did someone tell you stories in the night?

F: Yes, I was told stories about the jaguars. My mother told us that we must not make noise or the jaguar might come. When I was a child, they said the jaguar is attracted to the noise. I took this very seriously, and even on the trail, we hardly made any noise, in case the jaguar would be nearby. I was always afraid in the night when my mother told me these stories. Because of this, I obeyed my mother in everything. She told us these stories almost every night, about the jaguars and the warriors. If we were not quiet, the warriors might come. We all stayed quiet. (T.88.16.ROS)

M: My grandmother told stories to me about the jaguar, so we would be scared and go to bed quickly. Yes, jaguars and owls. They also told stories to us so I would not fight with my sister or play rough with her. If we played rough, a snake would constrict and kill us. That is what they told us. They told us so we would go to sleep right away. (T.87.11.ALE)

Some Ashéninkas deny being told stories about the jaguar. They are, however, aware of the lore linking the jaguar and its punishment for bad behavior.

R: Did someone tell you stories at night?

M: No. Neither my father nor mother told stories to me. My father had two wives, so I was somewhat neglected.

R: Did they ever say that a jaguar would come and punish you?

M: Yes, they always threatened us with this. When we fought, my mother said, "A jaguar might come in the night and eat you. It is not good that you fight. You must remain silent." My mother also told me that the jaguar would come if I cried because I had to go to the bathroom. She said I had to be quiet or the jaguar would come. I was afraid, so I stayed quiet. I knew that jaguars used to live in that area, so I thought the best thing to do was to stay quiet. (T.88.14.ALB)

The Ashéninka believe that stories about the jaguar and similar agents of punishment effectively convince young children to adopt Ashéninka norms of human conduct. As a child matures, he learns that reference to the jaguar and other agents outside the parents serve as effective control agents.

Ashéninka values expressed in traditional stories

Anger

The Ashéninka view expression of anger as a negative character trait. Once, an Ashéninka man and his two-year-old son visited me, when, to my astonishment, the little boy bit his father's knuckle as hard as possible. The father grimaced in obvious pain, but he tried to smile as he gently and slowly pried the boy's mouth from his finger. Greatly relieved when freed, he said, "Sometimes he likes to bite." Acceptable Ashéninka rage does happen, but rarely, and only in special circumstances, e.g., when someone has been murdered, a careless child has broken something of value, or a child causes another child to bleed. An enraged Ashéninka will try to kill a murderer or whip the offending child with nettles until his rage has passed.

M: After this, I was playing with my brother in the house of my father. My father was getting drunk while we were playing on the porch. We both fell off the porch (five feet high), fell on some firewood, and started to bleed—me on the head and my brother in the mouth. Because my father was drunk, he grabbed his arrows and wanted to kill me. I lunged to the side, and the arrow passed through my *cushma*. I ran into a ditch near the river by my uncle's house. That is where I escaped to. My father almost killed me because I wasn't obedient. When my father told me to do something, I knew I must do it. From then on, I stopped playing so much. I told my friends, "If you want to play, I cannot because if something happens, my father will hit me." I didn't have anyone to play with any more. I was afraid that something would happen and my father would kill me. He punished me hard. (T.87.02.APR)

The Ashéninka must be pleasant in their everyday relationships; they must not complain or show anger and severe mood changes. Traditional stories often portray people who have the negative trait of unjustified anger. In the following story, the main character shows patience with his angry wife until he finally decides to leave her.

The deer family

Long ago there was a man whose wife got mad at him very often.

One day he went hunting. The man shot a monkey and brought it to his wife in an attempt to make her happy. But her happiness didn't last very long. She cooked it for him, and then they ate it. But soon she got mad again.

The husband lost his patience with her. He said, "I've married her for nothing. She's no good. She is always getting mad! I think I'll go marry someone else who doesn't get angry. It's good that I can go hunting and get meat, so that we can all eat. But it's no good for me to continue in this situation."

He went hunting again. When he arrived at the woods he saw a well-used trail. He thought to himself, "I think I'll go find out who lives there." When he arrived, he found himself in the manioc patch. He walked on to the house. He saw a girl. She stood very tall.

She greeted him, "What?"

He replied, "Nothing. How about your family?"

"They are in another *chacra* 'garden' cultivating beans." The man sat down. When the sun was setting, they came back. They saw the one who had come.

They asked the girl, "Who has come?" Father was tall; his *cushma* came only to his knees, and he had long feet. He greeted the man, "What is it, my son?"

The man said, "Nothing."

"Where are you going?"

"Nowhere, I've just come to see you."

They had beans cooked with peppers for supper. The father had asked the man before eating, "Do you eat beans?" "Yes, I do," the man had replied. They also ate soup made of *pikoka* leaves. Everyone went to bed.

Early the next morning, the man and the father went to the *chacra*. They saw many trees weighted down with fruit. They went over to the beans. The father said, "These are a different kind of beans; they are *hiriki* beans." They went back to the house. The man was shown everything there was to see. Well, he stayed there several days.

One morning he decided to go back home. The family said they were going to the *chacra*. The man replied, "I think I'll go home." "Do you want to take some beans?" "Yes, I think that I will. Give me some!" The father gave him some which he put in his bag. "If you tell anybody about me I'll be mad at you," the father said.

"Okay, I won't tell."

"What are you going to say when you get home?"

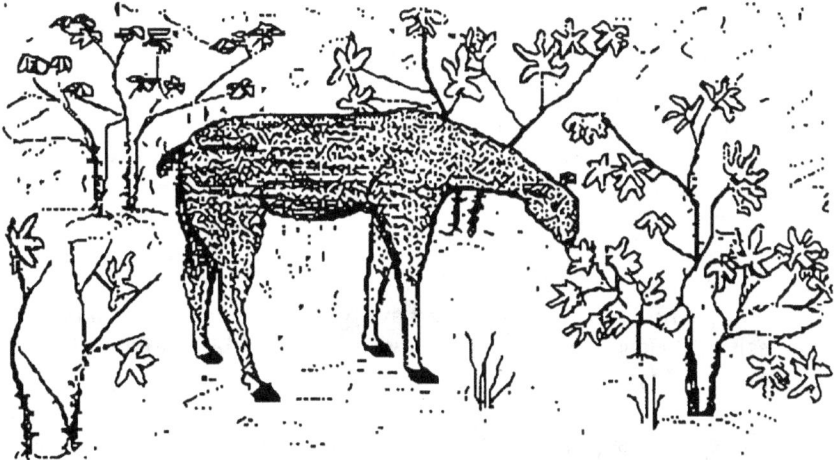

Figure 3.5 The deer family

"I'll tell them that I went visiting and got some beans from the people."

"Okay, you tell them that. Do you have a wife?" inquired the father.

"Yes, but my wife is no good; she is always mad at me. And that's why I came here. If she hadn't been mad at me, I wouldn't have come. I became impatient because she was always mad at me!"

The father of the deer family asked, "Would you like to come here?"

"Yes, I would like to stay here."

"Then maybe you can marry my daughter when you return."

"Well, perhaps."

They left and went into the forest. When they reached the edge of the forest, the deer said, "This is where I will leave you."

The deer turned around to go home. When the man got to his house, his wife was mad at him. She wouldn't talk to him. She didn't even say, "Have you come?" Nothing!

When he got inside, he sat down. His sisters were there. "Brother, where did you go?" his sisters asked.

"I went and slept in the forest. I saw the people who live there."

"We've been looking for you these past days. 'What is brother doing? He should be coming,' we said."

"I stayed there for a long time. I was going to come back here to stay but it's no good. They gave me these beans." He brought his shoulder bag around to the front. There was fertilizer all mixed up with the beans. The man picked the beans out and threw the fertilizer away. The deer father was outside listening. When he heard this he went and slept.

The next morning the man said to his sisters, "I am going hunting." His sisters waited and waited for him to come home. But he didn't come.

"Where could our brother have gone?" they asked themselves. "He's gone now, and we won't see him anymore." Finally, his sisters saw him coming.

He said, "I am coming to get all my things. I am going to live alone. It wasn't good for me to get married. I am frustrated over marrying her, for she always is getting mad at me."

His sisters cried, "Don't go!"

"Nothing doing, I am leaving now, and I am not coming back." His brother-in-law tried to follow him, but he couldn't find him. When he arrived at the deer house, he married the deer's daughter.

Yes, I've heard it all as they tell the stories. That is all. (Kindberg n.d.:40–43)

This story contrasted the patient husband and the angry wife. In the end, the wife got her punishment of losing her husband and the man got his reward of a new wife. Stories like these present ideals of Ashéninka character.

Obedience

Ashéninka children are taught to be obedient to their caregivers and to avoid dangerous things. A widespread story tells of a boy who was disobedient and did dangerous things, resulting in his forever becoming the man in the moon.

Arooshi

Long ago, a boy named Arooshi was very brave but disobedient, teasing things that were dangerous. His father would say, "Son, don't tease dangerous things."

Arooshi answered, "Don't worry, nothing will happen."

Arooshi went into the woods and met a spider resting in his house. The spider's bow and arrows were in the corner. Arooshi said to him, "Brother-in-law, are your bow and arrows dangerous?"

The spider replied, "Yes, they are dangerous. I always hunt deer with them."

"Really? I don't believe you. Shoot me in the finger. I want to test it."

"No, brother-in-law. If I shoot, you will die."

Arooshi teased the spider. He picked up the spider's foot and said, "Shoot me, brother-in-law, so I can feel the pain. Then I will know that it can kill a deer."

The spider got angry with Arooshi. He strung his bow and shot Arooshi in the finger, *tsitok*. It bled, *tsiririri*. Soon, Arooshi was spitting blood, *tho, tho, tho*, and died.

Arooshi's father waited for him to return, but he did not. He looked for his son until he arrived at the spider's house. He found his son already dead. The father blew over Arooshi to resuscitate him and carried him back to the house.

Another day, Arooshi went into the forest. He encountered a rock that was about to fall. Arooshi said to it, "Sister, can you run? Chase me to see if you can catch me."

The rock answered, "Yes, brother, I run fast. If I run, you will die when I crush you."

"How can you run fast? Let me see your feet."

"No, brother, I won't chase you."

"Let's go, sister. I will run ahead and you follow."

"No, brother, because you will die."

"Let's go, sister."

"Why do you tease me, brother? Let's go, then."

The rock fell, *tzirek*. It chased Arooshi, *tok, tok, tok*, and crushed all his bones. When the rock stopped, all that was left of Arooshi were a few pieces of flesh stuck to the rock.

Arooshi's father waited for his return. When he did not return, the father went to look for him. He found the rock with Arooshi's body stuck to it. The father gathered the pieces of his body into a small pile and blew on it, resuscitating Arooshi. They walked back to the house.

Later, Arooshi returned to the jungle, where he met a hummingbird that was bathing. He said to the hummingbird, "Brother-in-law, are you bathing?"

"Yes," said the hummingbird. "Come and join me."

"Thank you, I will."

Arooshi came closer, putting his medal on a rock. The hummingbird said to Arooshi, "Brother-in-law, give me your medal."

"No, brother-in-law, it's mine."

Arooshi did not leave the water because he was having fun. The hummingbird flew off, carrying Arooshi's medal. When Arooshi left the water, he found neither the hummingbird nor his medal. Arooshi put on his clothing and ran to his father, saying, "Father, the hummingbird stole my medal."

"What? I don't know anything about this," said his father.

Arooshi made a hunting-blind to kill hummingbirds, so he could find his medal. He killed many, but did not find his medal. Arooshi became angry and thought, "Since the hummingbird stole my medal, I will find a better one."

That night, Arooshi saw the bright moon rise and thought, "How can I get to the moon? I want a piece of the moon for a new medal."

Figure 3.6 Arooshi

Arooshi went to his father and said, "Father, I'm going to visit the moon."

"Don't go. You'll never get that far."

"I'm going, even if it takes me a long time."

Arooshi left. It took a long time, but he finally arrived at the place where the moon lives. Arooshi visited the moon's wife who is named Mavitaro [Venus]. She said to Arooshi, "My husband will kill you. I don't kill people, but my sister does. Her name is Kinankaro [Mars]."

"Okay, thank you."

Arooshi hid in the grass to wait for the moon. As it got dark, Arooshi sharpened his ax, so he could chop off a piece of the moon. He saw the moon rising. Arooshi climbed the hill, *tok, tok, tok*, thinking, "Now I will chop off a piece." Arooshi grabbed his ax and climbed quietly up the hill, *ef, ef, ef*. He suddenly left his hiding place and gave a shout of challenge to the moon. The moon said to him, "Arooshi, I'm going to pick you up by your collar!"

Arooshi chopped at him in the forehead, *tyak*. The moon reached out his hand and grabbed Arooshi, *shepik*, around the neck and picked him up.

Arooshi's father waited at home for his son. After many days, he went to search for Arooshi. He looked up in the sky and saw Arooshi in the moon. His father went to visit the moon, saying, "Brother-in-law, give me my son."

"I can't."

"Brother-in-law, give me just a little of his fingernail."

"I can't give you anything. I'm going to keep him."

The moon would not give Arooshi back to his father. If the moon had given him a fingernail, the father could have resuscitated Arooshi, but the moon did not want to do it.

That is why we see a man in the center of the moon. It is Arooshi. He was disobedient to his father and teased dangerous things.

That is the story of Arooshi. (Translated from *Arooshi* by Alberto Pablo Ravírez (Anderson 1985).)

The themes of disobedience, danger, and bad consequences are repeated often in this story. The Ashéninka use the moon for their calendar and lighting at night. Reference to the man in the moon may remind children of the Arooshi story. All Ashéninka adults know at least the gist of the story and can point to Arooshi.

The story "The jaguar and the two women" referred to the danger of speaking with a stranger. Ashéninka children are taught to be suspicious of everything they encounter, in case it is the manifestation of a demon or has some other power that can hurt them. Ignoring such warnings and disobeying the advice of a parent can result in a fate similar to that in the following story.

Two women and a boa

Once, two sisters went to a lake. Their father told them, "Daughters, don't play with anything that you find near the lake. You could have an accident or the owner of the lake (the boa) may grab you."

The girls arrived at the lake. They walked along the edge of the lake, it being dry. They found a *papagayo* parrot calling, *aaa, aaa, aaa.* One girl said to her sister, "Let's catch the *papagayo* and make a pet of it."

They followed the *papagayo* to catch it. It flew to a branch that hung over the lake, *sapok, sapok, sapok.* One girl said, "Sister, reach for it so it will return."

The girl got a pole, but could not reach it. The lake did not overflow its bank, though it always overflows when people pass by it. One sister said, "I don't think the lake is going to overflow this time, but if it does, we'll run."

They caught the beautiful *papagayo,* put it in their basket, and left the lake and went to the house of their uncle. They stayed a little while and returned to the lake with the *papagayo.* One girl felt her basket get heavy. When she looked to see what had made it so heavy, she saw a huge boa. She called her sister, "*Eee!* Sister!"

Figure 3.7 Two women and a boa

She wanted to run away, but the boa wrapped around her, *pok.* It was like someone had tied her up. Her sister came running to cut the boa, but she felt something grab her feet, *shepik.* She couldn't cut it. The lake overflowed, *tok, mooo.* The lake grew and, *pok,* carried off the two girls.

When their father saw that the girls did not return, he went to find them. He went to the uncle's house and said, "Brother, have you seen your nieces?"

"They left a while ago carrying a *papagayo* in a basket. Let's look for them."

They went to look for the girls. When they came to the river, they saw the *papagayo* flying. The uncle said, "That's the *papagayo* that my nieces had. Let's trap it."

The *papagayo* escaped to the center of the lake. The father
said, "Brother, let's shoot it with arrows."

When they shot it, they saw the *papagayo* convert itself into a
big boa. The boa fell, *tok.* The lake began to overflow and almost grabbed the men, but they escaped. They stood on a hill,
watching the lake. After a while, the lake returned to normal.

Another day, the man returned to the lake and saw his
daughters in the middle of the lake. He called to them,
"Daughters, come! What are you doing in the lake? Take care
that it doesn't carry you away."

They were on their way to their father when the lake overflowed again, *tok*, and carried them back. They were
completely lost, being carried off by the lake. (Translated
from *Apite cooya ipoña noonque* by Alberto Pablo Ravírez (Anderson 1985).)

The Ashéninka like to make pets of colorful birds. This story tells of the
danger of capturing a pet. Another lesson in this story is to obey a parent's
warning to avoid lakes, because one never knows when the lake will suddenly rise and carry one away.

Children are taught to be obedient to their parents whenever asked to
do a chore around the house. Parents typically yell at a disobedient child.

R: Do you remember being yelled at by your mother?
F: I only remember that I was yelled at by my mother when I was disobedient. She told me to do something I did not want to do, so she
yelled at me. My mother said something like, "What can you be
thinking of that you cannot bring me water." But when my mother
was happy with me, she did not yell. (T.88.17.LAU)

Disobedience is always punished in Ashéninka traditional stories.
Sometimes, a warning not to do something is accompanied by the promise
of a negative consequence.

The man who disobeyed his grandfather

Long ago, a man disobeyed his grandfather. His grandfather said to him, "Grandson, when you make your *chacra,*
you must not look at the parrots. If you do, weeds will grow
in your *chacra.*"

The man did not obey his grandfather. He laughed at him
and said, "Grandpa, how do you know that when you look at
a parrot, weeds will grow in your *chacra*? You are teasing me.
I'm going to my *chacra*. I want to watch the weeds grow."

Figure 3.8 The man who disobeyed his grandfather

Then the grandfather blew and said, "You fool, grandson, all your life you have been disobedient to the advice given to you. Now you will see weeds in your *chacra*."

When it began to get dry, this man made his *chacra*. He burned it and cleared it. He planted manioc, and it began to grow. The next day, he saw that weeds were growing all over his *chacra*. He weeded rapidly, but he could not keep up with them. He could not plant more manioc and could not eat the manioc that was planted.

This is what happened every time he planted a *chacra*, because he disobeyed his grandfather.

That is what happened to the man who disobeyed the advice of his grandfather. (Translated from *Apaani Ashéninca ithainquiri icharine* by Alberto Pablo Ravírez (Anderson 1986b).)

This story combines the themes of disobedience, lack of respect, and the power of older people to curse someone who behaves badly.

Disobeying others' warnings brings negative results in many Ashéninka stories. The fear of the jaguar and a fear of other consequences associated with disobedience strengthen the relationship between child and adult.

This type of story supports the role of the adult as a socializing agent to make the child more willing to receive instruction.

Respect for privacy

The Ashéninka value their own and others' privacy. They do not ask for an inventory of another's possessions, and they do not ask about another's business.

R: Why is it that the small children do not bother me when I am eating by myself?
F: We always tell children not to watch other people eat, saying, "Only the dogs watch people eat to see what they will give them (laughs)." When I was young, I was afraid to get close to people because my mother told me that others would kidnap me, that they came to steal small children. When someone came to visit, we hid until the people went away. We never watched others eat; it was not our custom. I do not tell my children to be as afraid of people as I was. I do tell them not to watch other people eat, but to wait for them to finish eating and then play with them. (T.88.13.VIC)

Whenever I asked for information about another person, a common reply was, "Why don't you ask him yourself?" Ashéninka children are discouraged from being too inquisitive; asking too many questions is considered pestering. The following story tells how continuing with persistent questioning brings bad outcomes.

The flood (part 2)

The flood also changed the manioc to what we see now in the jungle, what looks like manioc but is not. The children of the shaman stayed on the raft. The shaman had a young daughter. One day, the daughter said to her mother, "Mother, I'm a woman now."

"Fine."

The mother made a little hut for her. The daughter sat in the hut with nothing to eat. She took a bit of mud and began to form manioc out of it. When it dried, she cooked it. When done, she ate it because there was no manioc. All the food had disappeared with the flood.

A big grasshopper we call *oretsi* was in the house with the girl. This grasshopper changed into a person for the girl. Her mother did not know anything about him because they talked quietly. Since the grasshopper was a person, he said to the girl, "Step on my stomach. If you step on my stomach, manioc will come out."

Without thinking, the girl stepped on the stomach of the grasshopper and a big manioc came out, *sopirek*. Since she could not cook it in her little hut, she gave it to her mother. The girl said, "Mother, here's some manioc."

When the mother saw the manioc, she was thrilled and said, "Daughter, where did you get this manioc?"

The daughter replied, "Why ask me questions? Just cook it."

The mother cooked the manioc, and everyone ate it because they had been eating only dirt. The grasshopper appeared to the girl again and said, "Step on me again."

Figure 3.9 The flood

She stepped on him and bananas came out.

"Step on me again."

This time, *pitucas* came out. She continued stepping on his stomach and all the different kinds of food came out. She put them all outside her hut, giving them to her mother. Her mother said to her, "Where are you getting this food, since you don't have anything in there?"

The girl had an older brother. He said to her, "Sister, where did you get the manioc?"

The young girl got angry and would not tell them. Her mother said to her, "If you can get manioc, then maybe you can get cuttings of manioc, bananas, *pituca*, *daledale*, *sachapapa*, and other plants."

The girl replied, "Yes, I'll get them for you."

She went into her hut again. The grasshopper again appeared and said, "Step on my stomach."

She stepped on it, and out came cuttings of manioc. She stepped on his stomach again, and out came other plants. She gave them to her mother. She said, "Take these things that you asked for. Wait, and I'll get you some *pituca* seeds."

The girl returned to her hut. She stepped on the grasshopper's stomach, and out came *pituca* and *sachapapa* seeds. When her mother received the seeds, she took them to plant. The brother prepared the garden for planting the manioc, *pituca*, bananas, *sachapapa*, and *daledale*. There was nothing, however, to eat unless the girl stepped on the grasshopper's stomach.

The brother continued asking the girl about the manioc, though he had planted it and it was growing. She grew tired of his questions. The mother said to him, "Don't bother your sister. Don't ask her any more questions."

The girl said, "I don't have a place where I get the manioc; a grasshopper gives it to me."

He said to her, "Who is this grasshopper? How can it give you manioc?"

"Don't ask me any more questions."

The brother kept asking, "Where do you get the manioc?"

"Don't ask me any more, brother. The grasshopper *oretsi* gave me the manioc and all that we eat."

When the grasshopper heard her tell this, he became embarrassed and never returned. She waited, but he did not return. There was nothing to eat. The grasshopper stayed as an insect, though he wanted to marry the girl. The mother looked for the grasshopper, too, so he would give her daughter more manioc. They had nothing to eat since the previous night.

The girl was angry with her brother and said to him, "Brother, you kept pestering me with your questions. Now you bring us manioc to eat!"

That is the way they all scolded the brother who had asked the questions. The manioc continued to grow. Since the manioc was not ready to eat, they returned to eating dirt.

When the girl left her hut, she sang a song of blessing over the manioc. The manioc continued to grow and was soon good to eat. It multiplied, and now everyone can eat it.

The brother of the girl continued to plant more manioc stalks. Large manioc *chacras* ended the famine. There were bananas, manioc, and all the plants that we know today. We would not have anything to eat if it were not for the girl and the *oretsi* grasshopper. (Translated from *Ooncantacari quipatsi* by Alberto Pablo Ravírez (Anderson 1985).)

This and other stories tell of secret, magical things that must not be revealed to a third party. In this story, the mother of the woman had the correct response of not inquiring about the gift of food, but the brother had the incorrect response of insisting on discovering the secret. The attitude promoted in this story discourages personal aggressiveness in social relationships.

Honesty

The Ashéninka are well-known for their meticulous honesty that, at times, causes them to suffer in their economic relations with mestizos. The following is an outsider's account of the Ashéninka reputation for honesty.

In some areas, patrons give things to the Campas to get them in debt, and then oblige them to work. Only because the Campa is honorable enough to pay off his debts does this system work. Very rarely does a Campa fail in the end to pay work debts or trading debts. He does not forget promises. Because of this, he has difficulty understanding how outsiders can make promises and never give another thought to keeping them. If the Campa has something that someone else in the community needs, he usually lends it to him at no charge or, in the case of food, it is shared. (Kindberg, personal communication)

The Ashéninka give many different explanations for not stealing. They generally believe that thievery is offensive, shameful, and the thief will always be discovered and punished. The following interview tells of the bad consequences of stealing.

R: Parents tell stories about this?

M: Yes. You must not steal because if you steal from a witch, he knows instantly that you stole from him. He can bewitch you and you will die. You can be bewitched or shot with an arrow. It is worse if you steal something to eat and someone has put poison in it. With these thoughts, children don't touch anything belonging to another. (T.87.01.ABC)

Ashéninka honesty goes beyond not taking something from among another's possessions. They will not even touch something that has accidentally fallen on the trail, in case they might be accused of taking it. The proper action when finding something lost by another is to leave it there and to let everyone know what was found and where they saw it.

R: What were you taught about stealing?

M: When our parents take us to another home, we see the things that are thrown around and are told, "Do not take the things you see around here. If you want something, ask the owner for it." I never took anything that was not mine. (T.88.04.ELI)

R: What were you told about stealing?

F: My mother said that if I found something, I should not touch it. I was very young. They always told me that. I never touched something belonging to another. (T.88.08.FLO)

R: How did your mother teach you not to steal?

F: For things like stealing and honor, my mother was very strict in controlling us. She said that when she was a child, it was disgusting to think that a child would take things that were not his. This person was severely criticized. My mother said that it was not good to touch the things that are not ours. If we find something lying on the ground, we must not touch it. She said, "Leave it there. When the owner comes, he will take it away. It should stay there." (T.88.20.JOS)

R: Did anyone tell you not to steal?

F: My mother and father always told me, "You must not touch the things of your playmates when you visit them, not even the things that have fallen to the ground. You must not touch them, but tell the owner that it is on the ground, saying, 'Whose is this?' Otherwise you might learn to steal." They said this a lot. (T.88.13.VIC)

The Ashéninka directly ask for something from another. They might ask for medicines, food, or tools. The person who owns the item must give it to the person who asks for it, unless the owner talks him into letting him keep his own things. The free sharing of possessions makes theft especially offensive.

Traditional stories tell of thieves and their unhappy end. The following stories are typical.

The thief and the tar baby

Once, a man had the bad habit of stealing chickens. He painted his face with carbon so no one could recognize him.

But the owner of the chickens thought of a way to discover who was stealing his chickens. He said to his wife, "Who is stealing our chickens? Why don't we see tracks and feathers?"

In the evening, he took ashes and scattered them around the door of the chicken coop. When he went to sleep, the thief came and took another chicken, not knowing of the trap.

The next morning, the owner of the chickens went to the coop. He saw the footprints of the thief. He said, "It's a person who's stealing my chickens."

Figure 3.10 The thief and the tar baby

He became very angry. He went to the jungle and gathered some sap from the *thonkitziro* tree. He cooked it, mixing it with the sap of the *jopo* tree, until it was very sticky. Then he made it into the form of a person.

In the evening, he put the tar man at the door of the coop. When the thief came, he saw the tar man. He spoke to it, thinking that it was the owner of the chickens, but it did not answer. He came closer. He tried to knock it down, but it stuck to his hands. He could not get it off.

The thief screamed in vain, but he could do nothing. No one gave him anything to eat, so he died. That is what happened to the man who stole chickens. (Translated from *Icantacota coshintzi* by Alberto Pablo Ravírez (Anderson 1986b).)

The thief

A man made a habit of stealing. He did not like to hunt with arrows or with a rifle—he only liked to eat chickens. That is how he lived.

When he felt hungry, he stole chickens from other people. He stole chickens every day, and no one knew who it was. Every time he stole a chicken, the owner said that a jaguar had eaten it. He continued stealing chickens, though once he was almost discovered. They trapped him, but he managed to escape. One owner of chickens finally figured out who was stealing. He put two chickens in the same door of his house. This was a trap to catch him, but the thief was smart, and did not go to steal them.

The thief went to the house of another man who had many chickens. The thief was in the chicken coop and made the chickens begin to squawk, *petapeta, petapetajaaa.* The owner heard the noise, went quickly, and locked the thief inside. He was locked inside and did not know how to get out.

The owner got all the chickens out of the coop. He put a light up to the coop and saw the thief. The thief pretended to be a jaguar, *jaaam, jaaam, jaaam.* The owner of the chickens became angry. He made sure the door was locked really well, *shoi, shoi, shoi,* and set fire to the coop, *tziririri.*

As the coop burned, the thief continued growling like a jaguar. Soon, embers began falling on his shoulders and he could not endure. It burned his entire body. He began to scream desperately, "*Eee,* you're burning me!"

Then the owner said, "We aren't going to save you. Go ahead and burn!"

When the fire got hotter, it burned his whole body and he died.

The father of the thief was sitting in his house, waiting for his return. He did not know what had happened. In the morning, the owner of the chickens recognized the thief. He said, "This is the man who kills chickens in other areas. It is not a jaguar; it is a man. Finally, the thief is dead. Now we must go to his father."

The owner of the chickens went to the house of the thief's father. When he arrived, he said, "Where is your son?"

The father answered, "He went to visit his uncle."

When the man heard this, he became very angry and said, "You're lying to me. He didn't go to visit his uncle. I found him in my chicken coop and burned him. He died because he was stealing my chickens."

When the father heard this, he became despondent and said, "It's good that you burned my son, because he was a thief."

Figure 3.11 The thief

The father of the thief was very sad. The next day, he went
to a ridge where *palmiche* palms were and built a house. He
did not notice that his house was on a trail that a jaguar always took, and he did not know what would happen. That
night he went to sleep. In the middle of the night, a jaguar
came and ate the father of the thief. It also ate his wife and
son.

That is the story of the man who had the habit of stealing.
(Translated from *Icantacota apaani Ashéninca coshintzi* by
Alberto Pablo Ravírez (Anderson 1986b).)

Though I know of children who have stolen things, family members are
shamed by such behavior. The family of a compulsive thief must move
away from others.

These stories and others are told to children to reinforce the value of
honesty. The following interviews refer to similar accounts of bad things
that happened to thieves.

F: They said that long ago, people who stole chickens had their hands
cut off. They said that if we stole things, people would cut off our
hands. Then what would we work with? We would have nothing to
eat. "You would die of hunger," they always said. After they said
this to us, we never touched the things that were not ours. When we
saw cooked meat, my mother always said, "Do not touch it if it is
not yours. Wait until I come, so we can eat it together, so you will
not learn to steal." I had to wait for my mother when she went to
the *chacra*, so we could eat together. She did not let me eat by myself. (T.88.13.VIC)

R: Did your parents teach you not to steal?
M: My mother always said, "It is better to ask for something than to
steal it. The day they catch you stealing something, they may kill
you. They can catch you and kill you." They told me the stories of
the thieves from past times. I was afraid to steal. Also, there was a
person who had stolen something and the villagers took him to
Puerto Bermúdez, where he was punished by the police. My mother
told us what he went through, how the police captured and hit him.
This scared me. (T.88.23.ABC)

R: In that village, was there someone who stole something?
F: I did not see it, but my father told me of a case of someone who
stole something. He was castigated and hit by others. They hit him
with sticks and did not give him anything to eat for part of the day.
(T.88.04.EVI)

The Ashéninka take great pains to avoid the appearance of stealing, but they are also direct in asking for something they want. Though the Ashéninka are trained to be nonassertive in social relationships, they are taught to be direct in expressing their desires. A child should not pester an adult who is working, but a child is expected to tell an adult when he wants to learn a skill or borrow materials to practice a skill. Children are taught through stories and example to display a balance between assertiveness and nonassertiveness that is uniquely Ashéninka.

Generosity

For the Ashéninka, stinginess is another character flaw that is discouraged. A person who does not share is considered bad. Ashéninkas must be generous in sharing what they have, whether it be meat after hunting or a shotgun for a neighbor to use. The following story tells of people's disgust with a person who is stingy, and of his unhappy end.

The stingy man

Once, there was a stingy fat man. One day, he went hunting and shot many doves. He gave one to his wife and kept the rest for himself. The man wrapped the doves in leaves. He ate them at night when his wife was asleep. When he wanted to eat, he put his wrapped doves in the coals and went back to bed. When the doves were cooked, he got up quietly, dug the doves out of the ashes, put them in his bed, *sherok*, and ate them. After eating them all, he went back to bed.

The wife of the man did not know that whenever he went hunting, he shot many doves, but gave her only one. He always said to her, "Never look in my bag."

One day, the man went to hunt near a stream. He shot many birds with his arrows. He gave two birds to his wife and kept the rest in his bag. While his wife slept that night, he roasted the other birds. He always did this. He never gave his wife and children sufficient food to fill their stomachs.

Another day, the man went fishing and returned with many small anchovies. Since he did not treat his wife well, he kept the biggest portion of them for himself. This time, the man would choke on the bones of the fish.

The next morning, he said to his wife, "Sweetheart, cook me some manioc."

She obeyed, because she did not know how stingy he had been with her. She said to him, "Here it is."

The stingy man was sitting in a house a little ways away. He secretly took an anchovy and put it in his manioc. After he did this, he began to eat, saying, "*Jiii*, friend, what kind of manioc is this? It's so delicious, *ijiii, jai, jai.*"

"What?"

"Friend, what kind of manioc do you grow?" (We always say, "Friend, what kind of manioc do you grow," and make a swallowing sound in our throat to show how much we like the manioc.)

The stingy man continued to eat his manioc. He took a large anchovy. He ate it while his wife ate her manioc with only a little salt. He was very happy with his anchovies.

To show he was very happy with his manioc, the man tried to make the swallowing noise in his throat, *koiii*, but a big bone stuck in his throat. He stood up, *tankorek*. He was frightened and yelled, "*Ajai!* What do I have stuck in my throat? It must be a manioc core."

"How can you choke on a manioc core?"

Figure 3.12 The stingy man

He could not swallow the bone, though he coughed with force, *kajaa*. He said, "You don't think I'm choking?"

"You can choke on manioc?"

He could not wait. He tried to cough up the bone, *kajaa, kajaa*. His wife asked, "What's happening?"

She called, "Neighbor, my husband is dying because he's choking on a manioc core."

The stingy man left the manioc where he put his anchovies. He tried again to cough up the bone, *kajaa, kajaa, kajaa*. His neighbor arrived as the man was about to die. He said, "Friend, what happened?"

The wife answered, "Your friend has a manioc core stuck in his throat."

"Give him raw sweet potato leaves to eat and some liquid to drink."

She gave him these things, but they did not do any good.

The neighbor said, "Let's see what he swallowed."

The neighbor took the manioc and split it in half, *kontarek*, and found a big anchovy. "Friend, it's an anchovy you have stuck in your throat."

His wife came running to see the anchovy. She said, "Well, I don't think I'll be your wife any more. Your children are starving while you eat fish. Go ahead and suffer! Choke some more, so you will die!"

The man continued to cough, *kajaa, kajaa*. The neighbor ran to the man's bag. He found two more packages of anchovies.

"Here are more. Friend, how could you be so stingy with your wife? Why don't you share with her?"

The wife picked up the packages of fish and took them to her house.

"Neighbor, come eat. Leave my husband to suffer."

They ate until they finished all the fish. Then the neighbor went back to the choking man. He took sweet potato leaves, chopped them up, and gave them to the man to eat. He ate them and then put his finger down his throat so he would vomit, *chaak, thopak*. The bone came out. Blood came out too, and the man was very ill. His wife said to him, "Look, whose going to boil your water now? I hope you suffer."

She said to her children, "We're going to leave your father because he's worthless."

They left the stingy man. His wife remarried, but no one wanted to marry the stingy man. (Translated from *Shirampari shampitsi* by Alberto Pablo Ravírez (Anderson 1985).)

The value of generosity is being challenged by a changing economic world. Ashéninkas are beginning to have conflicts among themselves when one individual or village has more money than others and is reluctant to share. The side without money typically accuses the other of being stingy. Though values may be changing in Ashéninka society, the ideal expressed in the traditional stories is unreserved generosity.

Humility

The Ashéninka show a reserved personality to others. Men and women are expected to be humble and not boastful or showing off. In traditional communities, as in pre-colonial times, an Ashéninka man earns high status by becoming a powerful shaman, a consistently skillful hunter, or a warrior. Instead of having one chief for the whole group, headmen of different family groups had similar status. A headman is only headman in very specific contexts, such as in a hunt or war. In most contexts, married men have equal status, which they show by their humility. Women are considered of equal status among themselves, though others admire some for their skillful weaving.

Many villages have parallel modern and traditional power structures. A chairman and officers are elected at village meetings. Those chosen for these positions are often the most bilingual and skillful in writing documents to government offices. Shamans and headmen are still respected in certain contexts, but village and regional officers are of high status in other contexts. The shaman learns his skills through traditional apprenticeship and a testing period, but the political representative receives most of his training and testing in a school taught by persons outside the culture. This has not upset Ashéninka society but it is a significant change. Ashéninka culture has not been particularly affected because the persistent values of humility and equality continue. Those leaders who become proud or haughty lose respect, their position, and status. The value of outward humility is expressed in the following popular stories.

The proud man and the wasps

A young man who was very vain said to a young woman whom he liked, "Hey, I found a wasp nest."

He said to his potential father-in-law, "I found the large variety of wasps in a hollow log."

The woman's father said, "Fine, son, go and smoke out the wasps so we can eat the larvae with our manioc."

He said to his daughters, "Go with the young man."

"Okay, father, we will go with him."

When they arrived at the hollow log, they saw the wasps flying around the hole of the heavy log. The man started to enter the log, but one woman said, "Don't go in; it is full of wasps. Get some dry palm fronds to burn them."

But the man said, "Don't worry, I always do it like this. I'll throw them to you."

The women began to giggle. The man was showing off so the women would want to marry him. He entered the log and was stung all over his body. He grabbed the larvae and tossed them to the women. He got all the larvae as the women continued to giggle. The wasps stung him all over, even his eyes and ears. He stayed calm, saying, "Let's go back to your father."

When they came close to the house, he screamed, "I was stung by the wasps, and I think I will die!"

His whole body swelled and he died. He died without getting a wife. That is the story of the vain man who entered the wasp nest and was killed. (Translated from *Shirampari shamerentzi ipoña sani* by Alberto Pablo Ravírez (Anderson 1986b).)

Figure 3.13 The proud man and the wasps

The vain man and the *pifayo* palm

A young man was vain and wanted to impress a woman. He wanted to marry her, but she did not want to marry him. He went to the father of the woman and said, "Father-in-law, I want to marry your daughter."

"Fine, you can marry her, since you are in love."

Later, the man said, "Father-in-law, along the trail I found a *pifayo* palm with ripe fruit."

The father said to his daughter, "Daughter, go with my son-in-law to pick the *pifayo* fruit."

So the man went with the woman and her sister. When they arrived at the thicket where the *pifayo* palms were, the girls began to tease the man. Because he was vain, he said to the women, "Sisters-in-law, in my village we always climb a *pifayo* tree."

The girls replied, "How can you climb one [the *pifayo* palm is covered with two inch thorns and nobody touches it with bare hands]? Don't you get poked with the thorns?"

He said, "I always do it. Come and see."

He took a strip of bark from another tree so he could climb it. As he began to climb, the needles of the *pifayo* made the noise, *chemiririri, chemiririri, jmmm, jmmm.* When he arrived at the cluster of fruit, he grabbed it. The girls laughed at him, thinking that this was his way of picking *pifayo* fruit. His whole body was full of needles. One woman said, "Sister, we must marry him, because he always climbs *pifayo* trees."

Then the man yelled down, "Sisters-in-law, here comes the bunch of *pifayo* fruit!"

He let the bunch of *pifayo* fruit fall to the ground. He became nauseated. He began to fall, but halfway down, he got stuck on the thorns of the trunk and died. The women took a stick and pried the man loose. When they looked at him, they saw that his whole body was full of thorns. The thorns covered him as if they were his hair or fur.

These women were very frightened. They ran home without the *pifayo* fruit. When they arrived, they said to their father, "The young man died because he climbed the *pifayo* tree."

When he heard this, the father went and found the man dead on the ground. He said to his daughters, "Your brother-in-law climbed the *pifayo* tree because you teased him."

They answered, "No, he said to us, 'I always climb the *pifayo* tree.'"

That is how the marriage plans of this man were destroyed. (Translated from *Shirampari shamevairentzi* by Alberto Pablo Ravírez (Anderson 1986a).)

Figure 3.14 The vain man and the *pifayo* palm

The young woman who chewed corn

A young woman went to visit her uncle, staying several days. One day, her uncle said, "Niece, I want you to make some corn *chicha* [alcoholic beverage made from corn] for a party."

She replied, "I'm not used to grinding corn to make *chicha*. I will chew it instead."

She gathered many ears of corn and pealed them, *shaari, shaari*. She wanted to finish the chewing of the corn in one day and add water the next day before the party. She said, "Now I'm going to chew the corn fine as dust, like a moth does. I won't leave one kernel that isn't ground up."

Later, her sister-in-law said, "Is it true what you say?"

The girl answered, "It's true, sister-in-law."

In the morning, she chewed corn without stopping to eat. All day she continued to chew, *piche, piche,* until the evening, because she wanted to finish quickly to impress a young man. She almost finished chewing all the corn, but her jaws were getting very sore and she could not eat. That is why she died without ever getting married.

When her uncle saw that the girl had died, he immediately called her mother [his sister] and father. When her father arrived, the uncle said to him, "Your daughter is dead."

Her family examined her and saw that her jaw was swollen shut. They said to the uncle, "We think you killed her."

He replied, "No, I didn't kill her. Look to see where I hit her. Here is the corn that she chewed. That's why her jaw is swollen shut. That's how she died."

The father looked all over the body to see if there were any bruises. She had just died like that. Her uncle was very sad and did not have his party. He was sad because of his niece, and he felt ashamed.

That is the story of the girl who chewed corn. She wanted to be like a moth, but she died. (Translated from *Apaani cooya onaatziri shinqui* by Alberto Pablo Ravírez (Anderson 1986b).)

Figure 3.15 The young woman who chewed corn

In all three stories, young men and women were "showing off" to impress others. They not only lacked humility but showed a disregard for danger, which resulted in their deaths before reaching their goal of marriage.

The Ashéninka strive for expertise in the skills they learn, but they must not boast about their expertise. A quiet competence is the ideal character of the mature Ashéninka who reflects these ideals in storytelling and in direct actions.

Conclusion

Ashéninka traditional stories present an ideal world in which those who live by the ideals of Ashéninka culture are successful and those who deviate from Ashéninka ideals experience a tragic fate. All have their lesson or moral, and many have multiple lessons that repeat societal values and reinforce the explicit teachings of adults.

The stories are presented during social interaction with a caregiver, internalized as the child matures, and become a part of the spiritual life of the individual. Traditional stories present Ashéninka beliefs and values that form a part of the cultural context for socialization. This context helps the individual set goals for personal development and structures a framework in which adults and children work together to pass knowledge from one generation to the next. The next chapter, records the voices of individuals navigating through the Ashéninka world with the motives to survive physically, to grow into social acceptability, and to reach personal fulfillment.

4

The Motivations for Learning

My father told me, "Make your chacra so you will have something to eat. If you do not work, there will be no food." He wanted me to plant all the foods. He told me to do this so I would not have to buy food from the neighbors. That is why I decided to learn. DAV

My mother said, "You must get accustomed to planting things, so when you are big, you will not be ashamed for having to go to another person to get food." I liked to go to the chacra. ROS

I wanted to be like my brother-in-law who was an excellent hunter. Whenever he went to the river, he brought back fish. Whenever he went hunting, he brought back game. I wanted to be like him, doing like he did. ABC

In those days, we did not know what money was or what it was worth, and didn't know our numbers. My brother said, "Go to school so you will know how to count money." DAV

They said we would continue to be exploited if we didn't go to school. We needed to know our rights. SAM

This chapter examines the different motives a child or adolescent has to learn those things Ashéninka adults need to know. Learning traditional skills depends on and interacts with (1) anticipation of future physical need, (2) social acceptance, and (3) identity formation. New technologies and modern changes in the physical and social environments change what children will and "should" learn; for example, socioeconomic changes strongly influence the decision to learn reading and math skills.

In this chapter, individuals tell how they decided either to learn or not to learn a particular skill. They tell how their cultural surroundings and social interaction with others influenced decisions regarding learning. Adults do not expect their children to become exact replicas of themselves; but rather, adults try to orchestrate a child's experiences, so the child will decide for himself to learn social norms and instrumental competence. Though the focus here is on the individual, it must be remembered that individual decisions interact with the cultural context and others involved in the process of socialization.

The next three sections discuss three different motives for learning: anticipation of future physical need, social acceptance, and identity formation.

Anticipation of future physical need

Food

Ashéninkas believe they must work hard enough to provide for their own and their family's physical needs. The major source of food is the family *chacra*, for which a new plot of land is cleared of trees, planted, cultivated, and gradually harvested every year. A family that cannot keep up with their food needs is considered to be in poverty, whereas the family that produces more than their basic needs can host manioc beer parties and have surplus produce to trade for other goods.

Infants accompany their mothers to the *chacra* and toddlers are expected to help. The smallest carry back a stick for the fire or a piece of fruit in a miniature basket. Parents expect a child of seven or eight years to dig up manioc, cut weeds with a machete, and carry heavier loads. It is usually hot work, but children are told to work hard in order to prepare to satisfy their food needs in the future. In the following interviews, adults tell how they were admonished to work hard in preparation to meet their own future physical needs.

R: Did your mother take you to the *chacra* with her when you were young?

F: Yes, I went with her a lot to the *chacra*. She would say, "Let's go to the *chacra*. If we do not go to the *chacra*, you will not learn to maintain a clean *chacra* and you will not have anything to eat." (T.88.18.JOS)

R: What else did your father teach you about working in the *chacra*?

M: He taught me to plant manioc. He told me, "Make your *chacra* so you will have something to eat. If you do not work, there will be no food." He wanted me to plant all the foods. He told me to do this so I would not have to buy food from the neighbors. That is why I decided to learn. (T.88.08.DAV)

R: What did your father teach you when you were young?

M: My father died when I was little. My mother taught me everything, like how to plant a *chacra* so when I would have a wife, I could provide food for her.

R: Who taught you to make a *chacra*?

M: My mother taught me. She said, "You must have a *chacra* so you can eat." She taught me to use an ax and to stack the sticks for burning. My mother said, "You must learn to plant manioc because otherwise you will not have anything to eat when you get older." This is how she motivated me to want to work in the *chacra*. I was about twelve years old when I started using an ax. (T.88.12.LOP)

Use of coca

Parents promote coca use by children, starting at about twelve years old, when they begin to be productive workers. Ashéninkas have traditionally chewed coca leaves, which are activated by lime, an alkaline substance. Many consider coca to be a necessity. Those who chew coca are said to be stronger and more productive when working in the *chacra*. J. G. (1868) noted that the Ashéninka chewed it often, at all times of the day. Sinclair (1895) writes, "Of the sustaining power of coca there can be no possible doubt; the Chunchos seem not only to exist, but to thrive, upon this stimulant, often travelling for days with very little, if anything else, to sustain them" (p. 32). The Ashéninka say that coca helps women to stay awake, so they can spin longer into the night, and helps men not to feel their hunger on a long trip or hunt. In the following interviews, the admonitions to chew coca were all justified by saying that the person's physical needs would be satisfied. Though the parents made the case for chewing coca, most interviewees made the individual decision not to continue the practice.

F: I used coca because my mother wanted me to. When I passed puberty, she said, "You should chew coca because it will help you to be more alert and not be sleepy or lazy. With coca, you will not be half asleep, but awake and adept at doing any activity in the home." But I said, "I do not want to chew it." My mother said, "You must chew it so you can do the work of the *chacra* or the home." She chewed a little and said, "This is sweet; try some." She gave me some, and I discovered that it was sweet. I chewed it until about six years ago, because that is when I became a Christian believer. (T.88.19.JOS)

F: I learned to chew coca.
R: How did you learn?
F: My grandmother had some and said, "Chew some coca so you will not be sleepy."
R: Did you like it?
F: No, because the lime burned my lips and mouth. I did not want much because it burned me, and I still got sleepy. (T.88.08.FLO)

R: Did you ever try coca?
M: I was taught how to chew coca from my father, but when I tried it the first time, I burned my mouth with the lime and never tried it again. They say that coca is good because you won't feel hunger if you chew it. But soon after, the Adventists came and I didn't try it again. I was about eight or nine years old. (T.88.11.ABE)

R: Have you tried coca?
M: Yes. I was about thirteen years old. I took it by myself. I got it from my uncle and it made my tongue swell up so much that I could not eat manioc for about two hours. After that, I did not want to try it again. I ate coca, lime, and *chamairo* all at once. But my uncle was accustomed to it. He told me, "If you chew coca, you will not be hungry." I didn't like it. (T.88.12.LOP)

M: He said, "You need coca so you will not be hungry or weak and can work in the *chacra*." I did not want to, but I tried it. I planted it and became accustomed to chewing it. I liked it, though at first I did not. I started gradually by chewing just a little. (T.88.13.GRE)

R: Have you tried coca?
M: Yes. (laughs) My father gave it to me, saying, "It is good to chew coca so you will not be hungry. If you do not chew, you will die of hunger. Wherever you are, you will not feel hunger if you chew coca." I was motivated by my father, but I did not like it because it burned my mouth. (T.88.14.ALB)

Neatness

A neat house is another Ashéninka social value, with various reasons given for the need for neatness. In the following interview, the need to avoid snake bite is given as a reason to keep a neat house.

R: Did your mother teach you to clean the house?
F: My mother said, "You must do the cleaning, like cleaning up the trash around the house and clearing the grass from around the house. If it is not left clean, a snake could come and bite someone. It is very important to do this because we do not know of good medicines for snakebite. That is why the house must stay clean." (T.88.21.JUA)

This has a sound basis in fact because snakes often make homes in abandoned or unoccupied houses. I treated one child who was bitten when lifting a mat in a house that had been vacant for only a week. I also found a snake among my personal goods when I returned to the village after an absence of many months.

Health

Boys are motivated to learn to be shamans for the practical purpose of curing those near them. Shamanism is attractive to Ashéninkas because its practice gives the shaman a sense of defense against both physical and spiritual dangers. They have knowledge of native medical treatments for maladies of the spirit, as illustrated in the following story.

The man who slept alone in his *chacra*

A man slept alone in his *chacra*. In the middle of the night, a big rat came and grabbed the man, leaving him paralyzed.

In the morning, the man returned to his house and said to his sons, "I went to my manioc field where I met a big rat that grabbed me."

His wife teased him, saying, "The rat went to visit you because you were sleeping alone."

Then the man's feet began to stiffen and he could not walk. He was very sick for several years. One day, a shaman visited him and asked, "What happened to you?"

He replied, "Years ago, a rat grabbed me, and I began to be paralyzed. I've been this way since."

The shaman tried to cure him by blowing over him, which is our custom. In the night, when he was asleep, the shaman had visions of what happened to the man. In the morning he said, "Oh! The rat sickened your soul. You wanted to rescue it, but you couldn't conquer it."

The man got worse and was about to die. Another shaman came with medicinal plants used especially against rats. He bathed him in a mixture of these plants and the bark of the *shimiro* [a species of tree with a fragrant bark]. Then the man got well. (Translated from *Ashéninca jimayi apaniroini irovanequi* by Alberto Pablo Ravírez (Anderson 1986b).)

Numerous stories mention shamans' successes in healing the sick, saving the world from destruction, and performing assorted historic deeds. These stories and the prestige given the position make study of shamanism attractive to young men.

The process of becoming a shaman can be unpleasant because novice shamans become nauseated by the ingestion of tobacco juice. The following interviews show that for some the long-term physical benefit of becoming a shaman is reason enough to study to be a shaman and to undergo short-term discomfort.

R: How did they try to teach you?

M: They said, "You can cure other people. You could be like a doctor." I could cure some and make the vomiting go away. Sometimes nothing else can cure someone. When we use tobacco, they get well. (T.88.05.ARM)

R: Have you tried tobacco?

M: No, I was afraid because it is very bitter. Many times others wanted me to try it, but I always avoided it. I was afraid because it can make you nauseated. My uncle tried to get me to use it so I could cure others, but I was immature. I was about twelve years old when he tried to get me to try it, saying, "We are going to get you to use it so you will be qualified to cure." But he gave it to my cousin who got nauseated and vomited. This made me afraid. I ran away to my sister's house and hid. I hid from my uncle. My sister asked me why I came and I told her. She didn't say anything. I still want to be a doctor. (T.88.23.ABC)

This final interviewee found another way to become a person who cures others. He was chosen to be trained as a paramedic and now receives a government salary to care for the sick in his village.

Learning to swim

The Ashéninka often travel by raft or canoe, frequently through danger-ous rapids or rain-swollen rivers. These vessels sometimes capsize and all must try to make it safely to shore. Drownings are common. Since 1970, two Ashéninka school teachers have drowned in accidents. Parents en-courage their children to learn to swim so they will be ready for an acci-dent on the river.

R: Did you learn to swim?
F: Yes, my mother taught me to swim. If not, I would have problems in an emergency when the river is high. My mother went with me and motivated me by saying, "It is important to learn to swim for when the river is high." I wasn't afraid. None of my children were afraid—they were all anxious to learn. They were usually about ten or eleven years old when they knew how to swim well, but about seven or eight years old when they first tried it. (T.88.07.LOL)

R: Did you teach anyone to swim?
M: When I was a boy, I tried to teach other children. I told them that they should learn, so they wouldn't drown if they went on a trip. (T.88.11.ABE)

R: How did you learn to swim?
F: I know how to swim because my mother taught me. She said, "You must learn to swim or you will drown in an emergency." (T.88.21.JUA)

R: How did you learn to swim?
M: I saw my brother swim and tried to do like him. It was like now when the stream is low. My brothers told me, "You need to know how to swim so you won't drown in rainy season." (T.88.05.ARM)

Skills and crafts

Children learn to make things like clothing, baskets, arrows, and houses that are useful for them. Parents often speak of the utility of a skill when trying to motivate their children to learn.

R: Did you teach your children to weave baskets?
F: My older daughter, yes, but not my younger daughters. I am start-ing to give them the first words to motivate them to want to do it. I tell them, "You must gather the materials. Weave this so you can learn. This will be useful to you in the future." (T.88.21.JUA)

R: How did your mother teach you to spin cotton?

F: I learned to spin when my mother said, "You must learn to spin because it is very important to be clothed. It would be a disgrace if you became an adult and did not know how to weave clothing and could not supply clothing to your husband." That is why I wanted to learn to spin and weave. (T.88.03.MAR)

R: How did your mother motivate you to want to learn to spin?

F: My mother taught me to spin when she said, "You must learn to spin cotton because you should not wait around to have someone give you clothing." She said that I could learn to make those things. (T.88.15.MAR)

R: Do you teach your children to spin like you were taught?

F: I teach them the same, with the same advice, "You must spin because who can give you gifts of things to wear? You must spin to have clothing." They like to spin cotton.

R: What did your mother say to motivate you to want to spin?

F: She motivated us because, in those days, they did not have clothing, such as shirts, pants, and blankets like we have today. She said, "You must weave because we must have clothing and have something to keep us warm at night." I also was taught how to make bracelets. (T.88.21.JUA)

The Ashéninka are aware of their need for food, health, physical intimacy, tools, and other things that help them survive in their physical environment. Parents know the skills necessary to satisfy these needs, and they motivate children to value these skills by relating physical needs to the skill itself. Parents' admonitions make sense to children in light of traditional stories, personal experience, and contemporary oral histories.

The case for learning these skills is strong until changes in the physical environment or social situation develop. A social sanction against coca chewing or shamanism may weaken the case for practicing these skills, and a network of roads may decrease the urgency for children to learn to swim.

Social acceptance

The need for social acceptance is another motivation for learning instrumental skills and proper social behavior. Rarely does anyone live alone. All young people assume they will have a spouse and family when they reach adulthood. Traditional stories portray ideal family relations as the norm, with any deviation from the norm becoming a story theme. The Ashéninka have their expectations of what the ideal husband or wife will be: someone who shows instrumental competence and behaves in an upright Ashéninka manner.

Social acceptance within the family

The need for social intimacy is another motivation for learning. In the following interview, mastery of hard work, hunting, and shamanism are cited as traits that attract women; a man lacking these skills will have difficulty in keeping a wife.

M: I used to practice hunting a lot. Probably the most important thing for us is hunting and a good garden (so they don't say we are lazy). I practiced these things a lot. We don't do it to win a woman, but because we know that if we cannot do these things, we will suffer when we have a family. We won't have food and would need to be supported by others. We see some families like that and we say they must be lazy. There are problems in the marriage because the woman is often deceived in thinking the man can hunt and work. Divorces happen for this and because of unfaithfulness....

A man has two wives, before and now, because he is a good hunter, has a big garden, or is a good shaman. The women think these men are the most attractive. (T.88.01.SAM)

R: How did your father motivate you to want to hunt?
M: The words of my father were, "Son, you must get accustomed to hunting in the forest because when you become an adult and have a family, you will have food in the house." (T.88.14.ALB)

R: Did your father say anything to motivate you to want to hunt?
M: He said, "You must get accustomed to going hunting because if you don't, when you are married, it will be hard to get enough to eat." (T.88.22.MAC)

The same theme is repeated in many Ashéninka stories. In the following story, a man's incompetence is discovered, causing him to lose his wife.

The man who did not know how to hunt

Once, a man did not know how to hunt. He shot arrows, but never hit anything. This man had a wife and daughter.

One day, he went to hunt. In the middle of the jungle, he entered his hunting blind and saw many doves. He shot at them, *tak, tak, tak,* but missed them all. He went out to gather his arrows and then went back into his blind. He stayed there until night, but did not shoot any. He left and the doves flew away, *peta, peta, peta.*

Then the man went to where there was an abundance of bamboo and the squirrels that eat bamboo. *Satak, satak,* he shot his arrows, but did not hit anything. He threw down his arrows and chased the squirrels, trying to catch them. He growled, *jaaam, jaaam, jaaam,* like a jaguar. The squirrels escaped and went into a hole in the ground. The man dug in the ground until he caught one. The squirrel bit him on the hand. The man did not drop it, but hit it, *pok,* until he killed it. He grabbed an arrow and jabbed the squirrel. He was very happy as he returned home. He entered his house and called his wife, saying, "*Eee!* Light the fire, I killed a squirrel."

He hid his hand in his clothing so his wife would not see it bleed. He gave the squirrel to his wife, saying, "I shot many squirrels, but I brought only one back."

His wife said to her daughter, "Your father shot a squirrel. Let's roast it."

They quickly roasted the squirrel. When it was done, his wife began to eat. The man did not eat. He was rolling on the floor in pain from the bite. It was still bleeding. Though his clothing was wet with blood, he did not say anything to his wife. She said to him, "Here, have some squirrel."

He answered, "Give it to the children. I will shoot more."

Then his wife and children ate it all. She said to her daughter, "Thank you, daughter. We have eaten the squirrel your father shot for us."

In the night, the man called to his wife, "Give me a little squirrel meat to eat. I'm hungry."

She answered, saying, "Why do you ask me after it's gone? You told us to eat it."

The man became angry at his wife and said to her, "Don't criticize me. The squirrel bit me on the finger."

The wife began to laugh, "*jiii.*" Then she asked, "Where did it bite you?"

He showed her. When she saw the wound, she quickly applied medicines until it was healed.

Another day, a man arrived who was a good hunter. He gave the family a *paujil* bird that he had shot along the trail. He said to them, "Friends, eat this *paujil.*"

The hunter gave the *paujil* to the wife to cook. Everyone ate it. They also drank manioc beer. Later, the hunter talked with the wife and said to her, "I want to marry you. Leave your husband who doesn't know how to hunt. All he does is hit your children, and he never brings home food."

The woman replied, "Very well. Let's escape now."

When they saw that the husband was really drunk, the hunter escaped with the wife and children. The next day, the man searched for his wife and children, but could not find them. Eventually, he found them on the trail. The two men fought, and the man who could not hunt was killed.

That is the story of the man who lost his wife because he did not know how to hunt. (Translated from *Cayetsi* by Alberto Pablo Ravírez (Anderson 1986a).)

A boy who hears this story considers the poor hunter to be a pathetic individual who cannot even get a squirrel without almost dying in the effort. The strain on the family is obvious and the woman appears justified in leaving her husband. A boy fears growing up to be such a poor hunter.

Parents often remind children of the family role they are destined to fill and encourage them to prepare for that role. In the following interviews, interviewees tell of their parents' relating the learning of a skill for the future role of the woman or man of the house.

R: Did you go with your mother to the *chacra*?
F: I went with her a lot. She said, "You must get used to going to the *chacra* because when you have your husband or mother-in-law, they might say, 'You are lazy; you do not know how to work in the *chacra*.' Or, they might say, 'Since you do not know how to work in the *chacra*, you should go back home to your mother.'" (T.88.17.LAU)

R: What other things did your father teach you?
M: He always gave me advice, saying, "While you are young, you must learn to make your field and your house." He always tried to motivate me, saying, "Son, you must first make your garden, buy your pots, have your own house, and buy material for clothing and bedding, so when you are ready to have a wife, when you bring her home, you will not be found to have nothing there but your food and house." (T.88.06.GER)

R: Did you go with your mother to the *chacra*?
F: I went with my mother a lot because we weeded and put sticks around to prevent animals from eating the crops. I was never lazy

and always wanted to go with my mother. I still like to go to the *chacra*. I was about six years old when I began, and I still went at twelve years old. Mother said, "It is good that you go with me so that you will be accustomed to it when you have your husband. If you don't know how to work well, you won't have anything to eat." (T.88.07.LOL)

F: My mother always encouraged me with a relevant example. She would say, "You must make good baskets because when you have a family, you will need something to carry manioc and other things in." She also said, "Make a good fan, because if you don't, what will you fan your fire with?" She explained that this would be very useful in the future. So, I was motivated to learn to make these things for when I would have my husband in the future. (T.88.18.JOS)

M: When a boy is ready to marry, he is ashamed if he doesn't know how to hunt right. If he is not a good hunter, his wife will leave him right away. The man needs to feed his family. If not, he is worthless and is like a woman that doesn't know how to hunt. Sometimes, the woman knows how to hunt better than the man. This is why the boys have to become good at this. He also has to know how to prepare his field, build his house, etc. This is so he can live in the house of his father-in-law and work for him. He will be ashamed if he must be supported by his father-in-law. This is no good if he wants his own home. The boys have to work hard to do this, and the father must teach them the techniques. Some fathers say, "Son, you must prepare this garden by yourself. I won't help you." So the boy does it himself, preparing himself well. (T.87.08.MRC)

R: Who taught you?

M: My father and my grandfather always gave me the advice that when older and having a family, I should know how to hunt and be able to feed them. My father also said that besides hunting, I should always go with him to the *chacra* because when I have a family, I should have a *chacra*. I always went to the *chacra* with my father. (T.88.10.ABE)

F: I said to my older sister, "Let's spin, because mother says we should. It would be shameful if we didn't know how when we have our husbands." We didn't even know what a husband was. (T.88.18.JOS)

Social acceptance outside the family

The Ashéninka also want acceptance by those outside their own family. Parents urge their children to learn skills so they will not be embarrassed because others see their incompetence. In the following interviews, conformity to the norms of self-sufficiency and neatness are important.

R: Did someone teach you to cook?
F: Yes, my mother taught me. She told me, "You must learn to cook because cooking is important for your future home."
R: Did someone teach you how to clean the house?
F: My mother taught me to sweep. She said, "You must learn to sweep. It would be a shameful thing if visitors came and found the house full of trash. This would not be good." My mother talked like that and that is why I learned to clean. (T.88.17.LAU)

R: Did your mother take you with her to the *chacra*?
F: Yes, she always took me with her. When we came back, we spun cotton. She taught things like how to plant yams, *pitucas*, and other plants. My mother said, "You must get accustomed to planting things, so when you are big, you will not be ashamed for having to go to another person to get food." I liked to go to the *chacra*. (T.88.16.ROS)

Sloth is shameful to the Ashéninka. In the following interview, a grown daughter was admonished by her mother to teach her daughters so as to motivate them not to be lazy.

R: How old were your daughters when you started taking them to the *chacra*?
F: I took my daughters to the *chacra* at the age that I was taken. My mother said, "You must always have your children go to the *chacra* with you. If you do not, when they get older, they will not be accustomed to working and will be lazy." (T.88.16.ROS)

R: Who taught you to cook?
F: When I was small, I was given a small pot to cook with. I would cook something and give it to my grandmother. She said, "Don't eat what you have cooked or you will grow up to be lazy." They taught me to peel and clean manioc. (T.88.08.FLO)

The Ashéninka have standards for their models of a well-kept house. In the following interview, the reasons for learning to keep a neat house are to please God and to be distinct from animals noted for their sloppiness.

R: What did your mother teach you about keeping the house clean?

F: My mother taught me to clean the area around the house. The reason for cleaning it of trash is that this pleases God. When the house is clean, God is happy and might come—not personally, but he can come. This is why my mother had us clean continually around the house and put the trash in a basket in one place, and always throw it away in a place far from the house. Now you find houses that are dirty, but in the old days, it was almost a sacred thing and people always had very clean houses that were neat.

R: How did you teach your daughters to keep their houses clean?

F: I tell them about the same thing that I was taught, that they should clean the house because we are humans and should have clean houses, not like the animals, such as the armadillo that likes to live near the trash. I tell them that they must sweep the house every morning. If there is trash or grass too close to the house, some insects or other dangerous thing could do us harm. (T.88.19.JOS)

The worst social sanction against an Ashéninka is the accusation of being a witch. In the following interview, a person studied to become a shaman to protect himself from such accusations.

R: Did you ever learn to drink tobacco?

M: When I was a teenager, the shamans told me that I should learn. They were not from my family. I practiced it.

   I was motivated to be a shaman because someone earlier had accused me of being a witch, so I wanted to have power to get back at those who accused me. I was about ten or twelve years old when I started learning to be a shaman. That is when they threatened to kill me and accused me of being a witch. (T.88.11.ABE)

Weaving requires much patience because the threads break, knot, or tangle. Women are thought to have more patience than men. A lack of patience is a social defect that is typically attributed to men, as told in the following interview.

F: Once, my daughter started a small bag and I left to do something else, but when I returned, I found the bag cut off the loom. Maybe she did it because she was frustrated and could not do it by herself. She cut it. She knows how to spin, but does not know how to weave.

R: What did you think of that?

F: I was disgusted and said, "Why did you cut it? Where are you thinking of going? Why are you in such a hurry? As a woman, you must have the patience to weave. You are acting like a man, in a hurry to go do something else." (T.88.16.ROS)

The Ashéninka expect to conform to the ideal of social and instrumental competence. Reference to admirable traits, such as patience and self-sufficiency, and to a child's future role in society are used to encourage children to learn specific tasks and norms of behavior. Proper learning of these brings social acceptance.

Identity formation

The Ashéninka prepare their children for independence and self-reliance. They traditionally lived in isolated, small family groups, marrying soon after puberty. Though parents actively teach social and instrumental skills to their children, parents also expect children to be self-motivated and self-learners. Ashéninka children do not learn passively, but are active learners in accordance with their personal goals.

From birth, children are reminded that someday they will become adults and will fill an adult role in society. Adults talk to infants about the adult-like things the child will eventually do. The following is a short example of forward-looking chatter.

R: How little are infants when adults start talking to them?
M: Even with the newborns. Sometimes their mother will talk to them. If the baby is a boy, she will say to him, "You will be a man. You will cultivate my field," though he is a baby. This is a custom that shows affection. (T.87.07.ABC)

Parents orchestrate children's activities so work becomes an early habit. A person accustomed to hard work fits in with Ashéninka society better than one who is not a good worker. A person's enthusiasm for work is also a reflection of the parents' child-rearing competence.

R: What did your mother tell you to motivate you to want to go out to the *chacra* to work?
F: I accompanied my mother a lot to the *chacra* when I was small. She always said, "We must go to the *chacra* so you will learn how to work, so when you are an adult, no one will say that you did not learn to work." (T.88.15.MAR)

Parents also orchestrate a child's experiences to condition their bodies for hard work. A parent who properly raises a child instills the habit of work by training the child's body to make it strong enough for common tasks. In the following interview, a man tells of his father's concern for his son's physical adequacy.

R: What did your father say to you to motivate you to want to work?

M: He said, "Son, you must work. If you do not work, when you become an adult, you cannot work. If your hands are not in condition
to work hard and long, you are going to have many blisters and
your hands will peel. That is why you have to learn to work at such
a young age." I was eight or ten years old. (T.88.22.MAC)

Life expectancy was lower fifty years ago than it is now. Frequent epidemics of measles, flu, and malaria afflicted the Ashéninka, who lacked
antibiotics; accidental death was common, and continues to be. Parents
prepare children for independent living, because life is seen as fragile; a
boy or girl might unexpectedly need to fill in for a sick or dead parent. The
urgency to achieve adult competency is expressed in the following
interviews.

R: Did he criticize you or make fun of you when you didn't do something right?

M: No, no, no. He was only insistent; he didn't make fun of me. He insisted until I arrived at perfection. "Do you know why?" he told me,
"If I die, you will never do anything well, so you have to take advantage of this before I die. Learn to gather firewood because, if I
die, you must bring the firewood. Learn to bring water because, if I
die, who will bring water? Make a hunting blind over there because,
if I die, who will bring birds to eat? Learn to dam up the stream to
dry it up because, if I die, who will dry up the stream so you can eat
carachama fish? Learn to make a hunting blind up in a tree because,
if I die, who will bring birds to eat from up in the trees?" He also
told me not to get married early because I didn't have my cultivated
field. He told me that when I had a cultivated plot, a house, and I
knew how to hunt, then I could get married. I needed to know that
in case my father died. He was very insistent. (T.87.04.EUS)

R: Did you teach your daughters to spin cotton?

F: Yes, they know how to spin. I taught my older daughter to spin, saying, "Daughter, learn to spin; take advantage of learning to do it
before I die because when I am dead, no one else can teach you." I
said the same to my two daughters. They were interested and happy
to learn to spin cotton. (T.88.21.JUA)

Adults expect children to want to do the tasks of adults and to behave as
adults. Parents are not surprised when the child takes the initiative in trying adult-like things. Though some children need encouragement to try
coca, in the following interview, the father shows little reaction when his
son wants to try it.

R: Did someone teach you to chew coca?

M: I saw how my father chewed coca. He chewed coca during certain labors he did. I saw how he did it. My father didn't say anything to me, but I saw him doing it and I asked him for some. He didn't say anything to me, but just gave me the coca to chew. I was about ten years old. Though the lime burned my mouth, it seemed very sweet to me, and I liked it. (T.88.22.MAC)

When asked if they remembered one person whom they admired and wanted to be like, many wanted to be like their mother or father. The responses to what they admired in others varied greatly, showing that they do not share a common view of the individual ideal. The following interviews tell why a child wanted to be like a parent or grandparent.

R: Which women were the most admired by you when a young woman?

F: My mother, who was a good weaver. She knew how to weave everything well, and I wanted to be skillful like her when I got older. (T.88.03.MAR)

R: Did you have someone you admired when you were young?

M: Yes, a person who hunted in the forest and always brought back meat for the family. My grandfather was like that, and I wanted to be like him. I practiced hard to be like him. Unfortunately, there is not much game around here any more. (T.88.04.ELI)

R: Did you have someone you admired when you were younger?

F: I wanted to be like my mother, because she was good at weaving baskets. (T.88.04.EVE)

R: Did you have someone you admired?

F: I admired my mother, because she could do so many things. She was a good worker, very strict, and I wanted to know everything that she knew. I respected her a lot. I was a bit afraid of her because of her manner. I can now do everything that my mother taught me to do. (T.88.19.JOS)

Others admire acquaintances, distant relatives, or a group of people who mastered a particular skill. In the following interviews, people tell of wanting to be like individuals who were different from their parents.

R: Who did you admire when a child? At what did you want to become expert?

M: It was one of my uncles who worked hard in his garden. He worked in the hot sun and stayed strong and did not get tired. I always wanted to be like that. (T.88.02.RAM)

R: Did you have someone you admired when you were young?
M: Yes, I admired those who knew how to drink tobacco, to be shamans. I thought it would be good to do this when older. I drank just a little and I changed my mind, because I did not like it. (T.88.05.ARM)

R: Did you have someone you admired?
M: Yes, those who knew how to make good arrows, because some men in those days made very colorful, well-crafted, and creatively designed arrows that others admired. I wanted to do that when older, though I didn't meet my expectation. I do know how to make the whistling arrows with the snail shells. I did this in the Pajonal. It is beautiful to hear the men shoot many whistling arrows simultaneously. (T.88.14.ALB)

R: Did you ever have someone you admired?
F: When we arrived at this village, I saw that some women had very clean houses and clothing. I wanted to be like that. (T.88.15.MAR)

R: Did you have someone you admired when you were young?
F: When I was small, some people had bands made of very beautiful and colorful feathers. I wanted to learn to weave these things. I said to my mother, "Mother, I want to spin a lot of cotton so I can make one of these." My mother tried to make one, but we could not get the feathers. (T.88.16.ROS)

R: When growing up, did you have someone you admired?
M: In those days, we lived only with our family. I wanted to be like my brother-in-law who was an excellent hunter. Whenever he went to the river, he brought back fish. Whenever he went hunting, he brought back game. I wanted to be like him, doing like he did. I could not be like him because I was in school and had to give up on my desire. (T.88.23.ABC)

Though parents train children in basic skills, proper social behavior, and the work ethic, parents also expect children to grow into adults who have unique qualities and characteristics. Parents encourage children's independence and participation in an adult role. Children have particular preferences of what they enjoy and aspire to, and they set their own motivations for learning independent of their parents' efforts. Such individual preferences are particularly relevant to socialization in the present period of rapid change.

New technologies as a change factor in learning traditional skills

Change is coming quickly, though irregularly, to most Ashéninka areas. Roads pass through villages, wild game is disappearing, and families want an economy that is more than subsistence. These changes bring new challenges to Ashéninka socialization.

Some traditional skills are not as important as in the past. One interviewee tells how his father saw no point in teaching him to hunt.

R: Tell me about what your father said was the way people taught in the past.

M: My father did not teach me because civilization had entered. He said, "I am not going to teach you because with civilization, we will not use arrows or shoot guns because there will not be any animals to hunt or even the jungle to hunt in." (T.88.06.GER)

Other men are perplexed by their sons' lack of motivation to learn to hunt. They blame the schools, preserved meats that can be bought, and their love of recreation. Older people accuse their children of not being as interested in hard labor as before. The formation of villages and greater social contact has put a higher value on recreational activities that take away some time formerly dedicated to hard labor with the family.

M2: Before, they liked to hunt; but now, in the school, they are exposed to salmon and tuna fish. Before, they didn't have these things and the parents insisted that they learn to make a hunting blind and learn to hunt alone. The hunter brought home the meat but did not eat it. Our custom is for the son to eat the meat of the father and the father to eat the meat of the son. The youngest son cannot eat what he has killed or it will ruin his aim. Now they play soccer day after day, every afternoon, and they only care about the ball. Later, they eat tuna fish that their father has bought and the chicken that their mother has raised. They are no longer concerned about hunting for their meat. In my case, when we are in the garden, we don't have anything to eat, so we hunt. Others do not do this. (T.87.05.EUS)

M: I am teaching my sons, but I am not teaching them as well as I was taught, because they spend more time in school. I showed the secrets of good hunting to my sons, but they do not practice as much as I did, because they are in school and doing homework so much. I do little to try to motivate them. (T.88.22.MAC)

These interviewees do not mention the increasing dependence on shotguns. Since the times of the rubber boom and the Peruvian Corporation, Ashéninkas have frequently been paid with guns and ammunition. Greatly more efficient than a bow and arrow, the shotgun allows a person with mediocre hunting skills to get wild game. Increased use of shotguns and a denser population (including mestizo colonists) have depleted the available game by overhunting and by destroying the food sources of wild game. Young men often work contracts to get the money for a shotgun and ammunition. The bow is quickly becoming a tool used only by those who cannot afford a shotgun. Hunting with a shotgun is said to be much easier than with a bow and arrows, as told in the following interviews.

R: Who taught you how to use a shotgun?
M: My father. I accompanied him. He let me shoot it when I was twelve years old. An animal came into the *chacra* and my father said, "Shoot it." I had good aim with the shotgun, better with that than with an arrow.
R: Do you now hunt with a shotgun?
M: Yes, when I have cartridges. I also hunt with a bow and arrows, especially fish. You cannot kill big animals with arrows, only the small ones. (T.88.04.ELI)

R: Don't your children have their own bows and arrows to play with?
M: Yes, but they are just toys that are very little and do not have points. I never had that because I was in school. I was in school and could not go into the forest to hunt. I got my arrows when I was twelve or thirteen years old to hunt fish, etc. Only when I was fifteen years old could I go into the forest to hunt by myself. At twelve years I was making my own arrows.
R: Did you learn to use a shotgun?
M: Yes, my father taught me to use it when I was ten years old. He took me to the *chacra* where there was an animal eating the manioc. At 5 p.m., my father took me to the garden and had me aim. I hit the animal in the head. (T.88.08.DAV)

The lack of motivation to learn hunting skills makes the present generation more dependent on the outside economy that, in turn, gives them less time to practice hunting.

Near the end of the nineteenth century, metal pots were introduced, another technology that the Ashéninka adopted on a grand scale. Older women remember learning to make clay pots. Metal pots became more practical, however, and mothers stopped teaching their daughters to make traditional-style pots. In the following interview, a woman tells of the disadvantages of using clay pots.

R: Did you have your own pot?

F: I had a clay pot, a little one made for me by my mother. My mother made me my special little pot. When we lived at the headwaters of the Nazareteki River, my mother taught me to make the small pots. A special clay can withstand the baking process needed to make them. I learned to make pots and plates, but the plates often broke when I carried manioc on them. I was ten or twelve years old when I started to learn. I needed to learn to fire the pot just right, so it would be strong. I had to fire it with the wood of the *pona* tree. If I used ordinary firewood, it would just smoke and not last. My father made the fire for me. My mother and I made and fired the pots at the same time.

R: What did your mother do when you broke your pots?

F: I was punished a lot by my mother. Once, my mother sent me to bring water with one of these clay pots. I stepped on a slippery spot, slipped, and broke a basket full of pots. I was punished when she saw that all the pots were broken. I was hit with a stick and not given water to drink for a couple days, so I would be reminded that I broke all the pots. (T.88.18.JOS)

Women preferred to use metal pots even more than men preferred to use a shotgun. No one I met in the Pichis or Perené areas knows of anyone who still uses a clay pot, though some in the Ucayali area buy decorative clay pots from the Shipibos for water storage. The disadvantages of clay pots, cited above, made acquisition of metal pots a high priority. These were typically acquired from patrons or merchants through labor in the outside economy. Once families had enough metal pots to meet their needs, the reason for making clay pots or teaching others pottery disappeared. In an isolated location, the family of the person in the following interview used clay pots until they were replaced by metal pots about forty years ago.

R: How old were you when you learned to cook?

F: I was very small because I saw very small children putting bananas into the fire to roast them. I did not know about metal pots like I have now; I learned to cook with clay pots. My mother made me a special small pot with which I could cook. I never learned to make this kind of clay pot. (T.88.21.)

Few young women learn to weave clothing, though all learn to spin cotton. Men wear store-bought shirts and pants; women wear the traditional-style clothing made of store-bought material. Older women and young women who live away from roads and schools now weave the traditional clothing mostly for ceremonial use. Men will change into their *cushma* to relax in the evening, to wear to a manioc beer party, or to attend a regional political meeting. In the following interview, a young-adult daughter tells that she had to find work as a maid in an urban area to earn the money to buy clothing.

F: I left to learn to cook, iron, etc. We don't have irons here. I didn't know how to iron when I left. I learned so I could later teach my sister. Also, I needed money to buy clothes. My father didn't have enough. I wanted to help my younger brothers and sisters, too. That is why I left to work. (T.87.18.AMA)

Weaving the traditional Ashéninka *cushma* takes about a month, while a small bag may take a few days. All girls learn to spin, few learn to weave a bag, and fewer still find the time and desire to weave a full *cushma*. The following interview tells of the difficulty a mother has in getting her daughter to learn to spin and weave.

R: Have you taught your daughter to spin cotton?
F: Yes. My other daughter does not want to learn because she is in the school. I always try to teach her, but she does not want to learn. I do not know why. She does not yet know how to weave. She will learn when she is older, around thirteen to twenty years old. (T.88.08.FLO)

A few older women sell or trade *cushmas* for profit. In the following interview, a mother believes this motive is sufficient for her daughter to want to learn to weave.

R: What did you say to motivate them to want to weave?
F: I said, "You must learn to weave because when you know how to weave, other people will want to trade your weavings for things that you want. Also, it is a shameful thing for a woman not to know how to weave. When you have a husband in the future, he will not have his bag if you do not weave one for him. If you do not know how to spin, you cannot make his bag." This is why my daughters were interested and learned. (T.88.17.ROS)

Spinning cotton is tedious work that gets little positive reinforcement. A girl typically spins for years before being judged ready to learn to weave. Weaving is a difficult skill that requires patience. Girls who spend many hours in school have little time to practice spinning cotton, and they know that being clothed is no longer dependent on learning to spin and weave because they have the option of store-bought clothing. The expectation that clothing will be bought makes labor in the outside economy more important than ever. Children make many of their own decisions regarding what and how they learn, and some girls are openly resistant to learning to spin, as a thirty-year-old woman relates here.

R: Do you and your mother still spin cotton?
F: Yes. A week ago, we spun a lot of cotton. My sister, who is eleven years old, is real slow at learning these things. She still does not know how to spin. She is just learning and does not like to do it. She says, "I am a student and I will not spin." My mother says, "Spin cotton," but she answers, "Huh, I'm not going to learn to spin. I'm a student." But now my mother has insisted on it enough that she is starting to want to spin a little. Many no longer teach their daughters to weave. (T.88.13.VIC)

Some traditional skills have become obsolete because more efficient technologies are affordable. Older adults differ in their adoption of these new ways of doing things. Some continue to work in a strictly traditional manner, others use the new technologies when they are convenient, and others have completely abandoned most traditional practices. The adult bias toward the traditional technology, and local availability of the new technology are opposing influences in parents' insistence that a traditional skill be learned. Children have their own ideas on the importance of learning traditional skills, and adolescents increasingly choose to be more dependent on the outside economy, spending less time on learning traditional skills.

Social stigma as a change factor in learning traditional practices

Some traditional practices, such as coca chewing and shamanism are learned less often today by adolescents because of changing social norms. Ashéninkas are aware of outside views of traditional practices, and they are less willing to learn practices that have a social stigma.

The highland Quechua have a stereotype of what they think a jungle Indian is. The stereotype is often expressed in traditional Quechua dances performed at festivals. In these dances, men wear masks representing monkeys and jump around in an exaggerated manner, making animal sounds. Outsiders sometimes have the degrading stereotype of the Ashéninka as animal-like or uncivilized. At the end of the eighteenth century, near the height of the British Empire, a sharp distinction was popularized between people of European descent and indigenous peoples of the tropics. Sinclair (1895), a British adventurer, expresses the predominant stereotype popular at the time, much of which is still common.

> These Chunchos, or "Campas," are evidently the remnant of a very barbarous and low caste race of untameable savages, recognising no laws, and killing each other with as little compunction as we kill our rodents....it does seem strange to see this magnificent land left to a few Chunchos, who are really little better than the monkeys that grin on the branches above them. Practically, it is no man's land, for it has never been taken possession of, the present nomadic tribes recognising no laws, no government, no God....But though Markham speaks of these Chunchos as "untameable savages, barbarously cruel, showing the greatest hostility to the advance of civilisation"—and, locally, we were told they have already massacred and eaten several European planters. (pp. 35–37, 39)

The Ashéninka culture was only one of many different indigenous cultures of pre-colonial Peru. These ethnic groups recognized different markers of identity, such as physical markings, clothing, language, and the name by which they called themselves. The coming of the colonists, however, created a tension between the technologically advanced mestizos and the Ashéninka. The mestizos saw the Ashéninkas as being inferior and animal-like, which motivated Ashéninkas to hide or modify their most salient markers of identity in situations of contact.

One Ashéninka practice that is commonly stigmatized by the outside culture is coca chewing. The young adult population chews less coca than older adults. Though once socially desirable within the closed Ashéninka society, coca is less acceptable today because of the influence of mestizos, missionaries, and teachers. In the following interview, a boy's initial disappointment with coca was followed by permanent abandonment of the practice after he started school.

M: I tried it just once. The others wanted me to try it. Those who liked to chew coca were sitting together. My father always said, "With coca, you do not get hungry. With coca, you are more enthusiastic about working." I wanted to try it, but it burned my mouth. The lime burned and I did not try it again because I could not eat. I was about eight or nine years old. I just told everyone that I wanted to try it out in the open, so they gave me some to try. I had it in my

mouth for about an hour when I felt the pain of it burning my
mouth. At lunch, I felt even more pain, and my mouth had sores. I
didn't want to do it anymore. I told the others, "I am not accustomed to chewing coca." They said, "It's your fault because you put
in too much lime." They insisted that I should learn to chew coca,
saying, "Some day, when you are far away, you will be hungry and
have nothing to eat. With coca, you can tolerate the hunger until
you get to where you are going." I did not want to listen to them
anymore. They laughed at me because I could not eat. My
brother-in-law laughed at me the most. I got angry at them because
they did not explain to me how to use the lime. (laughs) I put a lot
in my mouth. I gave them the silent treatment. They said, "By all
means, you must learn to chew it." I said, "I will not chew it anymore." When I went to school, I stopped using coca and nobody
tried to get me to chew it anymore. I told my family, "If you insist
that I learn to chew coca, I will stop going to school, because I cannot have it there." So they stopped insisting that I chew it.
R: Why couldn't you have it in the school?
M: Because the teacher often said that we could not have it. There were
always some children who had some hidden and chewed it at recess, lunch, or after school. The teacher punished them. This is
another reason I did not want to have coca.
R: Why did these children have coca in the classroom?
M: Because chewing coca was their custom by that time. Once you
start, you always want to have your coca. (T.88.23.ABC)

The discomfort of learning to chew coca and the social stigma attached
to it by outsiders have decreased the motivation of Ashéninka children to
begin chewing it.

Though the mestizo culture has its own traditional beliefs and people
who function as shamans, mestizos attach a stigma to traditional
Ashéninka beliefs, taboos, and shamanic practice. Few young men admit
learning to be shamans (*sheripiyari* 'tobacco drinker'). As with coca, interviewees say they did not want to be shamans because the tobacco made
them sick.

R: Did someone teach you to use tobacco?
M: Yes, my father chewed tobacco and told me that I should, too, but I
did not, because it made me dizzy and nauseated. My father tried to
teach me, saying I should be a shaman, but I had already separated
from him because my father went to work. Yes, I was taught to suck
on tobacco when I was about sixteen years old. (T.88.13.GRE)

R: Did you try using tobacco?

M: (laughs) He knows about this.

R: Did you ever want to try it?

M: I tried it once, but it was very bitter and I never tried it again. I was about fourteen years old.

R: Did anyone try to motivate you to want to be a shaman?

M: My father motivated me. He always said, "Son, let's learn to drink tobacco because it is really good," but I never paid attention to him. (T.88.14.ALB)

Another possible explanation of the decline in the number of shamans is increased contact with missionaries, teachers, and modern medical practitioners. These people may perpetuate the stigma attached to shamanism, but they also promote different methods of healing. Most organic sickness is now treated by modern medicine, leaving the shamans to treat only those illnesses that do not respond to "chemical medicines". The lack of motivation to learn to be a shaman can be explained as a combination of the avoidance of stigma, the physical distress of training, and the perceived decrease in the need for shamans.

The surface disappearance of coca chewing and shamanism, and the decrease in facial tattoos, traditional dress, and speaking the Ashéninka language ease Ashéninka entry into the outside economy. After entrance, success in the broader economy is believed to depend on a person's mastery of skills learned only in school.

Socioeconomic changes promote learning reading and math skills

In the late nineteenth century, Ashéninkas began to increase their participation in the outside economy. They cut trees, harvested crops, and gathered rubber in exchange for metal tools, guns, and clothing. Though many non-Ashéninkas exploited them, others treated the Ashéninka with respect. Some believed that education would help bridge the cultural gap between the Ashéninka and mestizo, and give them skills to protect themselves from being cheated.

The motivation for learning reading and mathematics came initially from the urging of outsiders, plus the Ashéninkas' realization that they lacked important skills used by more successful people. In the following interviews, interviewees tell how the motivation for going to school began with outsiders.

R: In those days, why did you want to have an education? What was the use of education then?

M: The missionary told us that if we learned to multiply, when we bought something, we would know its value. (T.87.13.FRA)

R: How did they get the idea that education could help them?

M: A mestizo who was pretty good taught us, saying, "You work a lot to get almost nothing." He asked us how long we had worked and asked us how much we had made, because we didn't have anything. We worked hard but had almost nothing. He told us we needed a school so we would know how to write. That is why the Ashéninkas asked for a teacher.

R: Where was this?

M: Here in the whole area.

R: Who was this mestizo?

M: Someone who came from Pucallpa. He first came and talked to us. He wasn't boastful. He was a worker for a patron but knew how to figure accounts. He told us how to figure them. The Loretanos from Pucallpa act almost like us—he cooked and everything. He even fed us. He is the one who gave us this idea. (T.87.14.CAR)

M: When the missionary came, an Ashéninka leader said, "Get your children educated." But my father said that if we went to school, we would just sit around and get lazy and learn to steal and tell lies. He said he would not let us go to school. For me, a measles epidemic came and my father died of it. My mother lived and I was a bit older. The teacher said to me, "You can go to school." I answered that I was then too old to go to school. He said that it was easier for older children than younger ones. He said that I would better understand the explanations of the teacher. My mother lived near Huachiriki, near Pichanaki. The teacher got me excited about school. My mother no longer had power over me; it was my father who stopped me from going to school. So I said to my mother, "I want to go to school to see if I can learn." She said that was fine, so I went to school here in Marankiari. This is were I met Chaiña [one of the first teachers]. He had just arrived from Puno. I registered. It cost fifty centavos in those days. Chaiña asked me if I knew anything and I said that I did not. He told me that I would learn from him. I studied and learned. I finished fifth grade of primary school, and that is as far as I went. From that time, I started looking for my wife and children. I resolved that they would be educated. I wanted my children to be educated, so they all finished their secondary school. This is my plan for myself. (T.87.21.ROB)

M: My teachers also told me that I should keep studying and I could be something. So I got more excited. (T.88.01.SAM)

R: Why did your mother send you to school?

F: The teacher in Cajonari said, "Send your child to school so she can learn to write." So I went, though I didn't know why. I said, "What is this stuff?" I never understood why I was there. I played with the other children at the school.

R: You were never discouraged at school?

F: No. I went to school for four years. (T.88.08.FLO)

R: Why did you send your children to school?

F: I put them in the school because, at least in the case of my son, the teachers that came to the village said that we needed to put all our children in the school so they could learn something and not be like their parents who did not know anything. I thought that my children should learn something, so I sent all my younger children to school. (T.88.17.ROS)

Some of the first schooled Ashéninkas came from mixed parentage, with the father usually being mestizo and the mother an Ashéninka who worked as a maid in the household of the man. These children were more exposed to the mestizo social value of education and had the advantage of knowing Spanish when entering school. Many of the Ashéninka political leaders came from this kind of background. Contact with those who sent their children to school often led other Ashéninkas to send their children.

R: Why did your parents want you to go to school?

M: My father was not interested, but my mother sent us to school, working to get money to send us....

R: Why did your mother send you?

M: So we would know more than she. She was adopted into a mestizo family and saw that their children would later have jobs. Sometimes we didn't want to go because of the distance, but she would take us. (T.87.01.DMG)

The above statements were from one who attended school for many years. His mother decided to make schooling a priority, despite the difficulties of sending children to school, which included the fear of witchcraft and the lack of money to buy school supplies. Other parents heard the urging of outsiders but did not find these convincing enough to merit sending their children.

Many parents are unclear on why they should send their children and have little commitment to making economic sacrifices to keep a child in school. Though attending a village school is becoming a social norm, some families let their children quit school early.

R: Do you want your children to go to school?

M: Yes, so they will learn things. For example, I want my child to work so he will not steal.

R: Is it also important that your daughters go to school?

M: Yes, but sometimes not. I am now aware that my daughter is not finishing. She says, "Father, I cannot do it. I want to study, but I do not know it." I also do not have enough money to pay for her materials. Now she is working in the *chacra*, waiting for her husband, so he can take care of her and let her go to school. I do not take good enough care of her so she can go to school. There is no work for my daughter. (T.88.05.ARM)

Literacy runs in families. If at least one parent is literate, almost all their children study in school for many years. When the parents are not literate, school is especially difficult for the first child. Subsequent children tend to fare better, as young parents mature and younger children get help from the older ones. A woman tells how her younger siblings were more successful in school than she was.

R: Why did your parents want you to go to school?

F: My father put me in school because he wanted me to learn and to help him in case he needed my help in something. But I could not, because he put me in school and then took me somewhere else where I could not go to school. I could not learn that way. My younger siblings have done better. I suffered much in school because I could not learn the things being taught. I thought it was a lot of time spent in school, entering at 8 a.m. and leaving at 12 p.m., and then doing other things. That is why I learned little from the school. (T.88.17.LAU)

Some parents, especially widows, transfer decisions about their children's schooling to others. In the following interviews, others made the decision for children either to study or drop out of school.

R: Did you or your daughter go to school?

F: I did not, but my younger daughter went for a little while, but she did not stay because she was incapable of learning. I sent her to school because I thought she could learn. I have another daughter. Since my younger daughter could not learn, my other daughter said, "Let's take her out of school so she can help you in the *chacra*." (T.88.20.JOS)

R: Why did you bring your children here to go to school?

M: I am not the one who wanted to put my children in school. It was really my older brother who knows things and says, "They must go to school to learn something. If not, we will be cheated of our money for not knowing how to count." (T.88.22.MAC)

The most common reason for sending children to school is to give children the skills necessary so they will not be cheated in the outside economy. Especially important when contracts were made to exchange money or goods for days worked, Spanish skills offered protections against exploitation.

R: When you first went to school, why did your parents send you?

F: I remember my father telling me I needed to learn to read and write. He said, "When you become an adult, you can keep account of your work debts." (T.87.01.ABC)

R: When your father sent you to school, did he say why he wanted you to learn?

M: Yes. In those days, there was much exploitation and the Ashéninkas were fooled. We needed to stop being cheated for not knowing how to keep accounts. (T.87.08.MRC)

R: How is it that you went to school?

M: Because my father educated me. He was interested in my knowing something, because he didn't know anything yet. But when the mestizos came, there was much exploitation. My father didn't know how to handle it when he sold his chickens and other things. They cheated him a lot. Because of this, my father was interested in sending me to school to learn. (T.87.13.EDU)

R: Do you have any idea of why he didn't want you to be like him? What is wrong with being nonliterate?

M: Well, maybe not to be exploited by the mestizo people who came to the village. My father gave me many examples, telling me that certain people keep exploiting and robbing them, especially of the things they produce. The mestizos do this. (T.87.13.)

R: Why did they send you to school?

M: I have an older brother who told me that I should go to school so I could make more money when older. He said that the times were going to change, and we were going to need money in the future. In those days, we did not know what money was or what it was worth, and didn't know our numbers. My brother said, "Go to school, so you will know how to count money." (T.88.08.DAV)

The above interviews were primarily of first generation literates. These were among the first Ashéninkas to learn to read, do math, and speak Spanish—skills useful in common economic situations for that era. The contact situation, however, had changed by the time their own children reached school age.

Successful first generation literates typically sent their children to school not simply to learn basic skills for participating in the outside economy, but primarily for a transformation of self. These parents adopted schooling as an important shaper of identity for children—an identity socially acceptable to the outside society. When asked, "Why do you send your children to school?" these parents mention the specific skills taught in the school, but they dwell on the more general goal of being better people or having a better life.

R: What is going to happen to those who don't send their children to school?

M: I think they are going to stay exploited in indirect ways by other people because they don't know their rights. If they are women, they don't know how to defend themselves from their husbands. And the husbands are less prepared to confront modern life. We don't know how to defend ourselves and get out of messes. That is what I think. (T.87.06.MUS)

R: Why did he want you to study? Did he ever say?

M: The only thing he said to me was that I had to study because he did not want me to be illiterate like him. That is all he said. My father is illiterate, not knowing how to read or write. He said that if I didn't go to school, I would be illiterate just like him. Not to follow in his footsteps, he sent me to school. (T.87.13.EUL)

R: Did your father tell you why he sent you to school?

M: Yes. He sent me to learn. He said he didn't want me to be like him. He said, "I am always the little teacher who teaches you everything I know, but I want my children to have a better education. I am sending you so you will be something in life. "

R: Like what?

M: Education can be used in our work. He told us that if we didn't learn, our lives would be just like his. With education, we could have a business, or other work that is easier for us.

R: Did he think that if you learned, you would move out of the village or work in a town like Tarma?

M: My father's idea was that I learn more than he, and learn to do something. He didn't care if I went to the city to work. (T.87.21.ROB)

M: I never thought I would have a life like I've had. I first went to school because they told me I could eventually have something like a job to support my family. They said we would continue to be exploited if we didn't go to school. We needed to know our rights. I tried to learn, and then got interested. I started when ten years old. When I started to realize that the marks on the page had meaning, I got real excited and wanted to learn more. I don't know why I was more excited than others, but maybe I had more opportunities than others. I see that I took advantage of the opportunities. (T.88.01.SAM)

R: What did he say was his reason for sending you to school?
M: My father said, "Son, you must go to school." At first, I did not want to go because I was afraid. Many times I returned home. Often when my mother or father took me, I cried. I always wanted to go back home. Little by little, I got used to it. My father always said, "Study, son, because I do not want you to be like me, who does not know anything. I do not want you to be ignorant like your mother. I want you to be another kind of person. Our village needs people who are prepared, who understand the laws, both of God and of man. You must always behave yourself in class, obeying your teacher." My father always told me this and, when I disobeyed, my father punished me. (T.88.06.GER)

R: Why do you send your children to school?
M: I send them to school so they will know how to write and read and learn. I want them to be teachers or something like that. I did not have enough money to study. Things have changed a lot and we need people who are not ignorant, who know how to read and write, to be secretaries for the future. I spend my money so my children can learn. This is for the future. (T.88.08.DAV)

R: Why did you send your children to school?
M: I sent them to school because the school started about the time I arrived here. There were also conversations among the adults in which they said their children should go to school and learn the things we never learned, so they would know Spanish and other things. Though they didn't learn everything, they learned something. (T.88.15.ALB)

R: Do you want your children to study?

M2: Yes, of course. I want them to know more than I.

R: Why do you want them to study?

M2: That they be useful in life or enter a profession and not be in the same place as I.

R: What do they lack here? What level of education do you want them to have?

M2: As long as I can afford to send them. (T.87.01.ABC)

R: Why did your parents send you to school?

M: When I was seven years old, a school was established in our village. Since the school was close, my mother registered me in the school. At first, I was afraid to go to school. The teacher was very bad. He punished us and hit us, so I was afraid to go. But my mother insisted that I go, saying, "You must go to school to learn, so in the future others cannot cheat you. You must have a job and not be like we who don't know anything. I do not know how to count money." That is how my mother motivated me to go to school. She said, "You must study and be a different kind of person." She compared me with people who had work, comparing us in the *chacra* with those who worked in town. She did not want me to follow her footsteps. (T.88.23.ABC)

Generally dissatisfied with their current situation, these parents want something better for their children than what they have. They believe education will improve the lives of the young, and this belief has taken on mythic proportions and it is taught to the children, much like the social values of honesty and hard work. Children from these families faithfully attend school because they know their parents expect them to do so.

Since the 1950s, the Ashéninka have had increased contact with the outside society. Groupings of families have formed villages, and individuals have become church leaders, political leaders, and school teachers. Colonization of Ashéninka areas by mestizos has pushed Ashéninkas to speak out for their interests and has put pressure on them to have leaders to deal with these new problems. All villages want a leadership that can communicate effectively with mestizos and wade through government bureaucracy, while still relating closely to those in the village. An Ashéninka school teacher tells of his hope that his children will some day provide leadership, partly learned in school.

R: Why do you send your children to school?

M: So they will be prepared for life. At this time, there are many changes and life is becoming more difficult. When one prepares more, he has more possibilities to have success in life. He can later defend himself in life. Our community requires that we have people prepared who can help the progress. We want to improve. (T.87.06.MUS)

Boys who attend school and learn the skills taught can be confident that they will be elected to a position in the village government. Prestige similar to that once earned through hunting prowess can come through showing competence in school-taught skills. The need for social acceptance that motivated boys to learn traditional skills now encourages them to learn in school.

Though girls are not elected to village office, many professions are available to them. Girls and boys can be teachers, paramedics, or secretaries in government offices. Ashéninka girls aspire to these positions in roughly the same proportion as do mestizo girls. As Ashéninkas participate more in the outside economy, both boys and girls are attracted to the professions. Educated parents often send their children to school for as long as the child wants to attend. This is especially common in families in which a parent is a teacher, paramedic, or pastor. Two Ashéninka professionals said the following:

R: Why do you want your daughter to be educated?
M: The mentality is changing. A person needs to be educated, prepared, so they can have a profession to improve their life. To be educated means that one can help his fellow Ashéninkas, to the level he can arrive. (T.87.08.MRC)

R: What do you want your children to do?
M: Yes, I have the same hope for my children that my father had for me—even more. I want my daughter to be something, to make her living from her learning, that she have a profession.
R: You don't want her to work in farming?
M: It depends on her luck. If she marries a man who is a farmer, she must work in the *chacra*, but if she marries someone with a profession, she has to try hard to be a professional so they are equal. This depends on her. I, as her father, have to give her guidance so she is not crazy and gets married before she completes her education. This is my job as her father. (T.87.21.ROB)

A professional has high prestige without being elected to village office. Though salaries are low, they provide a sense of economic security, supplementing the income from the *chacra*.

Ashéninka children take much of the responsibility for their own learning in school, as they do in the learning of traditional skills. Many village leaders have stories of how they took the initiative for continuing in school. Others tell of how their desire to continue their education was interrupted by a lack of money or family responsibilities.

M: I interrupted my education because we didn't have enough money. I had five years when I didn't go to school. I was always motivated to study. I had a plan in which I would work and use my savings to study somewhere else, but that wasn't enough; it was only enough for clothes and food. I also lacked my personal documents, so I had to travel often to Oxapampa to get them. I had trouble, because I didn't have a birth certificate. Once, I wanted to go into the army so I could get my documents, but when I got there, they took only some of us. I was rejected from the army because I had a high number. I am now teaching myself. I cannot study much because of all the work I have to do. (T.88.01.SAM)

M: My brother was about twenty years old and I was about seven years old. He does not know how to read very much. He only advanced to third grade. I finished all my primary school in Cahuapanas. My father sacrificed much to send me. I wanted to continue but could not. I want my son to continue his education, but there is not enough money. (T.88.08.DAV)

Conclusion

As with traditional skills, not all the motivation to learn in school originates with the parents. Children need to have competence in skills that are becoming increasingly important to village life, and to form an identity that they believe will make them more socially and economically successful. They see these skills practiced when the school teacher and village leaders conduct business with outsiders, when their parents obligatorily vote in national and local elections, and when they dream of someday having a profession that uses many school-taught skills. In this sense, many Ashéninka children have a strong self-motivation for study in school. They make the decision to learn according to the cultural reality they understand. This is particularly important in light of rapid economic change and intensive contact with a different culture.

Parents present ideal expectations to children through traditional stories, motivating talk in learning situations, and talk that speculates on the future. A part of socialization is the individual continually assessing the cultural situation and social presentation of the Ashéninka world by others, making decisions regarding what part or version of the world the child wants to learn. In this chapter, I focused on the individual in the process of socialization and the individual choosing to identify with the socializing world. In the next chapter, I focus on an aspect of socialization that is more social—the expert presentation of the Ashéninka world to the novice. The dominant model of presentation is apprenticeship, the expert and novice working together in a way that results in the child becoming expert in various activities.

5

Teaching and Learning Strategies

First my father made the arrow. I was next to him, watching how he did it. With this as a foundation, I learned to make arrows. EDU

My daughters started cooking when they were about five years old, doing the same as I showed them. They had their own small pots. ROS

My mother guided me by taking my hand and helping me pull the cotton. Eventually I didn't need help. Sometimes I messed up, but my mother never got angry at me; she just helped me with a lot of patience. I got it right by her showing me the right way. LOL

This chapter explores the variety of activities in learning situations. No study of socialization can focus on only the child as learner or the adult as teacher; socialization includes the broad range of activities in which children learn in many contexts and with different models. Ashéninka parents typically take responsibility for socializing children, spending much time directly transmitting expert knowledge. Yet Ashéninka learning broadly falls into two categories, that which is guided and that which is not. In nonguided learning, the child learns by imitating adult roles in dramatic play, solitary experimentation, and collaboration with other children. In guided learning, an adult structures the learning situation and presents and sometimes models the knowledge to be learned.

In this chapter, the focus is on the strategies used by both teacher and learner to accomplish goals. Both are active participants in the process of socialization, with their respective roles changing as the child progresses from novice to expert.

Nonguided learning

Dramatic play

Nonguided learning is characterized by individual motivation and initiative. Psychologist Rogoff writes of the active role that motivated learners' play in learning activities.

> Children's own eagerness to participate in ongoing activities and to increase their understanding is essential to their learning in social context. Children observe, participate in, and manage social activities in which they advance their skills and understanding. (Rogoff 1990:191)

In nonguided learning, the participation of others is minimal, but adults may provide the necessary tools and model the skill. A little boy who imitates his father by playing with a toy bow and arrows is an example of nonguided learning. A father gives a boy his own bow when the child shows an interest in hunting and displays the motor development to handle it. In the following interview, a father tells how his nephews tried to get his five-year-old son to play with a bow and arrows.

R: Have you given your little son a toy bow and arrow yet?
M: Yes, he often goes and plays with his cousin who made him a bow out of ordinary sticks. His cousin is about eight years old. My son likes to play with it, but not so much. He gets bored and throws it down because he is only five. (T.88.23.ABC)

The father recognizes that if the child is too young, he will quickly lose interest.

Parents often manufacture miniature tools for their children to use in their play. Little boys typically receive a toy bow and arrow when four to eight years old. They pretend to be hunting, shooting at fruit, frogs, or objects near the house. Ashéninka men remember receiving their first bow and arrows.

R: Don't your children have their own bows and arrows for play?

M: Yes, but they are just toys that are very small and do not have points. (T.88.08.DAV)

M: Parents make miniature tools for their children. A father doesn't allow his son to play with the father's bow. The child cries, so the father makes him a bow to play with. When it breaks, the father makes him another. (T.88.01.SAM)

M: At first, he made me a bow from a stick and arrows without points. As I got older, he made me bigger bows. I practiced a lot—this was my life, going into the jungle until I lost all my arrows. I then returned for more. I saw how my father did it, so I copied him. I also taught my sons, all of them. I start to teach them to shoot animals at about ten years old. I gave them toy bows at about six years old. Little by little, they will have good aim. Whenever we saw a new animal, my father taught me its name. (T.88.05.ARM)

Though the bow and arrows are considered toys, fathers or another relative occasionally give tips to the child on how to hold the bow. Young boys are prohibited from going hunting on their own, and are expected only to shoot at nearby objects. Fathers do not expect them to be expert at this young age, though some boys successfully find edible game, such as frogs, fish, and other small animals that wander near the house. If a boy kills an animal, he is expected to follow the same dietary restrictions as expert hunters, not eating the game that he himself has killed.

R: At what age did you begin to practice with a small bow and arrow?
M: I began to shoot it like a toy at four or five years old. I practiced and practiced until I was good. But my father always prohibited me from eating what I shot.
R: Who made your first toy bow and arrow?
M: Since my parents didn't love me, an uncle made my first bow. He also showed me how to hold my hands, aim, and shoot. (T.88.10.ABE)

Besides being prohibited from wandering into the forest, little boys are told not to break household objects or to do injury to domestic animals or other persons. In the following interview, the informant mentions that small boys sometimes get into trouble for shooting at their sister or others.

R: When you were small, how did you learn to hunt?
M: I learned when I was four years old. My father made me a small bow and arrows. I started by shooting at birds. I practiced and went to the forest with my father, where we made hunting blinds. I started going with him when I was four years old. My father told

me, "Don't shoot at your sister; only shoot at animals." Some little boys shoot at their sisters, but I did not. (T.88.13.GRE)

R: Who gave you your first toy arrow?
M: My brother. I was about nine years old. It was made out of good materials. Before that age, my mother did not let me use an arrow and bow because I could accidentally make problems with the other children. (T.88.23.ABC)

A boy's target practice becomes dramatic play when the child begins to follow the social rules of expert hunters. A boy may accompany his father or older brother on a hunting or fishing trip. These trips are typically for a couple of hours near the home to shoot fish in the stream or birds eating wild fruit beneath a tree. Though the boy may not shoot at animals for several more years, he observes his father's movements and strategies, which he later imitates in his play. According to the following interviews, a boy may accompany his father on a hunt when about eight years old.

R: Who taught you to hunt and make an arrow?
M: It was my older brother. I watched how he did it. I learned after he shot the animal, watching and learning. I did not have my own bow until I was eight years old. He gave me a small bow. I did not have a big one until I was older and made a large one for myself. I started hunting with my brother when I was eight years old. I also went fishing with him. (T.88.12.LOP)

R: How did you learn to hunt?
M: I was about eight years old when my father started taking me to the forest and taught me about hunting. He showed me how to hold and position the arrow. He first showed me the *trompo*, an arrow with a large blunt end. He had me use a special small bow. (T.88.14.ALB)

R: Did your father make you a small bow when you were a child?
M: Yes, he made me one. I was about eight years old when I started hunting with him. My father did not let me play with a toy bow and arrow until I was eight. I made my sons bows and arrows, not with real materials, but with plain sticks for them with blunt practice arrows. When I was younger, my father didn't want me to practice around the house. When I was about eight years old, he made me the things I needed to go hunting with him. (T.88.22.MAC)

Fathers expect their sons to practice with the bow for many years before they are ready to hunt. In 1988, I observed a twelve-year-old boy (M-D) with Down's syndrome. He did not speak or walk until about nine years old. His speech and motor development were far behind that of his younger siblings and nephews, so his father waited to give him a toy bow and arrow until he reached the level of motor development and understanding of a four-year-old. He is still in the stage of dramatic play when using the bow, waiting for his father to judge him ready to hunt alone in the forest. In the following interview, M-D's father tells that he treated M-D comparable to the treatment his older brother and younger nephew received.

R: Did you teach your sons to hunt?

M: Yes. I taught them the same way that my father taught me, but of course, I let them use small arrows until they got older. I told them the things that my father told to motivate me. I gave one son his first bow when he was four years old. When he was about thirteen years old, he was pretty good. I also taught M-D, who has his own bow. He does not go hunting with me, but he practices with his bow. He likes to practice a lot with the bow. He always wants to go hunting with me, but we do not let him because he might have an accident and get hurt. My grandson [age five] has the little bow that M-D also uses, and both practice. (T.88.14.ALB)

Dramatic play is more common for boys than for girls because girls are expected to stay in the company of their mother, the two working together throughout the day. The most common opportunity for girls' dramatic play, however, is to care for younger children. Cooking is another activity learned by dramatic play. Though mothers give occasional instruction and feedback about cooking, the girl is free to select, cook, and serve whatever she wants.

Adults do not teach skills that can be effectively learned without instruction. Children observe and practice roles they see in the adult world. Children typically "grow into" many roles they imitate, or they may suddenly be put "on stage", as when a boy goes on his first real hunting trip or a girl gives birth to her first child.

Solitary experimentation

Several interviewees learned to swim by observation and solitary experimentation. They took the initiative in deciding to learn to swim, selected the location and time for practice, and determined the standards for successful performance.

R: Did someone teach you to swim?

M: I learned this by myself. My father and mother didn't let me go swimming because they were afraid that I would drown. When I was a bit older, however, my sister said, "Let's learn to swim." So we secretly went to experiment. That is how I learned, by practicing. I always practiced in shallow water. (T.88.02.RAM)

R: How did you learn to swim?

M: I learned by practicing on my own. I saw others swimming, but I was never in the water with them. I tried it by myself. (T.88.22.MAC)

Though these individuals were not formally taught, they did depend on the model of others when learning to swim.

Some boys do not have a father, grandfather, uncle, or brother who is present or is willing to teach basic skills. In the following interview, a boy tells how he needed to learn arrow making and other skills on his own.

M: No one taught me; I just learned by watching others. I learned to make arrows by watching. The first one was no good, but they got better and better as I practiced. I learned to make most things like a canoe, a house, etc., by watching. I learned these when about twelve years old and I could keep up with the adults. (T.88.01.SAM)

The speakers in the preceding and following interviews learned to make arrows through solitary experimentation. One had a mestizo stepfather who did not know how to make arrows, another lived with his widowed mother in a mission community, another had a father who lacked time to teach his son because of the time needed to pay back his debts to a mestizo, and one had a father who simply refused to teach him. These people made arrows because they needed them for hunting. They observed, experimented, and practiced on their own, as told in the following interviews.

R: Was he watching while you made arrows?

M: No. When I did it, he was at his work. When he came home, I said, "Look, father, is this how I am to do this?" He said, "Yes." He evaluated how I did. I was ten or twelve years old when I learned to make arrows. (T.87.21.ROB)

M: I learned by just watching others, even the feathers. It wasn't hard. At first, I wasn't so good, but with practice, I could do it well. I practiced a lot, constantly. Since my aim wasn't good, I lost many arrows, so I had to make more. (T.88.10.ABE)

M: I tried to make one, but the first one did not turn out the way my father's did. I cried and tried to do it many times until I made it right. (T.88.14.ALB)

Experimentation and play together often characterize nonguided learning. Ashéninka boys often imitate the activities of others, making miniature houses, canoes, or rafts. As the boy gets older, the things he makes get larger and more sophisticated.

R: Did your father teach you to make a house?

M: No, I just decided that I wanted to build my house. I was looking at our house when I was about five years old and got some sticks. I cut the sticks, put them in the ground, and tied them, but it didn't come out right—it was crooked, so I stopped. (T.88.05.ARM)

R: Do you know how to make a house?

M: Yes, I started by playing with some medium-sized sticks, imitating the work of adults. I was about seven years old. While my father was making a *chacra*, I made shelters out of banana leaves and sticks to make myself some shade. My father and brothers taught me, saying, "This is the way you put in the posts; this is how you put the poles; and this is how you tie the roof thatch." (T.88.23.ABC)

R: Did you learn how to make a raft?

M: Yes, this was easier than a canoe. My father taught me. I saw my father do it, so I practiced by making toy rafts from sticks. My first ones weren't very good, but they eventually got better. (T.88.11.ABE)

Parental and older sibling assistance in the learning of these skills was minimal, their main contribution being unconscious modeling.

The Ashéninka are good at improvising, capable of using many different materials and strategies to complete a task. Some of these strategies are learned from others, but some are learned from active experimentation.

Collaborative learning with peers

Peer collaboration is characterized by children experimenting, practicing, and playing together to learn a skill. This is not as prevalent as might be expected because Ashéninka children traditionally have little interaction with their peer group. Children rarely interact with their peers because they are taught that children beyond the family might be dangerous witches.

Many interviewees used collaborative strategies to learn to swim, usually with siblings and other children of their household, when they went to the water in the heat of the afternoon to cool off, bathe, and play.

Learning to swim is characterized by peer modeling, assistance, and playful practice.

M: My brothers taught me, saying, "You swim in this position." They showed me the movements to start with. I always went to the river with others. Sometimes my brothers taught me. I was about seven years old. (T.88.23.ABC)

R: How did you learn to swim?
F: I learned to swim by accompanying my older brothers and sisters. We played in the shallow places. I was about five years old when I learned. (T.88.04.EVE)

R: How did you learn to swim?
F: I know how to swim because my brothers, who have since died, taught me. I learned in the Pichis River in the afternoons. My older brothers showed me how. (T.88.15.MAR)

F: I had cousins who learned to swim before my sisters, brothers, and me. They showed us how to swim. I couldn't do it by myself, but only with the help of others who held on to me. I tried it in standing-depth water. (T.88.19.JOS)

Though interviewees tell of being taught to swim by others, the context is less formal than a situation in which an adult teaches a child. More capable companions may give some swimming instruction, but the primary goal is play.

If a boy cannot be taught to hunt by an adult relative, a "more capable peer" might try to help. In the following interview, the novice took the initiative to solicit aid from his more expert peer.

M: The first time I went to hunt, I made my own bow and arrows. I still did not have any idea of how to hunt. Since I was young, I had the mistaken notion that doves would just quickly come to me, so I did not even make a hunting blind. I just hid in thick forest and started to call them. They came, but since they saw me from far away, they flew away before I could shoot. I sought a solution to my problem. The next day, I asked my friend, "How do you hunt?" We were in school, so he said, "Let's go hunting this weekend." We went, gathered palm leaves, and he said, "This is how you make a hunting blind." He made it well. We sat inside and called the doves and partridges. He shot some. Then he said to me, "Now it is your turn to shoot." When a dove came, I took my arrow, but I started to shake all over. I was shaking for fear.
R: What were you afraid of?

M: Fear took hold of me. I do not know why, but we just get nervous sometimes when we are going to shoot. It was not because of my friend next to me. Though I was afraid, I shot the dove. When no more doves came, we returned home.

R: How old were you then?

M: Twelve or thirteen years old.

R: How old was your friend?

M: He was about fourteen or fifteen years old. Another day, I went alone. I made my hunting blind but not well, because I used the wrong kind of leaves. I did not know how to make it, but I eventually learned to do it right. (T.88.06.GER)

Peer teaching here follows a pattern similar to an adult teaching a novice. This differs from what is called "guided learning" in the next section because here the novice takes a prominent role in organizing the activity. Peer teaching can change to cooperative, playful practice, as in the following interview.

R: Did your father make you a small bow?

M: I wasn't loved enough by my father for him to make arrows for me, but I had older brothers and other relatives who showed me how to hunt and to make arrows. We became skilled by placing bananas or other fruits to shoot at in competition, to see who can hit them first. I learned because of the help of my older brothers. (T.88.10.ABE)

Peer collaborative learning is not as common as dramatic play or solitary experimentation. With increasing contact with the wider society, however, peer collaboration is becoming more common, especially for school-taught skills.

Guided learning

Rogoff describes what she calls guided participation.

Guided participation involves collaboration and shared understanding in routine problem-solving activities. Interaction with other people assists children in their development by guiding their participation in relevant activities, helping them adapt their understanding to new situations, structuring their problem-solving attempts, and assisting them in assuming responsibility for managing problem solving. (1990:191)

I use the term guided learning because I apply it specifically to the Ashéninka of this study. It is similar to guided participation but the emphasis here is on the prominent role of the adult in orchestrating many learning activities in several contexts. Guided learning is the formal presentation of knowledge by an expert to a novice, usually by an adult to a child. The goal of this kind of instruction is that the child will reach adult competence by having internalized the instruction. Ashéninka guided learning is characterized by the following:

1. Instruction is opportunistic, taking advantage of the context and child's interest.
2. The skill is demonstrated by the adult.
3. The adult starts the activity; the child gradually takes over.
4. The tools for the activity are appropriate for the size of the child.
5. The child takes the role of apprentice to the adult.
6. Standards exist for acceptable performance of the skill.
7. Practice is often solitary and persistent.
8. The adult gives feedback that typically highlights what must be done to improve skill performance.

The opportunistic character of guided learning

To teach a skill, parents typically take advantage of an immediate situation and a child's interest. In the following interview, a father takes his son hunting after the boy's expression of interest.

R: What did your father teach you about hunting?
M: Father went hunting every afternoon after working in the field in the morning. I asked, "Where are you going?" He answered, "I'm going hunting because there is nothing to eat." I said that I wanted to go, so he took me along. (T.88.05.ARM)

Children are willing to learn most skills before being taught by their parents; the parent chooses the most appropriate moment to begin instruction. Raft-making is not a difficult skill. The simplest rafts are two balsa logs tied with strips of bark. More elaborate and sturdy rafts use more logs that are nailed secure with hard palmwood spikes. Boys learn to make rafts when the need for a raft arises.

R: Did that ever happen to you, your father sending you to someone else to learn something?

M: Yes, for making a raft. My father didn't know how to make a high raft that is like a canoe. He didn't know, but my uncle did, so my father sent me to my uncle. He told me to learn from my uncle, so I went to his house. I learned how to prepare the balsa wood logs and how to nail it with hard palmwood spikes. I learned to turn it over and cut it in back and in front. It traveled well, like a canoe.

R: How many days did it take you to learn this?

M: Only two days. (T.87.02.APR)

R: Do you know how to make a raft?

M: Yes, my father taught me to make a raft because once, we needed to travel by raft. I took advantage of this by saying, "Father, so this is how you make a raft?" I watched how he made his raft. I was at least twelve years old. (T.88.23.MAC)

Adults rarely vary from their daily routine to teach. Children accompany a parent for most of the day, and the parent uses the task of the moment as a teaching opportunity. In the previous chapter, I showed how mothers use a trip to the *chacra* to teach a variety of attitudes and skills that are useful for work. Adults instruct children as they work, teaching facts, strategies, and explanations relevant to the current activity. When walking through the forest on a hunting trip, a father teaches his son about the significant flora, fauna, and landmarks as they are encountered.

R: Did anyone teach you the names and calls of the birds?

M: My father taught me the names of the birds.

R: How did he teach them to you?

M: He took me to the forest and when we encountered, captured, or killed an animal, he taught me its name. (T.88.02.RAM)

R: How did you learn the names of the birds?

M: My father taught me. He said this bird is named this and that bird is named that. He told me the names as he brought them to the house after hunting. I learned their songs by listening. (T.88.08.DAV)

R: How did you learn the names of the birds?

M: My mother and relatives told me the names as they brought them home after hunting. In the forest, they tell me the name of the bird when they see it. (T.88.12.LOP)

R: How did you learn the names of the animals and birds?

M: I learned them from my father whenever I went with him to the forest or up on the hill. When we encountered an animal, my father told me its name. When a dog went into the forest with us, it sometimes barked at different animals. My father took advantage to tell me the name of the animal the dog was barking at. (T.88.22.MAC)

Though women cannot be shamans, they make extensive use of medicinal and magical plants, especially to cure themselves and their children. Mothers teach their daughters about the plants, typically waiting for someone to have a particular illness as an opportunity to teach a cure to the daughter.

R: Did someone teach you about medicinal plants?
F: I learned these from my mother. My mother learned all the medicinal plants from her mother. She taught me whenever we needed to use one. When I felt bad with a headache, I said to my mother, "I feel bad with a headache." Then my mother would take me out to the forest and show me the plants, saying, "This plant is useful for pain, like the pain of a headache." If my sisters and I had another illness, she took us out again to find the plant. We learned them one by one, as the occasion arose. (T.88.19.JOS)

Opportunistic, contextualized learning is evident in the learning of most skills and values, with parents skillfully teaching something relevant to the situation.

The demonstrative character of guided learning

Adults typically demonstrate a skill before the child is expected to imitate it. A parent may unconsciously demonstrate a skill, such as when a child observes an adult handling a canoe on the river.

M: I learned to handle a canoe because my father always took me on the river with him. I did as he did. (T.88.23.ABC)

Girls learn basket weaving by mother and daughter weaving in parallel, the daughter imitating the mother step by step simply by close observation.

R: Did you learn by watching your mother?
F: I learned to weave by watching my mother make baskets; I imitated her, but doing a much smaller one. My mother said, "Very good, that is how you do it, like I do it. Watch how I do it and you do likewise." (T.88.18.JOS)

R: Did she correct you with words or by just showing you how to make a basket?

F: Speaking. At first, we had to get the palm fronds. Then she showed us how to fold them, telling us to do it like her. (T.87.18.CAM)

Spinning cotton and weaving are complex skills. A less demanding, related activity is the preparation of the cotton by removing the seeds and separating the fibers by pounding them with a stick. A woman tells that following her mother's example was easy.

R: How did you learn the preparation of the cotton for spinning?
F: The preparation of the cotton was done long before the spinning. This was not taught by my mother; I just observed how she took out the seeds and beat the cotton with a stick. After watching it enough, my mother said, "Now you try to do it." I tried and could do it at a young age. (T.88.03.MAR)

Arrow making is a complex skill. Baker (1983) gives a detailed description of the process of making arrows.

> The cane shafts have been peeled and straightened already. They are kept in bundles of perhaps two dozen, gathered by a loop of twine near one end. After extracting six from the group, Heraldo gives the bundle a quick, skillful spin and it arranges itself into a loose cone, a teepee skeleton, which keeps the shafts apart and dry. Next he takes a bunch of feathers and a roll of twine from the inside of the roof; the thatch and cross-bracing provide a convenient storage place for many items, the equivalent of our cupboards and shelving. When the feathers are carefully matched in pairs, he begins trimming and stripping them in the following pattern....
>
> His tool is an ordinary table knife that has been whetted against a smooth stone, and he is very adept with it. Bracing the slender spine of the split feather against his thumb, he turns the fine gray shavings from it, flattening it to fit against the shaft. After making a shallow notch in the top of the shaft, he picks up a tube made from a hollow section of bamboo. It contains a dark resin with which he begins to coat a length of twine, held taut between toe and one hand while the tube of resin is stroked along it. The resin comes from a tree, Heraldo tells me, and his mother spins the cotton twine. He dabs resin on the shaft and sticks the pair of trimmed feathers to it, then binds the fletching tight at top and bottom with the thread. He gives the feathers a twist, so that they spiral symmetrically around the shaft.

With the same knife, Heraldo splits a handful of long splinters from a chunk of the dark, hard chonta. The Ashaninka call the palm the Kiri, and it is the dominant presence in more than one old story. The chakopi arrow of the common sort is simply this barbed splinter pushed into the soft center of the cane shaft. Heraldo scorches both the paint and the haft in the coals. He says the fire hardens the tip, and the heated haft sinks into the cane pith, melting it to a sort of glue which hardens when the arrow is set aside to cool. The final touch is a few turns of the twine just above where the haft enters the cane, to keep it from splitting.

The whole process, excluding the time necessary for gathering the cane and chonta, takes no more than ten minutes. In a morning a boy can easily make twenty arrows. But it is not uncommon, Heraldo says, to expend all twenty in the afternoon, trying for the numerous and elusive small animals around the village—lizards, rodents, birds, snakes, fish, and monkeys. (Baker 1983:99–101)

As the child watches, an adult makes several arrows, modeling the movements and the final product. The boy imitates the adult, clumsily at first, followed by the adult again modeling the skill.

R: What did your father teach you?
M: He first taught me to work: to help him in the *chacra* to plant manioc, and to make arrows. He first did it as I watched. Once I saw him do it, I learned to make a good arrow.
R: How old were you when you learned to make arrows?
M: Seven years old. (T.88.04.ELI)

R: Did your father teach you how to make arrows?
M: Yes, I was about eight years old when my father taught me. I learned by watching him. I imitated him and made my own toy arrows. (T.88.22.MAC)

R: Did your father teach you anything?
M: He taught me to make arrows.
R: How did he teach you?
M: He gathered the materials, and had me watch how he made them.
R: How did he start?
M: I saw his model. (T.87.01.ABC)

R: Did your father tell you it was time to make arrows, or did you first go to him?

M: He said, "Son, come here to learn." He taught me everything.

R: What did he say to you, "Do as I do" or something else?

M: He told me to do it, though it would not be perfect, to make it just like he did.

R: Did your father help you?

M: Yes. First my father made the arrow. I was next to him, watching how he did it. With this as a foundation, I learned to make arrows. (T.87.13.EDU)

M: I was about thirteen when I learned to make my own arrows. My father taught me while he made his own arrows. I was there beside him, watching the shape and how he made the points. (T.88.14.ALB)

R: How did your father teach you to make arrows? Did he show you or did he explain?

M: No, I watched as my father made it. When he wasn't around, I did it the same as he did. I wanted to do the same as my father. He didn't say, "Do it." I just wanted to imitate him. Little by little, I learned from my father. (T.87.21.ROB)

Sometimes, instruction is both modeled and explained. An adult may explain and orally direct the child, who then attempts to imitate the skill as modeled.

R: Did your father explain how to do the work of making an arrow?

M: With words and with actions, saying, "This is how you do it."

R: Did you have to do it?

M: I had to do the same as I saw him do the example. Sometimes it didn't turn out right.

R: Did he show you anything while you were doing it?

M: Yes. He had examples, arrows already made to guide me. Sometimes you can't make something if you don't see the product. He always had arrows and other things. (T.87.13.EUL)

M: My father said, "Here is the arrow. This is how you make an arrow." He brought partridge feathers and said, "This is how you do it." He fashioned the feather as I watched. I understood and I did it too. (T.87.02.APR)

R: Who taught you to make a bow and arrows?

M: My brother and cousins. My cousin was an adult. When I was ten years old, I started to learn, but not well. I learned by just watching others. My cousin occasionally corrected me on how to attach the feathers and how to attach the *chonta* point. He explained it to me.

When he was making his arrows, I went up to him to watch how he did it. (T.88.23.ABC)

A child observes an adult repeating a skill many times, with the adult modeling the product and process, both visually and orally. Occasionally, the adult will "teach" by calling the young to attend, to listen, and also by making verbal note of error. Eventually, the child begins to imitate the adult, attempting to have a finished product that is similar to that of the adult.

Strategic assistance

Adults strategically interact with the child during the learning process. Adult help comes in setting up the materials for the task, starting the task for the child, or offering hands-on aid during the task. Parents typically provide the materials for learning a task.

F: Mother taught me when I was six years old. She prepared our first cotton for us. (T.88.18.JOS)

R: How did you learn to spin cotton?
F: My mother taught me when I was about five or six years old. I learned like my daughters are now learning. My mother prepared the cotton for me ahead of time. Sometimes my mother gave me only the bad cotton because she did not have confidence in my ability yet. (T.88.21.JUA)

Children often accompany the parent to gather the materials, learning where to find them in preparation for those occasions when they will try the task on their own.

Adults often partially complete a task that the child is expected to continue. For activities like basket-weaving, the first steps are the most difficult. A mother begins the first basket, and then gives it to the daughter to continue the repetitive movements that lead to completion.

F: Then I learned to do floor mats and other weavings. My mother started them, but I finished the work. (T.88.07.LOL)

R: Did you learn to weave baskets?
F: Yes, my mother taught me. My mother always started the basket and I continued it. I started with the most common *tampishi* vines that were not the best. (T.88.04.EVE)

Men weave the thatch for the roof and an occasional wicker crown for use at a party or political gathering. For a boy's first crown, his teacher begins the crown and then gives it to the boy to continue weaving the pattern.

M: My father told me how to start, how to hold it right. He started it, and then gave it to me to continue. When he saw me doing it incorrectly, he showed me how to do it right, saying, "This is how you do it" until we finished it. Another day, I tried to do it by myself. I didn't do it perfectly, but by all means it looked like a crown. (T.88.06.GER)

Adults assist children's learning by making sure that they have the tools and materials necessary to do the task. In the following interview, the father sharpens his son's knife so he can scrape the bow more efficiently.

R: Tell me about how your father taught you to make an arrow?
M: I was a child playing with my little brother. My father called me while it was raining. He brought a piece of hard palmwood and started scraping it. He told me, "Son, sharpen this knife." I didn't know how to sharpen it. After that, we had a knife that was very sharp to make the bow. He said, "Come here and sit." I sat by his side. I took the knife and he told me to make a bow. He knew how to make a bow, but I did not. He said, "This is how you do it. Make it like this." I watched how he handled the knife. I said, "Oh, now I understand. It has a better blade than my knife. Father, sharpen my knife for me." He sharpened my knife and I then started scraping my piece of palmwood. It turned out just like my father's. He said, "That is good. Now you have to scrape it a little like this." Little by little, it turned out good. (T.87.02.APR)

Adults also often arrange the surroundings to aid in the learning of a skill. In the following interview, a boy's grandfather arranged targets to help the boy practice archery.

R: You told me that it was your grandfather who taught you how to make an arrow. How old were you?
M: I was about twelve years old.
R: What was his technique for teaching you?
M: It was always with lots of practice. My grandfather made me targets. I shot at whatever I could for practice. At a certain point, my grandfather thought I was ready to go into the forest to hunt. (T.88.02.RAM)

Mothers may take the seeds out of cotton before the child spins it or split the vines before using them to weave baskets. Men may cut reeds to the proper length for a boy who is learning to make arrows.

R: How did your father, grandfather, or others teach you? Did some-one teach you how to make an arrow?

M: Yes.

R: How did they teach you to make it?

M: When I was small, my father first had me gather the materials.

R: How old were you?

M: I don't know, maybe four years old. My father sat near the fire. He scraped the reeds used to make arrows and made the canal for the string. Little by little, I saw him work and make good arrows. I watched how he did it. He said, "Here is an arrow, reeds, and a knife. Now let's see you do it just as I did." I had to do the same as my father. (T.87.04.EUS)

Girls learn to spin cotton when about six years old, but their motor co-ordination is not yet developed enough to spin without frequent mistakes. A mother helps her daughter by attaching the thread to the spinning tool and then handing it to her daughter to continue.

R: At what age did you begin?

F: When about four years old, I started learning to spin cotton. My mother took my spinning tool, which she always started, and gave it to me to continue. Sometimes, I had problems when the cotton broke or tangled.

R: What did you do when you had problems with the cotton?

F: When it got tangled, my mother said, "That is what happens. Keep trying." I kept trying and I saw it eventually done correctly. (T.88.03.MAR)

R: You told me when the tape was off that you learned how to spin cotton when you were about five years old. How did your mother teach you?

F: I always saw my mother spinning cotton. She gave me a little spin-dle and said, "Do it like this." She showed me how to do it while I watched. My mother hit the cotton and pulled the cotton out for me long and thin. The thread was wrapped around the whole spindle without breaking the thread. Little by little, I learned to spin. (T.88.13.VIC)

Some mothers literally take the hands of their daughters, as an exten-sion of themselves, to do the spinning motions and to give the daughter the sensation of spinning.

R: Before that age, what else did your mother teach you?

F: To spin cotton and do all the work in the house. I began to spin cotton when I was about ten years old.

R: What was your mother's technique to teach you?

F: She took my hands and guided them. My mother prepared the cotton ahead of time and helped me learn to spin. (T.88.04.EVE)

R: How did you learn to spin cotton?

F: I learned from my mother. My mother guided me by taking my hand and helping me pull the cotton. Eventually, I didn't need help. Sometimes I messed up, but my mother never got angry at me; she just helped me with a lot of patience. I got it right by her showing me. I used a smaller spindle than my mother. I began to spin cotton when five years old because I had nothing else to do, like go to school. (T.88.07.LOL)

Weaving clothing is one of the most complex skills to be learned. A mother sits with her daughter for hours, watching the daughter weave, monitoring her every move, and making sure that progress is made. When threads break or tangle, the mother is there to fix them so the work can continue.

F: Mother said, "Let's start weaving. Come and sit by my side so you can see how I make the lines. You must not move your eyes from what I am teaching you or I will take out your eye for not paying attention." So I sat there, paying good attention. The first thing I made was a shoulder bag. My mother prepared the thread and said, "Come and you make the movements." But there was a stick on the loom that I pulled by mistake, and my mother got very angry and hit me. My mother fixed it and said, "Now you must do this thread by thread. Grab it, like this." After a while, mother said, "It looks like you can do it by yourself now." That is how I learned. (T.88.18.JOS)

Strategic assistance comes in many forms. Such assistance is temporary and the child quickly progresses beyond the need for help. The taught skill soon becomes part of the daily routine, and the child can practice the skill independently.

Appropriate-sized tools

Ashéninka houses contain some cooking pots that are much smaller than others. When asked about the small pots, people say they are used by the little girls of the house. All the women told of using a small pot when a child.

F: I often cooked my own food. I used a small clay pot that mother made.

R: How old were your daughters when they started to cook?

F: They started cooking when they were about five years old, doing the same things that I showed them. They had their own small pots. (T.88.16.ROS)

R: Did you have your own pot when you learned to cook?

F: Yes, I had a special pot of my own that was small. My father bought it for me. It was a metal pot. I cooked my food in it. My mother told me what I should do. (T.88.17.LAU)

R: Did you have your own pot?

F: I had a clay pot, a little one made by my mother. My mother made me my special little pot. (T.88.18.JOS)

R: Do your daughters have their own pots?

F: Yes, they have their own, according to their size. (T.88.21.JUA)

Parents provide child-sized tools for their children to use in the tasks they learn. As the child grows, new, larger tools are made. Daughters are also given child-sized brooms and baskets, plus child-safe knives for cutting vegetables.

R: How did your wife teach your daughter?

M: She made a little broom for my daughter. In the morning, she got up and said, "Daughter, wake up." She got up and my wife told her to clean a certain area with her little broom. She told her to fill a little basket with the trash and throw it away. When she finished sweeping, my wife said, "Daughter, let's bring water." They went, my daughter taking her little pot. (T.87.02.APR)

R: How did you learn to cook?

F: At six years old, I was given small pots like these. It is more like real training and real work because we eat the food. I did not have my own knives, but I used the ones of my parents. They were dull knives because if not, we would surely cut ourselves. They were only sharp enough to peel manioc. (T.88.04.EVE)

Fathers make child-sized bows and arrows for their sons and give them shorter and lighter machetes and axes to use in their work. Men also make the spindles used by their wife and daughters. This is made from a long, smooth, slender piece of palmwood with a rounded stone at the bottom. Like other tools, the spindle is child-sized.

R: How were you taught to spin cotton?

F: My mother taught me to spin cotton when I was about eight or nine years old, because there was nothing else to do in those days. She taught me by having me watch her as she demonstrated how she turned the tool and pulled on the cotton. I started with a little spindle. I tried to do it, but it seemed difficult. (T.88.16.ROS)

R: Was the spindle the same size as your mother's?
F: No, mine was smaller because I was small. We always begin with small ones and when we know how to do it correctly, we spin with an adult-sized spindle. (T.88.03.MAR)

R: Did your mother teach you to spin cotton?
F: When I learned to spin, I was given a small spindle. My grandmother had a large spindle. (T.88.08.FLO)

R: Is the size of your daughters' spindles different from yours?
F: They are using their own, which are smaller than the one I use. (T.88.21.JUA)

Items made by a child are smaller than those made by adults. When a girl begins to weave, her first project is the strap for a shoulder bag. A boy builds many shelters and small houses before working his way up to an adult-sized house.

R: Did you learn to make a house?
M: My father showed me the way to make a house. It was difficult. I tried to make one many times. I practiced with small houses. Eventually I was satisfied with the way I did it. I did not help anyone to make a house, but made my own. I imitated my father. When I finished, my father came and said, "Very good, it is well made. This is how it should be for when you make your next house, which will be larger." I was about ten years old when I started trying to make a house. When I was sixteen years old, I finally helped my father make a large house, to make sure I knew how to make one. After that, I made my own. (T.88.14.ALB)

Adults gauge the size of tools and the tasks assigned according to the size and age of the child.

Apprenticeship

Apprenticeship is a process of a novice carrying out simple aspects of a task as directed by an expert (Wertsch and Stone 1985). By doing the task under expert guidance, the novice participates in creating the relevant contextual knowledge for the task and acquires some of the expert's understanding of the problem and its solution. The expert integrates explanation and demonstration by involving the novice in the learned activity.

Apprenticeship differs from other guided learning in that the basics of the skill are already learned and the adult and child interact more as adults. Among the Ashéninka, apprenticeship typically begins in adolescence, boys accompanying their fathers and girls doing more complex tasks beside their mothers.

The most complex skill learned by a boy is hunting. Once he learns the basics of archery, he accompanies his father to the forest to learn the characteristics of the animals, local geography, and strategies for a successful hunt.

R: How do you learn to hunt?
M: After you make your arrow, you practice in an open field, shooting at fruit.
R: Is your father with you?
M: The father sees you shoot and when you miss, he shows you the proper stance. After hitting the fruit with accuracy, the father says you can go after animals. He uses the same technique that he learned from his father and practiced. With this guide, we learn to hunt. (T.87.01.ABC)

M: Then my father said, "Okay, let's try to shoot the gourd again." He put it six meters away. He said, "You have to practice until you can hit it." I was practicing and practicing, and finally hit it. My father said, "Good, that is how you do it when you go hunting. If you see an *añuje* at its feeding place, shoot it. When you calculate that it is six meters away, shoot it." One day, he took me to the forest, and we came to the feeding place of some doves. We gathered palm fronds and made a hunting blind. At about 4 p.m., a dove came. To test me, my father said, "Son, shoot it! Shoot it!" Because I was only a child, I shot my arrow and missed. My father became angry and pushed me, so the dove flew away. I sat in the hunting blind, silent. He pulled my ear, saying, "Son, you have failed. What will we eat tonight?" I didn't answer. I sat there, crying inside the hunting blind. Soon, the dove came back. My father said, "Son, this is how you shoot it. Look at my hand." I watched him, and he shot the dove. He said, "Now do you see? This is how you do it also." I said, "Okay." About 5 p.m., another dove came very near. I took my arrow and shot it. (T.87.02.APR)

M: When I was in the forest, he made me practice. He was in the big hunting blind and told me to shoot the dove, to see if I could. I tried to shoot it, but failed.

R: What did he do?

M: The bird flew away, and he said, "When you aim, the bird sees the arrow." (T.87.21.ROB)

The novice hunter begins with a sense of inadequacy for the task, since his previous play with a bow and arrows does not fully prepare him for actual hunting.

The father opportunistically uses fishing or hunting situations to teach his son the "tricks" of hunting, such as where and when to find game.

R: How did you learn to hunt?

M: By making a hunting blind. I learned by going with my father. The first one I made was small. I was about twelve years old. It was far from home, in the *chacra* by the river. I went with my father when he went to hunt.

R: Did he teach you to identify the animals by their footprints or their sounds?

M: Yes. A bird likes to eat a certain fruit, so we made the hunting blind by the *pamaki* tree. My father told me this. This tree has fruit in October.

R: Do other fruits have their season?

M: Yes, *etziki*—it has yellow fruit. My father told me about it. He showed me how it looks. The *añuje* and deer eat this fruit. (T.88.04.ELI)

R: How did your father teach you to fish?

M: He taught me with a hook and line when I was about ten years old. At first, my father tied my hook. When I first tried to do it myself, I did it backward and wrong. My father laughed and said, "How did you do this? How are you going to pull in a fish with that? It will come off." (laughs)

R: Did he show you the best places to fish?

M: Yes, I accompanied him to the deep places.

R: Did he teach you about barbasco poison?

M: Yes, I was about the same age when I accompanied him, watching him use it. Once, he showed me how to fish with dynamite, but I never did it myself. (T.88.04.ELI)

The son learns strategic locations when hunting or fishing. He also sees his father use different techniques in specific situations, such as the choice of arrow for different animals and different means of catching fish, depending on the characteristics of the water.

Weaving provides clothing for the family and can be sold for profit. The average *cushma* takes about a month for an expert to weave, not counting the time to spin enough thread. Girls learn to weave when twelve to sixteen years old, many years after they begin to spin.

R: How old were you when you learned to weave?

F: I was about twelve years old when my mother taught me. Before that, she taught me all the preparation. The first thing I wove was a shoulder bag. Later, I made cloth that was about two or three meters long, my mother giving me instructions. After I improved, I made my first *cushma*. I am not sure at what age I made my first *cushma*, but I was a few years older than when I made my first bag. (T.88.21.JUA)

During weaving apprenticeship, a mother helps set up the loom and gives strategic assistance, so the simpler skills can be identified and practiced.

R: Was anything difficult when learning to weave?

F: The most difficult was weaving the first *cushma*, because the threads often get caught and break, and I did not know how to reconnect them. My mother came and reconnected them so I could continue. I needed help like that until I became more expert at about sixteen years old.

R: How did your mother help you learn to weave clothing? Did she say anything?

F: I was never formally taught, but my mother watched me to help me if my threads broke or something else happened. She was like my advisor. If I made a mistake, she said, "No, this is not how you do that," until I could work on my own. In those days, they said, "To weave well, you must always practice and be around someone who is an expert so you can become good at weaving." (T.88.03.MAR)

Learning to weave progresses from the expert carefully guiding the novice to the young person no longer needing assistance. Girls do not necessarily study under their mother; sometimes they learn from a grandmother or aunt.

The pressure and emotion of learning to weave can be intense. Most women remember the frustration of trying to get the threads right.

R: What do you weave from the thread?

F: Right now, I am making shoulder bags. Here is one that I just finished [holds up a bag].

R: Who taught you to weave bags and clothing?
F: My mother. I was about twelve years old.
R: Was it easy or difficult?
F: It was difficult to weave. This is the most difficult thing. To make it
    easier, my mother always gave examples and demonstrations of
    how to do it. She helped me when I had trouble, but she also
    laughed at me. Once, I became angry when she laughed at me. I was
    trying hard to learn, so why was she laughing at me? (laughs)
R: What did your mother say when you finally learned to weave
    correctly?
F: When I became skilled, she said, "Excellent, you know how to
    weave for when you are older and have a husband."
R: What was the first thing you learned to weave?
F: First, I learned to weave a small bag. A *cushma* is too difficult. I did
    not weave every day, but only occasionally. (T.88.04.EVE)

The intense emotions of learning to weave are one reason for starting with
smaller, easier projects and for learning from villagers outside the closest
kin circle.

More than skill is learned when an expert teaches a girl to weave.
Ashéninka aesthetics are taught also when selecting colors and patterns.
The Ashéninka values of intense labor and patience are cited in the fol-
lowing interview as another part of the learning experience.

R: How old were you when taught to weave?
F: I was about fourteen years old. My mother did not start the clothing
    for me, but sat close to me as I worked. She explained everything
    that I was supposed to do, like the width of the color stripes. I did it
    myself, according to my mother's instructions. The first thing I
    made was a bag, but it did not turn out good. My mother said, "That
    is how it is the first time; it will turn out bad, but you will improve
    after you do it many times."
R: What did your mother do when you made mistakes?
F: When I made a mistake, my mother said, "Why are you in such a
    hurry? Are you thinking of doing something else? Maybe you are
    lazy at weaving. You must have patience, since there is nothing
    better to do." She yelled at me because she did not like me to make
    mistakes.
R: How old were your daughters when they learned to weave?
F: They learned to weave when thirteen or fourteen years old, at the
    same age I learned. (T.88.17.ROS)

Women speak of teaching their daughters as they themselves were taught. Similarities include the age at which the novice begins and the initial setup of the loom and materials. In the following interview, one woman tried to teach a daughter to weave earlier than was usually the case.

F: I know they cannot do it earlier because I did an experiment with a small child. I had my daughter try to weave a bag strap, but she couldn't do it without getting the strings all mixed up. Both my daughters wanted to learn to weave, but the younger doesn't weave now because her babies are always bothering her.

F: So my younger daughter wouldn't break her threads, I doubled the threads together, just like my mother did for me. (T.88.18.JOS)

Ashéninka women gauge the readiness of their daughters for learning to weave according to the motor and emotional development of the child.

Standards of performance

Adults have standards of performance for children's tasks. In some situations, adults allow time for a child to improve his or her skill. In other situations, a parent may be insistent that the child meet their standards quickly. This impatient stance is especially likely in the preparation of food.

F: My mother taught me to prepare the manioc, saying, "If you make manioc, you must wash it well so it is not dirty." If my mother saw that my manioc was dirty, she said, "This manioc is no good to eat because it is dirty." (T.88.04.EVE)

R: Did your mother teach you to wash manioc?

F: Yes, she taught me, saying, "You must wash it so we do not eat manioc with dirt." Sometimes my mother yelled at me for not washing yams or the *daledale* vegetable good enough.

R: How did she yell at you?

F: She said, "This is the result of someone not paying attention when I give instructions. We do not eat dirt, but you cook it with all its dirt. You must clean it well." (T.88.21.JUA)

Only when small children have difficulty understanding adult standards do adults step in and tell explicitly what is expected.

Parents see the performance of their children as reflecting their effectiveness as good parents. The Ashéninka admire good workmanship and they teach this value with particular skills.

M: If I don't teach my children how to make good points on their arrows, they will keep doing it wrong. Someone will ask, "Who taught you to do it like that?" "My father." They would think that I was bad, that I didn't teach like I should. The arrow must be straight. I was taught how to make good arrows. I make good points. (T.87.13.CAR)

R: Did your father have patience?

M: Oh strong, he was strong. When I didn't do it right, he made me do it again. He was strong.

R: He was insistent?

M: He was insistent. He wanted me to do it just like he did. (T.87.04.EUS)

R: How many hours was your father teaching you to make arrows?

M: Sometimes we were there for three or four hours. It depended on how long it took to do the arrow well, because it takes time to do a good job. (T.87.13.EDU)

Children gradually internalize their parents' high standards, and they too come to have a concern for quality.

M: I tried to make one, but it did not turn out like my father's. I cried and tried many times until I made it right. (T.88.14.ALB)

The desire for good workmanship and skill directs a person's efforts to seek help from others and to practice new skills until expertise is reached.

Practice

The Ashéninka believe that anyone can attain the desired standard of performance with enough practice. Someone who is not skilled is thought to have not practiced enough.

R: What do you mean?

M2: Some people do not have good aim. They haven't become accustomed to it. I have one child, the oldest, who doesn't have good aim, but the younger one does have good aim.

R: Is the fault his or yours?

M: It is because he has not practiced.

M2: He says that he doesn't have any need for an arrow, but the other likes to hunt with a bow and arrow. (T.87.05.EUS)

Young girls practice spinning cotton for several hours every week. Though they initially need help, spinning eventually becomes routine.

M: After one day of watching, the girl needs to start doing it. She needs to practice until she is accustomed to spinning. This is her life, once she gets accustomed to it. (T.87.02.APR)

R: Did you do it well the first time?
F: No, I could not do it right until after many times of practice. (T.88.04.EVE)

F: With enough practice, I learned to do it. I prepared my own cotton, because it was easy. I watched my mother, doing as she did. My mother always gave me the crude cotton, and I prepared mine at the same time as her. It is not difficult; just take out the seeds, hit it, stir it, and it is ready. Spinning is not as difficult as weaving. (T.88.16.ROS)

Girls practice until they spin to their particular standards and gradually, after much hard work, the skill becomes routine enough that they do not need to think of it.

Feedback and criticism

Adults vary in the guidance they give. In the following interview, a woman tells of her mother's close monitoring to guarantee that she cook without error.

R: Did you learn to cook by just watching your mother?
F: I learned by watching what my mother did to prepare the food. It is not difficult. I never made mistakes cooking because my mother was always watching, making sure I did not make a mistake. (T.88.16.ROS)

In some circumstances, a child may be left to cook without guidance. Several women tell of embarrassing experiences when learning to cook.

R: How were you taught to cook?
F: I watched my mother cook. Once, I made a mistake by not washing the food before cooking it. My mother laughed because I cooked manioc with the peel and its dirt. I was ashamed for cooking it with the peel. Another time, my uncle brought an animal when my mother had left me alone. I cooked it with all its intestines and everything. My father came and yelled at me, saying, "You do not know how to cook!" He said, "When are you going to learn to cook? You might as well cook crickets if this is how you are going to cook. Get used to eating crickets." I wanted to cry because he threw it away, but I still wanted to eat it. (T.88.13.VIC)

F: Once, when I was young, I sometimes cooked manioc that was not completely washed. My mother made a joke of it when I cooked it wrong the first times. She said, "Look, this woman cooked badly. Someone should be her husband and see what she does." It was a joke, and she laughed. I felt ashamed when she laughed at me. I said, "Why do you laugh at me if you do not teach me how to do it?" (T.88.17.LAU)

R: Did your mother teach you to cook?

F: Yes, but when I learned to cook, I made the mistake of cooking the manioc without washing it. My mother yelled at me a lot for this. When my mother saw the dirty manioc, she dumped it out of the pot. She said, "We are the ones who are going to eat this manioc, but it is covered with dirt and worms. How do you expect us to eat this?" That is why she threw it out. When I saw her do this, I immediately cooked some more manioc, washing it better. I asked her, "Mother, is this how I am supposed to do it?" Mother said, "Yes, now it is good, otherwise I would throw it out again." I cried. My mother said, "You should be ashamed of yourself. Your father might come and see the dirty food that you cooked." That is why she threw it out and I had to cook it again.

R: Did you cook something else the wrong way?

F: Yes. Once, I cooked a dove with all its intestines. I was ten or eleven years old. When my father saw this, he complained to my mother, saying, "Why did you let this girl cook this? She doesn't know enough." My mother said, "Very well, she must learn with practice. Why are you so angry at me?" My mother said that I must wash it. I took it and washed it until the feces were all gone, but it still tasted bitter. I had to wash it with a lot of water, tasting it to make sure the bad taste was gone. I cooked it again, and we could eat it. (T.88.18.JOS)

These errors were intensified because they affected more than just the child. Parents sometimes criticize or laugh at the girl, making the child feel shame for not meeting her parents' standards.

Any one of several flaws in an arrow can make it useless. Fathers insist that arrows be made correctly, though they allow for some initial difficulty. Fathers typically give feedback regarding the adequacy of the arrow and how it can be improved.

R: He didn't intervene when you made the arrow wrong?

M: When he saw that it was wrong, he said, "You did it wrong. You have to change it a little here and a little there."

R: So he corrected you?

M: Yes. He corrected my mistakes. (T.87.01.ABC)

M: My arrow turned out wrong. It was crooked. Father said, "No, son, you messed it up. How did you make it so crooked? This is how you must do it. You must have a straight arrow so it will fly straight. You also must make it so it will not come out of the animal you shoot." I watched him. Again, I did it wrong. He told me, "You did not understand earlier. I told you to make a straight arrow. Don't you have ears?" I said, "Yes, father. I have ears. I understood you, but I need to practice more. I can't do it yet." He said, "Try it again." I tried it again, and it turned out fine. (T.87.02.APR)

M: I didn't arrive at the perfection of an older person in making arrows, but I thought I did it good enough. My father said, "You still haven't done it good enough." He was not content with my errors. He didn't say, "Oh, good." This is why I look at how some who teach in the school, saying to the child, "It is good," just so they won't discourage them by saying their work is not good. My father told me when something was not good enough, and told me to do it like him. I told him that it looked good enough to me, but he said that it did not look good enough in his eyes, that it was bad. So, I continued doing it for many days. Now I know how to make a good arrow. (T.87.04.EUS)

EUS is critical of modern pedagogy that focuses on the positive more than the negative in a student's work. The Ashéninka say little or nothing if a task is done correctly, often commenting only on the mistakes.

The Ashéninka use verbal means to correct someone learning a skill and to give advice on how to correct errors.

M: The teacher watches how the girl weaves. If she makes a mistake, she immediately corrects her. (T.87.02.APR)

R: What did your mother do when your thread broke?

F: When the thread broke, she said, "Don't put it in your mouth to wet it to put it together; just keep spinning." I obeyed and kept spinning. Whenever the thread got thick nodes, mother said, "Put your spindle down and pull on the thread until it is the thickness it should be." I did like she said and saw that she was right.

F: My mother always yelled at me whenever I made weaving mistakes because she wanted me to do a good job. My daughters didn't have any trouble, so I didn't have to correct them. (T.88.18.JOS)

Sometimes a mother gives physical feedback to her daughter by hitting the hands of a girl learning to spin or weave.

R: What did your grandmother do when you made a mistake while spinning?

F: She hit my hand. This made me afraid because I knew that if I did not learn, I would be hit again. I had to learn it. (T.88.08.FLO)

F: My mother hit me on the hand with the stone part of the spinning tool. She said, "This will help you learn to spin cotton."

R: When did she hit your hand?

F: She hit it whenever I did not spin correctly. It hurt and made me cry. It did not bother me too much, and I gradually learned to spin. (T.88.13.VIC)

F: She took a piece of balsa wood and hit me on my arms, elbows, and fingers, so the spindle would feel lighter. I think it worked. I pulled the cotton while my mother grabbed my fingers and pushed on them so I would grip the tool tighter as I spun it. I said I couldn't do it, so my mother bit me on the hand. She was angry because I could not do it. I cried and was afraid of being bitten again, so I tried hard and eventually could do it right. (T.88.18.JOS)

Girls typically respond to such punishment with shame and crying, but they must continue to practice until they master the skill.

Nontraditional learning

Many Ashéninka children attend school, but a parent who did not attend school is unable to help a child who is having difficulty. Though teachers help, children must occasionally use nonguided learning strategies to complete assignments. One person, who has completed secondary school, tells of his difficulty in completing an assignment in Spanish.

R: Were there other communication problems?

M: Mostly in the work of understanding the interpretation of the books, putting them in our own words. The words were difficult and we had to use the dictionary. I learned to use the dictionary, but a single word can have many meanings that often confused me. Now I know how to pick out the correct meaning. (T.88.04.SAM)

Students use nonguided learning strategies because the language of school is typically Spanish, and the teacher does not have time to work with students individually. Of those interviewed, the most successful in school were either those who had a literate parent or boys who learned most traditional skills in a predominantly nonguided manner. Those with nonliterate parents had great difficulty learning in the school.

M: At first, school was difficult, but it got easier. The most difficult was math, because I didn't know how to divide or add. Now I know a little more. Nobody in the house could help me because my parents did not know. The neighbors helped me a little, but not much. (T.88.08.DAV)

At school, children use peer collaboration and work together to try to overcome difficult assignments. If a "more capable peer" is in the group, help is more possible than is the case when all children have equal difficulty. In the following interview, the girl tells how her friends tried to assist her.

R: Could you understand the teacher in the school?
F: The teacher was an Ashéninka. No one could help me with my work. My mother and father knew nothing of my studies. But outside my home, I had a few girlfriends, but they did not help me much. They tried to help me by letting me see their notebooks and explaining things to me. (T.88.17.LAU)

When I observed an Ashéninka classroom, I saw the older children working in a group, helping each other read an assignment in Spanish. As one child read, the others helped him with the difficult words. Children encouraged and helped each other, replaying their patterns of learning together how to swim.

Handwriting is the school skill that most closely resembles a traditional skill learned by the Ashéninka. At least one Ashéninka teaches handwriting by taking the child's hand as he writes letters on the chalkboard, repeatedly demonstrating the writing of the letter, and closely monitoring the child as he makes his first attempts at writing alone. Other classroom skills are mental and less adaptable to demonstration. Math is a skill that many Ashéninka children struggle to learn. Math concepts and their use are minimal in traditional Ashéninka culture, so children need considerable guidance from others to learn them.[13]

R: Why do you explicitly teach them math, whereas you teach farming by having them watch you?

---

[13]Traditional Ashéninka numbers are: *tekatsi* 'none', *apaani* 'one', *apite* 'a couple', *mava* 'a few', and *osheki* 'many'. Those who have learned math in school can invent higher numbers in their language, but these are not used by nonliterate adults. The traditional solitary settlement pattern and subsistence economy did not call for complex numeration.

M: In the garden, I'm with them always, helping them, but math needs more attention, because you don't learn math by watching it, but by having it explained. It isn't like seeing how manioc is planted— learning by just watching. (T.01.SAM)

In the households interviewed, parents become partners with the teacher and student in school-taught skills. As schooling becomes the norm for more and more Ashéninka children, parents expect their children to learn math, Spanish, and reading just as they expect them to learn hunting and weaving.

R: Why do you help your children with homework?

M: I want to teach them many things. I don't want them to forget how to build a house or how to plant a garden. Our work has gotten bigger. Once, we just had to teach how to plant a garden and hunt, but now we have to teach math also. (T.88.01.SAM)

Parents contribute to the support of the school, help with its construction, give gifts of food to the teacher, purchase school supplies for their children, and make sure their children attend regularly. Literate parents typically go beyond this basic level of support, making sure their children complete their homework and helping them whenever possible.

R: Does your wife help the children with homework?

M: She only makes sure they complete their homework when I am away. Last year, they weren't doing their homework. When I found out, I tried to be home more to help make them do it. Now they are doing it more by habit, as a daily routine. They come home, eat, play a little, and then get out their homework without our having to remind them. I usually help them when they don't understand the homework. They suffer sometimes when I'm not around. (T.88.01.SAM)

R: Did your father help you with your homework?

M: Yes, he always helped me. When I didn't understand, he said, "Son, bring me your notebook so I can see what you did. This is not right. This is how you do it." He always bought me my A-B-C book in those days. I needed to know it, to learn it. If I did not learn it, my father pulled on my ear. He wanted me to know. (T.88.06.GER)

R: Do you help your children with homework?

M: Yes, sometimes I help them. I don't help them with math, but I do with reading. They have a lot of math and reading homework. I want my children to finish their studies and learn more. (T.88.12.LOP)

Schooling is rapidly becoming a routine activity in the lives of Ashéninka children and their parents. Some elements of guided learning are used to help children learn school-taught skills, but much must be learned in a nonguided manner.

Conclusion

Both adults and children actively work at the socialization of the child. In some situations, the child takes the primary responsibility for framing the learning task in nonguided learning strategies in which learning and play merge. The more common learning situation is one that is guided. The adult frames the activity by selecting the skill to be learned, and provides the necessary materials. The adult models the activity by demonstrating the finished product and the skill to be learned, expecting the child to pay close attention. The adult also gives strategic assistance to the child by repeating the demonstration, starting the task for the child, or taking the hands of the child to help through the movements of the skill. Throughout the learning activity, the adult adjusts the tools, instruction, and assistance according to the needs of the child. As the child learns instrumental skills, he is also being socialized into the Ashéninka ways of teaching others. People who were interviewed reported that they teach their children as they themselves were taught.

Absent from this discussion, however, is the spiritual component of socialization. The Ashéninka have a spiritual part of their world that is inseparable from their everyday activities into which children are socialized. The next chapter looks at how the Ashéninkas' concepts of spirits, witches, shamans, and magic are learned, and the ways these concepts affect the goals and processes of socialization.

6

Spirits and a Little Magic

He told me to avoid other children because some might be witches and contaminate me, making me a witch, too. They would kill me if I became a witch. I would be safe if I hung around adults because they cannot be witches, but one of the children might contaminate me. I did not have friends my own age. When I saw a new child, I said, "Oh, he is probably a witch." EUS

I learned by watching him make a hunting blind. He also told me the kind of food the different animals eat. He also taught me how to aim correctly. He knew everything about hunting. I wasn't very good, so he gave me a secret thing. He took a certain leaf and burned my hand with it. The next day, we went hunting and he said, "Shoot that bird." After that, I had good aim. ARM

Studies of socialization often ignore the spiritual beliefs of a society or culture. Belief systems figure prominently in socialization practices, for they offer both context and content. This chapter looks at how the spirit world is relevant to concepts of socialization among the Ashéninka.

Traditional Ashéninka beliefs describe malevolent spirits and witches in negative terms and shamans and magical plants in positive terms. Belief in malevolent spirits and child-witches strongly affects the social alignment of children and parents, causing children to spend much time with parents and little time with their peer group. Ashéninka shamans are a defense against bad spirits and witches. They traditionally have high status and are believed to receive instruction and special insights from good spirits. Many shamanic powers are available to most Ashéninkas, who have a collection of plants that have magical powers attributed to them.

Though many spirit beliefs endure in this period of change, some practices associated with these beliefs are changing. Schooling realigns the child-peer-parent relationship; increased contact with Spanish speakers has made Ashéninkas feel the stigma associated with shamanic practice, making this activity less popular and covert; and use of magical plants endures although their uses are changing with the times.

Ashéninka belief in spirits

The Ashéninka have a strong belief in a spirit world. Weiss writes of the Asháninka conception of the human soul.

> Every human being, every Campa, possesses a soul (*ishire*). It will survive his death and retain whatever may be required to identify it as the soul that had been his, although it may be transformed into a malevolent ghost or *shiretsi*, or have some other fate. (1975:428)

The Ashéninka have no consistent belief in the eternal destiny of the human soul, but they do have consistent beliefs about what can happen to the soul in the present life. The worst possible fate for an Ashéninka or Asháninka is to become "contaminated" by a demon. The Ashéninka believe that the human spirit can be transformed from having a human nature to having a demonic nature, usually an irreversible transformation. Those near the afflicted person feel particularly threatened.

> Ordinarily the sick person is not understood to be demon-possessed in the sense of a demon entering his body. But he is understood to have become demonic as a consequence of the attack he suffered. His soul has been transformed: if it was taken by the demon that attacked him, it has already taken on the form of a demon; if not taken, it will surely leave the body at death as a demon....It is altogether a distressful situation, and the Campas resolve it in the end by killing the sick person....
>
> Outright lunacy, violent in its expression, is similarly believed to be the result of a demonic attack. The victim, "broken" by a demon, becomes *kaviari* (insane, deranged, out of one's senses). The symptoms of lunacy, as enumerated by

my informants, include the following: eating such substances
as pieces of mat, dung, fingernails; exposing one's genitalia,
touching them, rubbing one's food on them, tearing off and
eating pieces of them; flinging oneself into the campfire to
suffer severe burns, waving an ignited firebrand about and
plunging it into one's mouth or genitalia, all without feeling
pain; speaking irrationally. (Weiss 1975:435)

The perceived threat of a kinsman becoming demonic causes an ex-
treme reaction, as described by Stahl, "They greatly fear sickness, killing
all who become delirious, believing that they are possessed of the devil"
(1932:34).

The Ashéninka know what symptoms prove that someone has been contaminated by a demon.

The departure from the body of the entire soul, as when it is
taken away by a demon, is understood to produce, not instan-
taneous death, but sickness leading to death, as the body,
bereft of its soul, falls into a torpor and ceases to eat....when
someone is gravely ill yet refuses to die, lingering on with re-
missions and delirium. For the Campas, such a condition has
only one explanation: the person was attacked by a demon,
who "broke" him, crushing his bones, then blew on him to re-
vive him. (Weiss 1975:434)

Beliefs about both malevolent and good spirits are taught through
many traditional stories. Knowledge of these beliefs is a part of being
Ashéninka. These also provide part of the cultural context, a sense of being surrounded by dangerous forces that an individual must be prepared
to confront with caution and a little magic. Change affects these beliefs
little because non-Ashéninka spirit beliefs can often co-exist with them.

Witches and social alignment

Witches and witchcraft in the Ashéninka (and Asháninka) case can be
looked at from two perspectives—what people say are their beliefs and
what people do with their beliefs. These two perspectives are necessary
because such beliefs have multiple applications. For example, children's
fear of being accused of witchcraft makes them avoid other children, but
adults may use the accusation of witchcraft to isolate an enemy socially.

Witches are believed to have some relationship to malevolent spirits,
many of which take animate form. Witches are typically children of six to

ten years old who are taught by a spirit mentor. The demon-mentor appears to the child in dreams, instructing the child to bury refuse from the person to be harmed. Weiss adds that a witch has continual contact with his teacher, "Human witches are understood to be in contact with their demon teachers, but on an intimate rather than ceremonial basis" (1975:479).

The Ashéninka think of witchcraft as similar to demonic activity. Weiss describes the Asháninka conception of and response to witchcraft.

> Witchcraft constitutes a special category of demonic activity. The Campa term for witch is *matsi*, and the Campas believe in the existence of both human and nonhuman witches. Nonhuman witches are the various species of ants and bees. These take food refuse and exuvia to their nests to practice witchcraft upon them, producing sickness in the individual from whom the materials came....
>
> Human witches are almost always children, usually girls, who bury such materials as pieces of mat, bones, and manioc cores around the house; these materials then enter someone's body and make him seriously ill. Children are seduced into witchcraft by any of a number of species of demonic insects and birds....
>
> When these demons appear to children for this purpose, they appear in human form. A child approached in this way is innocent but defenseless, and once it becomes a witch it is a social menace. When a shaman diagnoses an illness as being due to human witchcraft, he designates some child in the community, even in the victim's family, as the witch. The child is treated brutally and forced to dig up the materials it has buried. If the victim recovers, the accused child may be let off with a warning to cease and desist from further witchcraft; if the victim dies, the child is killed or traded to the Caucasians. (Weiss 1972:201)

A witch is "contaminated" by another witch, much like the soul is contaminated by a demon. Elick describes those who are typically pointed out as witches.

> The *matsi* is a person, usually female, often a child, who either deliberately or unconsciously uses her power to harm someone. She may be conscious of this maleficent power, the Campa believe, and use it to wreak vengeance for real or supposed punishments or slights, or she may not be aware of

> having the power. In either case her "death wish," often cou-
> pled with the ceremonial burial of something belonging to or
> used intimately by the victim, is sufficient to cause a person
> to become ill, usually with severe aches and pains, and with
> a fever. (1970:213)

The most defenseless people in society, including children, widows, or-
phans, or females in adulterous relationships, are often accused of being
witches. The mere accusation of being a witch can lead to the killing of
the accused.

> A person or creature one dreams about when ill is quite cer-
> tainly the causative agent. Thus if a sick or injured man or
> woman dreams about a particular person, that person is
> thought to be either a *matsi* or a sorcerer-shaman....A woman
> or girl accused of being a *matsi* seems to feel that the accusa-
> tion itself constitutes proof that she must be what they say,
> and she digs or sits by the patient hoping the latter's health
> will improve. If the patient dies, the kinsmen believe the
> death is due to the evil stubbornness of the accused *matsi* and
> will usually execute her, often with torture to weaken the
> *matsi* power. (Elick 1970:214–215)

The fear of witchcraft is strong enough that close relatives of the accused may kill the person, much as they would kill someone turned demonic. Stahl tells of people killing relatives accused of witchcraft.

> As the patient becomes worse, the witch doctor accuses some
> one about bewitching the sick one. Usually, it is a child six or
> seven years old, or a widow without a home. Warriors are
> immediately sent to bring the accused person, who is tied
> with a strong rope to a tree near the sick one's house. A stick
> is placed into the hands of the accused, and he is commanded
> to dig to find the thing that is causing the pain. If the patient
> recovers, the victim is released, after having been beaten; but
> if the sick one dies, the victim is immediately killed with
> clubs, or is choked to death, and the body thrown into one of
> the swift-running rivers. (I have known instances where a son
> has killed his own mother; and other instances where a fa-
> ther, because of his belief in witchcraft, has killed his own
> grown sons.) (1932:35–36)

Children and widows are the most likely to be accused of witchcraft.
From an early age, children are taught that (1) children do not know who

might be a witch; (2) a witch can be as young as five years old; (3) if contaminated by a witch, a child becomes a witch; and (4) if discovered to be a witch, a child will be killed by his father or another relative. Adults teach children to be wary of other children, telling them they cannot be contaminated as a witch if they are not touched. When visitors arrive, parents often send their children into the house, preventing any contact with the visitors. The following interviews illustrate parents' concern about witchcraft and the harsh penalty promised to those who are accused.

F: My mother told us that if we were with strange people, we could be contaminated as witches. If that happened, we would not live long because when discovered to be witches, we would be killed. We were afraid that we might be killed if we disobeyed, so when visitors came, we just rested and slept inside the house until the visitors left. (T.88.20.JOS)

R: Did your parents tell you to be careful of other children that might be witches?

M: My father always told me about witches. He said that witchcraft was real and I could not play with the children that came with their parents because I might become contaminated. If I got contaminated, I would be killed by my father because he did not like witches. (T.88.14.ALB)

R: What did they say would happen if you played with these children?

M: They said that we would abuse another person by committing a crime. We kill a witch. (T.88.12.LOP)

R: Did someone teach you about witches?

M: My father taught me, saying, "If an unknown person comes, they might contaminate you." My father said he would kill me if I became a witch. He showed me the stick he would kill me with. That is why I did not play with others. He told me this many times. Father said, "If you become a witch, you might kill me. If you kill me, then my brother will come and kill you." That is why we are prohibited from being with others. (T.88.13.GRE)

F: My mother kept telling us that if we played with many other children, we would end up being witches and someone would have to kill us. Many people kill others because they say they are witches.

R: How old is the usual witch?

F: Even old people, though they are infected as children. Some grow to be old. (T.88.13.VIC)

Besides telling a child that they would kill him if he became a witch, parents tell stories to their children so they will be wary of strangers and strange happenings. The following story is told as though it were first-hand knowledge.

F: Once, a young man came to marry a girl. At night, the man did not let the woman sleep, telling her, "Wake up; don't sleep." The man put juice from a certain leaf into her eye and she became a witch. The next day, she awoke and started acting like a witch. She told her brother, "I must be a witch now because I do not feel normal; I must have the spirit of a demon. Please send me away to live with the mestizo colonists." When her brother heard this, he told his father. When the father heard this, he got his weapon and killed the woman. (T.88.21.JUA)

This and similar stories reinforce children's consciousness of witches and strengthens social norms such as reserve and honesty.

The basic defense from witches is avoidance of unknown people, especially children. Buenaventura (1982) reports that when strangers are detected, women and children run to hide. Children are taught to hide from visitors, to ignore other children they meet, and to act reserved with a suspicious eye on those around them.

R: Did they say something about not being around other children?
M: They told me to be only with the people that I know, never with people I do not know because they could be witches and contaminate me. (T.88.23.ABC)

R: Did your father give you warnings about witches?
M: Yes. My father told me, "You should be very reserved and be accompanied only by your brothers and sisters and the other family members of our house. It is not good for you to be with other people because you could be contaminated by witches." I obeyed what my father told me. That is why I am not a witch. (T.88.22.MAC)

R: What did your parents tell you about witches?
F: My mother and father told us much about witchcraft. They said, "You must not play with strange people or be with people you do not know because that is how you become contaminated by witchcraft. You must not bathe with them because they can have a leaf with them that makes you into a witch. It is not good." (T.88.21.JUA)

R: Were you ever told to avoid other children?

F: My mother told me, "It is not good for you to mix with strange children whom you do not know because they might be witches. If the
other child is a witch, I will wink to let you know." My mother told
us these things, so we should not mix with other children. If others
come to our house, we should watch her to see if she winks to warn
us. She would know if the other children are the ones we should be
wary of. Whenever she did this, we went up onto the platform or
loft of the house and stayed there until the visitors left.
(T.88.15.MAR)

F: When visitors came, my sisters and I hid. We prepared our food in
our enclosed house and played there until the visitors left. We never
played with them because if they were witches, we could have been
contaminated. (T.88.17.ROS)

R: Were you warned against associating with other children?
M: Yes. Most parents prohibit their children from playing with other
children because they might be witches. The best defense is to stay
away. (T.88.11.ABE)

R: Did they say anything to you about not playing with other children
that were not of your family?
M: No, we never played with strange children, only with those who
were close to us. Our mother never let us play with strange children. (T.88.12.LOP)

R: Did your mother tell you anything else?
F: She told us not to be around strange children. We should only be
with people who are well-known or who are close relatives. I wasn't
permitted to be with strangers because we are afraid of witchcraft. I
didn't know why I couldn't do this, but I didn't ask why either.
(T.88.02.YOL)

R: Were you told that other children were witches?
M: I was told that witches were among us and that is why we needed to
avoid strangers and be only with those whom we know very well.
Even distant relatives might be witches and could contaminate us.
These witches could kill our parents if they came into our house.
R: Give me some words they used to tell you about the witches?
M: They said: "You must stay separated from strangers because if you
do not, they might contaminate you and do you harm."
(T.88.02.RAM)

To avoid accusation, children align themselves closely with the immediate family. Avoidance of social contact with peers reduces peer

comparison with others in the age group, and their behavior is then modeled for them mostly by adults and not by other children.

Beliefs about demons and witches are strengthened by traditional stories, parental admonitions, first-hand accounts, observation, and parental example. Though accounts by Elick, Weiss, and Stahl report that witchcraft was punished often in the past, interviews in this study indicate that most people take the necessary precautions to escape the accusation of being a witch. Though people take precautions, many are still accused by those who dislike them for some reason. The two accusations of witchcraft that I observed first-hand were against widows suspected of being involved in adulterous relationships with the husbands of the accusers. In both cases, the accusers' supposed medical problems did not respond to treatment until the accused women were beaten and driven out of the area.

Some fundamentals of belief in witchcraft have changed relatively little. Ashéninka children continue to be socialized to accept concepts of the human soul, demons, and witches. Small children know that from the age of six years they can be accused of being witches and if accused, they may be killed. In a village centered around a school, children continue to stay close to their families and away from other children. Most children are given instructions to avoid other children while in school and not to play with other children on the way home from school.

R: Did your parents tell you anything about children who might be witches?

F: Yes. My father always prohibited me from playing with others, saying that some are witches. I was told to avoid the other children in school because they could be witches and contaminate me. If I became contaminated, I might be killed by my father or mother.

R: Were you afraid of the other children?

F: Yes. I was not afraid, but cautious, on the watch in case someone was a real witch and wanted to contaminate me. (T.88.17.LAU)

R: Did you teach this to your daughter?

F: I think that even now there are witches. I tell my daughter that she should not be partying with others or associating with others because she could become a witch and then be killed when discovered. This is what we do if we discover that someone is a witch.[14] (T.88.20.JOS)

R: Do you think some children in the school could be witches?

---

[14]The woman referred to is an adult who has lived alone for several years because her husband left her.

F: I think there could be. I am real cautious about this because they
    look like normal people, but we are not sure what spirits they might
    have in their eyes or what demon may be in them. That is why we
    should stay apart and be very careful. (T.88.21.JUA)

R: What did you think when you saw children you did not know?
M: When I saw these children, I thought, "Nobody knows what these
    children might have in their spirit. It is better that I do not play
    with them. We are not sure." This is what I also tell my children,
    that they should not play with other children. (T.88.23.MAC)

School enrollment is increasing rapidly. The formation of new villages
and increased contact between children in the classroom make new strategies for avoiding others necessary. The following interview tells of cautious conduct between children in a classroom.

R: What were you taught about witches?
M: I was taught not to play with other children at school, but to sit at
    my desk calmly and not fool around with the other children.
R: Why did they tell you this?
M and F: To stay away from other children because they may splash wa-
    ter in your eyes and make you a witch.
R: Have you told the same to your children?
F: Yes.
M: Yes, I tell them, "When you are with other children at school, do not
    play with them or bathe with them."
R: Do you think other children here might be witches?
M: I *think* so, but I am not sure. That is why I am being careful.
R: Your children do not play very much with the other children?
M: No. But sometimes. Sometimes they work on their homework to-
    gether, but we watch them carefully. Long ago our ancestors taught
    us this. (T.88.08.DAV)

In the classroom, children often need to share books and check homework together. Most children group with their closest relatives when the
teacher permits. If a close relative is not available, a child typically becomes quiet and waits for the teacher to assign a partner. A teacher not
only presents the material to be learned but also must manage the inter-
personal dynamics of cautious children. Though modernization has made
living near the school important, most families live an average of ten minutes' walk away from the school. When the family is somewhat isolated,
children are told to come straight home after school. Even in a large village, people live either away from the village center or cluster their

houses in a family. This settlement pattern maximizes access to the school while minimizing contact with other children.

Before schools came to the villages, children associated only with their immediate family until wise enough to socialize safely with others. Children raised in this environment felt no peer pressure; parents and siblings served as their models. This social alignment makes socialization easier than if the parents compete with others for the child's attention. The following statement illustrates the child-parent alignment:

M: He told me to avoid other children because some might be witches and contaminate me, making me a witch, too. They would kill me if I became a witch. I would be safe if I hung around adults because they cannot be witches, but one of the children might contaminate me. I did not have friends my age. When I saw a new child, I said, "Oh, he is probably a witch." (T.87.04.EUS)

Ashéninka political leaders continue to believe in witchcraft and still accept traditional methods of punishing a witch. In 1979, at a congress of the forty villages in the Pichis valley, an invited non-Ashéninka guest was asked to speak. He told the assembled delegates of the beauty of their land, culture, and language, but he made the mistake of saying it was not good to continue beating and killing small children and women accused of doing witchcraft. After the speech, the leader of the congress stood and chastised the visitor for talking about something he knew nothing about. The leader spoke for several minutes, telling of recent incidents of witchcraft, saying that it is real and that the only way to deal with it is in the traditional Ashéninka manner. Other delegates supported his statements.

More intense contact with others does, however, decrease the number of reported incidents of witchcraft and subsequent punishment. The congress mentioned was in the Pichis region where contact with mestizos is much less than in the Perené, where children have been together in schools much longer. The following person lived in both the Pichis and Perené regions.

R: Did your parents think there were witches in the Perené village?
F: Not many there. I never heard of any there, but we hear of many around the Pichis area.
R: Do you teach this to your children?
F: Yes, my mother always tells them that the other children here might be witches and that they should avoid them. In the Perené we have almost forgotten this.
R: Do you also teach this to your children?
F: Yes. (T.88.13.VIC)

Beliefs regarding witches strengthen the bond between parents and children, but modernizing pressures bring some adaptive modifications of practices formerly associated with these beliefs.

Shamans and special insight

Shamans are often the heros of Ashéninka traditional stories, saving individuals or the world from danger. They are also a valued resource to heal those near them. Elick writes of the Ashéninka shaman.

> Some shamans rely heavily on materia medica to augment the effectiveness of their treatment. "Complete" shamans, however, are essentially psychotherapists who treat the ill by restoring harmony through manipulation of the psychological environment. The words, songs, and actions of the *sheripiari*, together with the respectful attention and "faith" of the onlookers, exert a powerful influence on the patient's mind. One of the most important acts of the shaman in this "psychodrama" is the symbolic removal of the disturbing agent from the patient's body. This is accomplished by sucking the affected area, sometimes after having anointed it with tobacco concentrate and "blowing" the area. (1970:215)

Shamans cure both physical and spiritual illness.

> The Campa *sheripiari* is, first of all, an intermediary between the seen and unseen worlds....He is the only person who can find souls that have wandered away or have been stolen. He can also cure by removing the harmful spiritual essences injected into someone by another shaman or by injurious forest spirits. He can often counteract the magic worked by witches (*matsi*) or demonic ants and bees. Thus the shaman is a central figure around whom the Campa build their sense of security in this dangerously unstable world....
> Another important function of the Campa shaman is to seek and bring back souls that have wandered away for one reason or another, or that have been trapped or stolen. Since depression and loss of appetite are some symptoms suggesting soul loss, it is obvious that the shaman's psychotherapeutic efforts might be most successful in this area of illness. (Elick 1970:204, 216)

Shamans often go into an altered state of consciousness to cure spiritual illness. To do this, Campa shamans mix a paste of tobacco juice and the ayahuasca drug. Those who actually become shamans are those who can best tolerate the mixture. The drugs free the shaman's spirit to visit and learn from the good spirits. While in this trance, the shaman's spirit may travel. The souls of other shamans may visit the shaman and, while he is under the influence of ayahuasca, be received by him. Conversely, his own soul may leave his body on a soul-flight to visit a distant shaman or to visit a distant settlement of good spirits. (Weiss 1975:472)

Swallows and other birds are spirit messengers to the shamans. These are good spirits that give knowledgeable insight, and shamans use this knowledge to cure patients. The following story tells of a shaman visited by familiar spirits.

The shaman and the swallows

Once, a shaman had spirit-mentors who were swallows. He called them his gods. When he heard the swallows, the shaman said to his family, "Listen to my spirit-mentors who are saying, 'Good morning, brother. Good morning, sister.' "

Figure 6.1 The shaman and the swallows

Others could not understand the swallows—only the shaman understood them. The shaman said, "When you see the
swallows, you must know that they are my brothers and that
they are gods." That is how our ancestors were. When he
drank tobacco juice, he saw an *unchala* bird or swallow in a
vision. They were his gods. When his wife heard the swallows, *shiii*, she answered them, saying, "Good morning,
brothers. God has blessed us because this is a new day." This
woman respected the swallows because the shaman said that
they were gods. When this shaman drank tobacco juice and
ayahuasca, he saw the swallows in visions. They were his
gods. (Translated from *Sheripiyari ipoña choriitzi* by Alberto
Pablo Ravírez (Anderson 1986a).)

Novice shamans receive their initial instruction from expert shamans.
They learn to mix the ayahuasca-tobacco mixture, the uses of other medicinal plants, and the steps of curing ceremonies. Fathers encourage
their sons to train to be shamans, beginning about twelve years of age.
Though much of a novice shaman's knowledge is learned from an expert
shaman, specific insights are learned from spirit-mentors while in a trance
or dream. The following interview tells of one person's failure to become a
shaman because his spirit did not pass a test while in a trance. If he had
learned to cure someone in his dream, instead of crying, he could have
been a shaman.

M: When I was a teenager, the shamans told me that I should learn.
They were not from my family. I practiced it and almost became a
shaman. A group of boys learned together. A leader of the group of
shamans taught us how to prepare the drink, put it in the container,
and everything. My father was there learning too, because he also
wanted to learn to be a shaman. Age wasn't important, but you had
to have someone knowledgeable in charge. The leader said that he
saw a swallow that flew into the house and dropped a peanut. The
shaman told us we all had to eat the peanuts the swallow brought. I
wasn't allowed to continue, however, because during my training, I
had a vision in which someone died of a gunshot wound, and I
started to cry. The leader said that I had failed by crying. I should
have cured the dead person in my dream and not cried. I was there,
learning for about two or three years. I was told that I couldn't cure
people because I had cried, so I left. That is when I found [the
Seventh-Day Adventist] religion. I dreamed because I drank
ayahuasca with tobacco juice. (T.88.11.ABE)

The novice shaman learns his most important lessons from the good spirits while in a trance.

Though belief in witches and malevolent spirits remains strong, few young men are being trained to be shamans. Preoccupation with earning money and the stigma attached to non-Christian religious practice have caused a drastic cut in the number of novice shamans. Most Ashéninkas, however, have a resource for counteracting the effects of spirits without a shaman—a plant that has both medicinal and magical uses.

Magic in daily life

The *ivenki* plant

The Ashéninka work persistently to teach and learn basic skills, yet people want a little extra luck to make them more successful with less effort. Besides guided instruction, Ashéninka parents give a little magic to their children. The main source of Ashéninka magic is the *ivenki* plant.[15] The *ivenki* plant puts magical powers within the reach of the average Ashéninka, despite gender, age, or social standing. Uses of the *ivenkis* are not hidden or secret cultural practices; most Ashéninkas willingly talk of the plant and its properties.

Ashéninka stories report that animals, stars, salt, and other important cultural objects were once human, but no stories mention the *ivenkis* as human or having a spirit. Though without spirit, the magical power of the *ivenki* resides in the plant, has only a specific application, and is transferred only through plant reproduction. For example, an *ivenki* used to cure snake bite reproduces other *ivenkis* to cure snake bite. Its effectiveness is temporary and is directed only at a specific activity. For example, when an *ivenki* is used to release a woman from a dietary taboo, it must be used before each meal.

---

[15]The plant *Cyperus piripiri*, called *ivenki* or *ovenki* in the Ashéninka language, is commonly translated *piripiri* in Spanish. This is a misleading term, however, in the Ashéninka context because *piripiri* is the word used for many different plant species and has different magical uses in different areas of the Amazon basin. I consistently use the word *ivenki* for this plant to focus on its Ashéninka uses and to avoid any confusion with the uses of the *piripiri* among other ethnolinguistic communities.

Cyperus piripiri is a cultivated plant that is not found in the wild. It appears as a round, dark green grass with a stem that is 2–3 mm. in diameter, growing 30–50 cm. in height. At maturity, it branches out 1–2 cm. at the top with small yellow seeds. Though it bears seeds, it is propagated by dividing the bulbs from which the stems sprout.

The bulb is the active part of the *ivenki*, being brown outside and whitish-yellow inside. Its shape is elongated, being about 1 cm. in diameter and 2 cm. in length. Many bulbs may be connected in a cluster. The bulbs are pithy, somewhat dry, and slightly bitter.

Only a few related species of *ivenkis* are found, but they have more than a hundred names and uses. Some *ivenkis* are used only by men; others are used only by women; and others are used by both. A woman's *ivenki* is used primarily for feminine activities, such as spinning cotton, and a man's *ivenki* is used primarily for masculine activities, such as warfare. A collection of the *ivenki* plants in a village shows that most look alike; differences in the appearance are due to soil composition, plant age, and the amount of sunlight.

The hunting and fishing *ivenkis*

A common use of *ivenki* is for hunting animals. One class of hunting *ivenki* improves the eyesight of the hunter and the other class attracts the animal. These hunting *ivenkis* are exclusively the property of men.

Table 6.1 The hunting *ivenkis*

Name	Translation	User	Method
oorivenki	falcon-*venki*	male	blow on hands
pakithavenki	large hawk-*venki*	male	eye drops
kovakitsivenki	small hawk-*venki*	male	eye drops
shirovenki	dove-*venki*	male	place on blind
tsimerivenki	small bird-*venki*	male	eye drops
koterivenki	*unchala* bird-*venki*	male	eye drops
opempevenki	toucan-*venki*	male	eye drops
sonkaarivenki	tinamou quail-*venki*	male	eye drops
thamirivenki	*paujil* bird-*venki*	male	place on blind
sankatzivenki	guan-*venki*	male	place on blind
shonkirivenki	bird species-*venki*	male	place on blind
chakamivenki	trumpeter bird-*venki*	male	place on blind
kenthorivenki	gray tinamou-*venki*	male	place on blind
shirontzivenki	bird species-*venki*	male	place on blind
manirovenki	deer-*venki*	male	change tracks
kitairikivenki	collared peccary-*venki*	male	change tracks
shintorivenki	peccary-*venki*	male	change tracks
kemarivenki	tapir-*venki*	male	change tracks

Name	Translation	User	Method
oshetovenki	woolly monkey-*venki*	male	blow toward
asankanentsivenki	pain in heart-*venki*	male	drink
shimavenki	*boquichico* fish-*venki*	male	blow on hands
mamorivenki	*sabalo* fish-*venki*	male	blow on hands
komayirivenki	*paco* fish-*venki*	male	blow on hands
kiyaarivenki	fish species-*venki*	male	blow on hands
kamathonkevenki	eel-*venki*	male	blow on hands

The following is the origin story of the hunting *ivenki*s.

The magic plant of the hawk

When the hawk was a person, he was a good hunter. He had many *ivenki* plants, so he ate the meat of birds every day. He never ate manioc without meat.

One day, a man arrived to visit the hawk. He asked the hawk for his *ivenki*, saying, "Brother-in-law, I've come to ask if you have the *ivenki* plant."

Figure 6.2 The magic plant of the hawk

The hawk answered, "Yes, I have the *ivenki* called hawk-*venki*. I also have *ivenki*s to hunt other animals."

The man asked for all the *ivenki*s of the hawk, and the hawk sold them to him. That is why some men have become great hunters. (Translated from *Paquithavenqui* by Alberto Pablo Ravírez (Anderson 1986b).)

Note that in this story, the hawk "sold" the man his *ivenki*s. These plants are passed on from person to person and are often traded. The new owner takes the bulbs and carefully plants them in a particular spot of sandy soil, making special note of where they are planted, one *ivenki* being tapir specific and a different *ivenki* being deer specific. The owner then knows where to find his *ivenki* for hunting tapir or deer.

An Ashéninka man attributes much of his hunting skill to his *ivenki*s. An important part of teaching someone to hunt is giving him *ivenki* plants and instruction in their use. Though a boy learns and practices the skills and strategies of hunting from his father, he still needs a little extra help from an *ivenki* plant. The following interviews tell of expert hunters giving *ivenki* plants to novices.

R: Tell me what your father said was the way people taught in the past.

M: My father told me how he was taught by his father, teaching directly. When the little boys were very small, they were taught to make little arrows. They had special plants that they applied to the boy so he would be a good hunter. My father was a great hunter, at least he told me so. My father has barely taught these things to me. I really do not know about the magical plants that help one to become a good hunter. He told me about these plants, for example the one he had for hunting deer, for partridges, etc. He had a different one for every animal. (T.88.06.GER)

M: For example, about fishing, when my son was about 12 years old, I told him that there was an *ivenki* to help him catch fish. I had him prepare his arrow, and then I taught him and gave him the *ivenki*. He went to the river and in the afternoon, he returned with his fish. He was happy and said, "Mother, I shot a fish." His mother took it and cooked it. He then said, "Father, how is it that you are so good at shooting birds?" I told him that my other *ivenki* was my secret. I said that if he wanted it, I would teach him how to use it. I taught him how to use it to hunt birds, and then he had good aim. This is what I taught him. Everything that my grandfathers taught me, I also taught my sons, so these things will not disappear. (T.87.02.APR)

M: I learned by watching him make a hunting blind. He also told me the kind of food the different animals eat. He also taught me how to aim correctly. He knew everything about hunting. I wasn't very good, so he gave me a secret thing. He took a certain leaf and burned my hand with it. The next day, we went hunting and he said, "Shoot that bird." After that, I had good aim. He taught me a lot and I practiced a lot too. (T.88.05.ARM)

R: How did your father teach you to have good aim?
M: My father taught me about the magic plants that we burn on our hands to give us good aim. He also told me that I wouldn't be as good as he. He then said that he had another *ivenki* that I needed to hunt because if I couldn't hunt, I wouldn't have anything to eat. (T.88.22.MAC)

Besides using the *ivenki* plants, a hunter must follow strict dietary restrictions. The following interviews tell of the importance of diet for future hunting success.

R: Were you prohibited from eating some animals while you were learning to hunt?
M: When I started learning to hunt when ten years old, my father prohibited me from eating the animal that I had killed for the first time because there is a belief that if I eat the animal that I have killed for the first time, I cannot kill that animal again, and will never become a hunter. That is why we have that prohibition. My father said, "To make you a good hunter, I will let you eat some meat that you get, but I will mix it with hot peppers until you are about fourteen years old." I was about eleven years old when I started hunting by myself. (T.88.14.ALB)

R: How did your father motivate you?
M: There are secret things that helped me hunt.
R: Did your father prohibit you from eating certain animals that you killed?
M: Yes, there were some prohibitions, like if I ate the first animal I killed, I could not kill that kind of animal again. I could try, but I would not be successful. I say the same to my sons. I tell them that they cannot eat that animal until they have killed it many times. (T.88.22.MAC)

Beyond improving the hunter's aim by applying *ivenki* to the hands, various *ivenki*s are used to improve the hunter's eyesight. This kind of *ivenki* is chewed and then placed with saliva in a swab of cotton. The hunter squeezes the cotton until a few drops of the saliva enter the aiming eye. The hunter then magically sees small birds as magnified. The following interviews tell of an expert hunter giving the novice an *ivenki* to help him have better aim.

R: Was there someone else who taught you something?
M: Yes, my great grandfather taught me to use the *ivenki* to have better aim. We chew it and blow it on our hands, on the arrow, and on the bow. Later, we put the juice of the *ivenki* in our eye. Then we go into the forest to see how our aim is. This is what my great grandfather gave me, and he went with me up into the hills. He said, "Shoot that toucan and kill it." I took the arrow, shot, but I didn't hit it. Since he had this custom, he took his arrow and shot it right away in the chest. He told me that was the way I had to do it. I tried again, but I didn't shoot anything. I didn't have good aim. Sometimes we have to know about magical plants to have good aim. (T.87.02.APR)

R: Did your father teach you to make an arrow?
M: Yes, this he did. He taught me how to make arrows, aim, and hunt. He also told me the secrets that came from our ancestors, the *ivenki* magical plants that help us aim. He taught me these things. He gave me *ivenki* to have better aim. With this plant, you can hit a bird from ten meters away. At first, you cannot hit anything from that far away. (T.88.13.EDU)

R: Did you ever ask your father for help?
M: I asked him why some people can hit birds from far away. He told me that those people have *ivenki*. This is one of our beliefs. If we have this plant, we don't need to wait until the animal gets close enough to shoot. (T.88.21.ROB)

Bad luck at hunting is attributed to bad aim, clumsiness, poor eyesight, or prey that does not appear. For these circumstances, the right *ivenki* can make the hunter successful. Anyone who excels at hunting is assumed to have one of these *ivenki*s, and the less skilled hunter is usually looking for an *ivenki* to change his luck.

The *ivenki*s used in war

Today's Ashéninkas are generally a peaceful people, but they were well-known warriors seventy years ago. Franciscan journals tell of the warfare between the Ashéninka or Asháninka and outsiders from the mid-1700s to the first part of the twentieth century. The Machiguenga and Caquinte people continue to mistrust the Ashéninka and Asháninka, remembering the slaughters of earlier times. Skillful warfare was once far more valued than it is today, but the importance of *ivenki* magic in warfare is remembered in several traditional stories. Fathers once instructed their sons in the skills of archery, defense, and strategy; and they gave them one or more *ivenki*s to give them better luck in a fight.

Table 6.2 The war *ivenki*s

Name	Translation	User	Method
tzisovenki	buzzard-*venki*	male	chew
amemporivenki	condor-*venki*	male	chew
sanivenki	wasp-*venki*	male	chew
atzirivenki	people-*venki*	male	chew
shoiritzivenki	*monje* bird-*venki*	male	rub on body
masontovenki	deaf/dumb-*venki*	male	rub on body
kitovenki	crayfish-*venki*	male	rub on body
parovenki	nightjar bird-*venki*	male	rub on body
chekopivenki	arrow-*venki*	male	blow toward

The following story claims that a war *ivenki* preceded the time when a man was converted into the wasp.

The wasp

The wasp was always angry when he was a person. He did not want anyone to come near to bother him. That is why he fought whenever anyone came.

He had an *ivenki* plant called wasp-*venki*. When he chewed it, he became more ferocious, always overcoming his enemies. It is that way today. Though he has turned into a wasp, whenever we get close, he might sting us. He was that way as a warrior and is that way today. When we come close to his home, he stings us and makes us run. (Translated from *Icantacota sani* by Alberto Pablo Ravírez (Anderson 1986b).)

Figure 6.3 The wasp

Other *ivenki*s endow the owner with special abilities, like avoiding arrows. One of these is the goatsucker *ivenki*.

The goatsucker bird

When the goatsucker bird was a person, some men hated him and wanted to kill him. But the goatsucker had his *ivenki*, so they could not hit him with their arrows.

One day, the men came to kill the goatsucker. They shot arrows at him, but could not hit him, so they returned home. Everyone heard of the fame of the goatsucker; he could evade all arrows.

One day, his brother-in-law went to visit him. When he arrived at his home, he said, "Brother-in-law, I've heard that you are good at evading arrows."

"That is correct," answered the goatsucker.

"Do you have something to give me so I can evade arrows?" asked his brother-in-law.

"Yes, I do."

"Then give me some, so I can evade the arrows, too."

"Very well, I'll give it to you."

The goatsucker showed his friend his *ivenki*s. He had different varieties, such as goatsucker-*venki*, *monje* bird-*venki*, and others. Then he taught him, saying, "If we chew this *ivenki*, we will be brave. It will not matter that they shoot arrows at us from close range; they will not hit us."

The goatsucker gave his friend some *ivenki*s. That is why our people like to make war so much between themselves, because they have goatsucker-*venki*, *monje* bird-*venki*, and other *ivenki*s to evade arrows.

These *ivenki*s came from the goatsucker bird and that is how we came to have them. (Translated from *Paro* by Alberto Pablo Ravírez (Anderson 1986a).)

Figure 6.4 The goatsucker bird

The Ashéninka are skillful at jumping out of the trajectory of arrows. They often shoot pointless arrows at one another for fun during a party or as a demonstration. To make this "dodging" *ivenki* effective, the bulb is chewed and the pulp is spit onto the hands. The saliva-*ivenki* mixture is then rubbed on the skin or clothing of the warrior. Once necessary for survival, warfare skills are used today for recreation.

The curing *ivenki*s

Men and women use many varieties of *ivenki* to cure physical and spiritual illness. Parents teach the use of these to their children at every opportunity.

Table 6.3 *Ivenki*s used for physical illness

Name	Translation	User	Method
marankevenki	snake species-*venki*	all	bathe
cheenkarivenki	snake species-*venki*	all	bathe
kempirovenki	snake species-*venki*	all	bathe
materinkevenki	snake species-*venki*	all	bathe
atsikaneentaantsivenki	stomach ache-*venki*	all	bathe
katsitsinivenki	gonorrhea-*venki*	male	bathe

The *ivenki*s that cure physical illness are used only externally; ingestion of *ivenki* through the mouth for physical illness is not practiced. For snakebite, the specific snakebite *ivenki* is chewed and spit into a pot of boiling water. After the broth cools, the affected part of the body is bathed with this water. In the case of vomiting, the vomiting-specific *ivenki* is prepared in the same way, and the abdomen is bathed. The *ivenki*s that cure physical illness are rare, few being found in Ashéninka villages. The *ivenki*s that counteract the damage done by malevolent *peyari* spirits or *matsi* witchcraft are more common.

Table 6.4 *Ivenki*s used for spiritual illness

Name	Translation	User	Method
pinitsivenki	*tilo* plant-*venki*	all	eye drops
inchashivenki	plant-*venki*	all	eye drops
matsivenki	witch-*venki*	all	drink/bathe
kentanentantsivenki	acute pain-*venki*	all	drink/bathe
peyarivenki	ghost-*venki*	all	drink/bathe
thaveretantsivenki	bad spirit-*venki*	all	drink/bathe
kemasaimpyantsivenki	hear voices-*venki*	all	drink/bathe
amparyaantsivenki	tree-person-*venki*	all	drink/bathe

Witchcraft is sometimes done by touching the clothing of a person with magical herbs such as the *tilo* plant (*pinitsi* in Ashéninka). Dozens of varieties of *pinitsi* have different uses, much as scores of *ivenki* varieties have different uses. The *pinitsi* plants, however, are used more secretively than the *ivenki*s. The most common use of *pinitsi* is to gain the favor of an unwilling lover. Those affected by *pinitsi* see the world as the perpetrator would like and require using *ivenki* eye drops to counteract its effect.

A more malevolent form of witchcraft comes from the burying of fish or bird bones from an animal eaten by the victim. As long as the bones are buried, the affected person experiences sharp pains in the chest and back, general weakness, and gradually failing health. A treatment with *matsivenki* or *kentanentantsivenki* may relieve these symptoms until the bones are found.

When a person comes close to a *peyari* ghost, or worse, has physical contact with it, he will have symptoms that include loss of appetite, depression, weakness, confusion, and vomiting. The only cure is one of many *peyarivenki*s. In such cases, a shaman or family member (often the spouse) cooks some *peyari*-specific *ivenki* and has the affected person sip it. If the damage done by the *peyari* is minimal, the person will recover. Yet, sometimes not even a shaman or an *ivenki* can save him. One reason Ashéninkas avoid sexual relations with strangers is for fear of demonic contamination. The following story tells how a man responded to the temptation of a female demon. It also tells that even proximity to a demon can cause illness that can be cured by an *ivenki*.

The man who went to hunt and saw a naked woman

A man went into the jungle to hunt. When he arrived at the river, he went upstream. There he saw a naked woman and thought, "Who is this woman?"

When the woman saw the man, she came closer to him. When he saw her up close, he noticed that her feet were short, like those of an animal, but her face was like that of a woman. He thought, "This can't be a person, it must be a demon."

The woman came closer, giggling, *iii, iii, iii*. The man said to her, "Why are you giggling? I don't know you. Go away before I shoot you with my arrow."

She replied, "Why do you want to shoot me? Don't you know me?" She continued giggling.

The man became angry and shot her in the abdomen with his arrow, *chek*. She screamed and jumped, falling into the river. She made a big whirlpool. The man said, "Oh! I've seen a demon. If I would have had sexual relations with this woman, I would have been killed. It's good that I shot her."

He returned to his house. He was very sad when he arrived. When his wife saw how sad he was, she asked him, "Why are you so sad?"

He answered, saying, "I met a woman at the river, but I shot her. She jumped and fell into the river, making a big whirlpool."

After his wife heard about this, she gave him *ivenki* to drink. She also bathed him with *ivenki*, and he got better.

That is the story of the man who went to the jungle to hunt but saw a naked woman by the river. (Translated from *Apaani ashéninca jiñiiro cooya caanquimerequiro* by Alberto Pablo Ravírez (Anderson 1986b).)

Malevolent spirits can take the form of physical objects, such as trees, animals, or people. If a man hunting in the forest thinks he sees another person, but discovers that it is really a tree, he may have seen a spirit. If a man hears voices, but upon investigation, finds nothing, he may have heard a spirit. Various stories still circulate about those who have died after such encounters. Having the proper *ivenki* on hand may aid in recovery after confronting these spirits directly.

Another common present-day use of the curing *ivenki*s is to guarantee a safe pregnancy and painless childbirth. Ashéninka cultural practice prohibits pregnant women from eating many sources of protein while pregnant. The Ashéninka believe that a pregnant woman who eats the meat of a large animal will give birth to a child with a head the shape of that animal. They also believe that ingestion of the bones of small fish during pregnancy (one of the only sources of protein in the rainy season) will cause intense labor pains at birth.

Table 6.5 *Ivenki*s used for pregnancy and childbirth

Name	Translation	User	Method
omotsivenki	womb-*venki*	female	bathe stomach
moithontzivenki	navel-*venki*	female	bathe stomach
shivavenki	small fish-*venki*	female	drink
meretovenki	small fish-*venki*	female	drink
shimpivenki	*carachama* fish-*venki*	female	drink
manirovenki	deer-*venki*	female	drink
kemarivenki	tapir-*venki*	female	drink

Many women pass *ivenkis* from one to another that allow them to eat a specific species of small fish or large animal. The pregnant woman cooks some *ivenki* bulbs in water and drinks a little of the broth. The woman is then free to eat the meat of a particular large animal or a particular small fish without fear that the child will be deformed or that the woman will have the sharp pains expected at childbirth. When a woman suffers from intense pain or the child is born deformed, those near the woman typically blame the misfortune on the woman having eaten meat without taking the necessary precautions.

Table 6.6 *Ivenkis* used to protect infants

Name	Translation	User	Method
tonkitsivenki	bone-*venki*	female	drink broth
asanavenki	fish species-*venki*	female	drink broth
shimpivenki	fish species-*venki*	female	drink broth
samotovenki	fish species-*venki*	female	drink broth
kiranavenki	fish species-*venki*	female	drink broth
kishoñaakirivenki	fish species-*venki*	female	drink broth
toniroshaavenki	fish species-*venki*	all	drink broth
shivavenki	fish species-*venki*	all	drink broth
koshivavenki	fish species-*venki*	all	drink broth
teparovenki	fish species-*venki*	all	drink broth
meretovenki	fish species-*venki*	all	drink broth
thonthovenki	fish species-*venki*	all	drink broth
ovavairentsivenki	food-*venki*	female	drink broth
oyevenki	rainbow boa-*venki*	female	bathe child
ovapathavenki	red clay-*venki*	female	rub on feet
kitsitharivenki	black clay-*venki*	female	rub on feet
shinavenkivenki	*lupuna* leaves-*venki*	female	rub on feet
toniromashivenki	*aguaje* leaves-*venki*	female	rub on feet
eentsivenki	child-*venki*	female	bathe child
athanarentsivenki	adultery-*venki*	all	bathe child

At the time of childbirth, a woman probably has an *ivenki* that is believed to lessen the pain. The childbirth-specific *ivenki* ("womb" or "navel") is cooked in water and used to wash the abdomen of the woman.

Another group of *ivenkis* provides protection to infants. One evening, my youngest child, who was ten months old, began to vomit. This caused excitement in the Ashéninka village, some women eventually inquiring of my wife as to what I, the father, had eaten, or if we were having marital problems. The Ashéninka believe that the actions of the mother and father have a direct effect on the health of an infant. The taboos in effect after the birth of a child regarding what can be eaten are as rigid as those in effect during pregnancy. Consumption of most fish, especially the small ones, and the ingestion of bones are strictly prohibited, unless the taboo can be counteracted by drinking the broth of the corresponding *ivenki*.

Besides breaking food taboos, other actions of the infant or parents can cause illness. If an infant urinates in water, the water boa (*oye*) is offended and bewitches the child. If the mother walks on certain clays or the leaves of particular trees, a child becomes ill, if the mother does not take the precaution of rubbing the proper *ivenki* on her feet. An adulterous parent causes an infant to become ill, with a child's daily *ivenki* bath being the only safeguard against becoming ill.

A young girl's socialization is incomplete without receiving a collection of *ivenkis* from her mother and instruction in their proper use. Every Ashéninka household has some *ivenkis*, especially if a woman is pregnant or has an infant in the house.

The other uses of *ivenki*

Other *ivenkis* aid the Ashéninka in their agricultural labors. An important part of learning to work in the *chacra* is to have and know the proper uses of certain *ivenkis*.

Table 6.7 The agricultural *ivenki*s

Name	Translation	User	Method
inchatovenki	tree-*venki*	male	blow toward
thamairitaantsivenki	clear weeds-*venki*	female	blow toward
pesaantsivenki	clear underbrush-*venki*	male	blow toward
inkanivenki	rain-*venki*	male	blow toward
ovaantsivenki	garden-*venki*	male	blow/burn
kanirivenki	manioc-*venki*	male	blow toward
kokavenki	coca-*venki*	male	blow toward

The first step in preparing a garden is the cutting of underbrush. Ashéninkas say that chewing on "clear underbrush" *ivenki* and blowing the pulp-saliva mixture in the direction of the area to be cut makes the work go faster. To help with the cutting of trees, a "tree" or "garden" *ivenki* is either chewed and blown in the direction of the trees or is burned; the smoke passing among the trees is said to make hollow spaces in the trees where the smoke passes. After the area is burned, a "rain" *ivenki* may be blown toward the *chacra*—said to make rain come sooner than normal. To accelerate the rate of growth of manioc or coca, the "manioc" or "coca" *ivenki* pulp-saliva mixture is blown on the cuttings of these plants before planting. Women's work of weeding is aided by blowing a "weed" *ivenki* toward the garden to be cleaned. Few families own more than a couple agricultural *ivenki*s, though they are recognized by most.

Table 6.8 The instrument *ivenki*s

Name	Translation	User	Method
ampeevenki	cotton-*venki*	female	rub on/wash
tampoovenki	drum-*venki*	male	rub on
sonkarevenki	panpipes-*venki*	male	rub on
pyamenivenki	bow-*venki*	male	wash
kirikivenki	*pifayo* palm-*venki*	male	wash
tonkamentotsivenki	shotgun-*venki*	male	wash

Though I am unsure of when the Ashéninka began to spin cotton, some traditional stories tell of when the Ashéninka were semi-naked and made clothing from tree bark. The spider is credited with being the originator of the skill of spinning thread. According to the following story, the spider woman could spin cotton because she had her *ivenki*.

The *ametyo* spider

Long ago, when the *ametyo* spider was a woman, she was accustomed to spinning thread every day. The other women did not know how to do it. One day, when she was in her house spinning alone, her granddaughter came to visit her, saying, "Grandmother, how did you learn to spin thread?"

Ametyo answered, "I have my *ivenki* to use on my hands so I can do it."

She took some *ivenki* and rubbed it on the hands of her granddaughter. Then she said, "Now that your hands have been prepared, you must spin thread constantly. If you rest, you will never learn to do it correctly."

Figure 6.5 The *ametyo* spider

That is how this young woman learned to spin like her grandmother, Ametyo. This spider uses its thread to trap animals. Whenever we walk through the forest, we see the webs it has left to catch flies. Flies are the primary food of the *ametyo* spider. She eats them as if they were birds.

Later, Ametyo the spider died, but her granddaughter took her place. That is how other women learned to spin cotton and weave. The *ametyo* spider passed on these things when she was a person. When she was a human, she loved to spin. (Translated from *Ametyo* by Alberto Pablo Ravírez (Anderson 1986b).)

Young women often have an *ivenki* to help them with their spinning. They either rub it on their hands, spit it on their hands, or wash the spinning tool with it. Other plants are also used to make spinning magic, especially the *ashipa* plant. The *ashipa* leaf is dried, burned, and the ashes rubbed on the hands of the girl who is learning to weave or spin.

M: A woman who knows how to spin and a girl who wants to learn have their *ivenki*. The mother blows it on her hand and on her cotton. In the morning at 3 a.m., they wake up and take the *ashipa* leaf and put it on their hands. Then the mother teaches her daughter how to spin cotton. (T.87.02.APR)

R: Did you teach someone else to spin?
F: I taught my two daughters. To encourage them to spin, I took a special leaf and burned it and put it on the hands of my daughters so they would have more skill and not say, "I can't do it." When I put the ashes in her hand, I told her, "You can't eat meat killed by a man for a week or you will become lazy." After a week, the mother goes to her daughter and washes her and then she can eat meat hunted by a man. (T.88.18.JOS)

R: Do you have a magic means of avoiding mistakes in spinning or weaving?
F: Yes, my secret is a leaf that we burn on the hands so weaving will not be difficult. However, that plant is not found here. I got it in the Apurucayali region, in the highlands. I gave it to my oldest daughter when we still lived there, when she was six years old. (T.88.21.JUA)

New values and tools are adding more uses for the *ivenki* plant. Young Ashéninka men aspire to be good singers, good drummers, and good panpipe players. By rubbing or washing a drum or panpipes with its specific *ivenki*, the young man should display more talent.

A hunter who returns empty-handed usually has an excuse for his failure, often blaming failure on his bow, arrows, or shotgun. If the weapon is not performing to his expectation, he tries to correct the condition by using the proper *ivenki*. For a shotgun, the man disassembles and washes it in the broth of the "shotgun" *ivenki*. After drying and reassembly, the gun should aim correctly and be more effective at killing game. The hunter believes that an *ivenki* treatment of his weapon gives it back some strength or effectiveness that was lost or taken away by a spirit in the forest.

The inventory of *ivenkis* used among the Ashéninka is more numerous than those mentioned here. A list of over two hundred *ivenkis* is possible, with many varieties having one use in one village and a different use in another. I even found some of what I call "vanity" *ivenkis*.

Table 6.9 The vanity *ivenkis*

Name	Translation	User	Method
eshikoiravenki	school-*venki*	all	bulb in bag
kamathavenki	crawl-*venki*	female	bathe child
kavaayovenki	horse-*venki*	male	rub on arms
pyarentsivenki	manioc beer-*venki*	male	chew

The proper *ivenki* can do almost any task: if a mother desires her infant to mature faster so she may become pregnant sooner, she can bathe the child in "crawling" *ivenki*; if a man wants to show-off at a drinking party, he can chew a "manioc beer" *ivenki* that increases the capacity of his stomach; and if a young boy desires to be stronger than his peers, he tries to find a "horse" *ivenki* that he can rub on his arms to give him added strength. In some villages, I found a "school" *ivenki* that is carried in a child's shoulder bag, said to make the child a better student.

The breadth and number of uses of *ivenkis* do not minimize their significance to the Ashéninka. In the most bilingual and integrated Ashéninka villages, *ivenki* plants grow outside almost every dwelling. The powers of the *ivenkis* are considered real, even by those who do not use them regularly. Parents continue to give the *ivenki* plants to their children to counter periods of bad luck.

Conclusion

The supernatural in the Ashéninka world significantly frames socialization. Belief in spirits and witches makes necessary the learning of strategies to avoid these beings. It also limits who a child can look to as a model or teacher because children are taught to avoid their peers, just in case one might be a witch. This leaves the parent as the best model and teacher.

Magic is an integral part of Ashéninka activities such as hunting, spinning cotton, warfare, and childcare. Along with expert instruction, parents give their children gifts of magic in the form of the *ivenki* plant. Parents teach the use of the *ivenki* plant to improve the child's success in everyday activities.

7

The Breadth of Socialization and Change

They don't really forget the Ashéninka language but try to deny that they are Ashéninka. From my point of view, they are the enemy. I don't like it! If I live ten or twenty years in Lima, I will return to my house and continue to be an Ashéninka. I will speak the Ashéninka language and do everything that is Ashéninka. I will eat like an Ashéninka and live like an Ashéninka. I don't need to act like something else. That is disgusting. ROB

My sons don't really go hunting with me very much because they are always in school. I go alone a lot. It's not like when I was their age. ARM

The multi-situated character of socialization

How does the history of the Ashéninka help situate the continuity or discontinuity of valued skills? Prior to the introduction of metal tools, an individual's skills at self-sufficiency were life and death matters. Men quickly adopted the metal axes and machetes that eased their labor, but this change had little effect on other aspects of Ashéninka life until the end of the nineteenth century, when the Ashéninka entered the market economy on a grand scale to earn money to buy not only metal tools, but also guns, pots, and clothing. In regions of intense contact, skills valued in earlier days, such as archery, weaving, and the manufacture of clay pots rapidly began to drop away. Increasing contact with Spanish speakers and dependence on the market economy prompted the Ashéninka to give more value to learning Spanish, organizing into villages to protect their claims to the land, and having their children learn school-taught skills to aid their economic competitiveness and to remove the stigma of primitiveness.

The oral literature of the Ashéninka retains the fundamental values that supported traditional skills and beliefs, as well as ways of learning to be a good member of Ashéninka society. Though Ashéninka traditional stories have various versions and not all stories are told everywhere, all interviewees report hearing the same kinds of stories from their parents and others. Stories are told to entertain, but most also have at least one "moral lesson" that typically addresses idealized Ashéninka conduct. Stories tell that deviance from reserve, humility, caution, honesty, or skillfulness usually ends in the death or humiliation of the person who does not conform to the norm. Elders tell these stories to encourage the young people to avoid being like the person who suffers and to prefer instead to exhibit correct conduct, skills, and ideals.

But learning is ultimately situated in the moment-to-moment needs of the individual. The motives that drive individual Ashéninkas to learn are anticipation of future physical need, the desire for social acceptance, and creative identity formation. Ashéninka children periodically experience hunger, cold, and sickness, and can easily imagine life if these conditions were to be chronic. Parents often remind their children that failure to learn valued skills could lead to physical suffering or even death. Children strive to learn to avoid being ridiculed, as Ashéninkas are quick to humiliate with laughter anyone who lacks skillfulness. The young people want to be like some adult that they know, and they practice to become expert at those things that make that person exceptional; extraordinary expertise at a valued skill brings heightened prestige. Participation in the market economy and schooling have changed many of the skills to be learned, but these modern shifts have not altered basic motivations for learning that include physical comfort, social acceptance, and a prestigious identity.

In the Ashéninka style of educational activities, Ashéninkas learn numerous skills and attitudes in a guided manner in which an adult consciously aids the child. Specific strategies for teaching the young have persisted for generations, including opportunistic skill introduction, demonstration, measured assistance, size-appropriate tools, apprenticeship, standards of acceptable performance, and feedback regarding performance. In guided learning, the adult organizes the instructional activity by determining when the child is ready to learn, arranging for the needed materials, and selecting times and places for instruction. Adult and child work together: the adult demonstrates and gives assistance whenever necessary; the child observes, practices, and requests help when needed. Skills learned in this manner include hunting, spinning cotton, weaving, and gardening. In nonguided learning, a child organizes the learning activities with minimal help from adults. This learning takes the form of dramatic play, solitary experimentation, and collaborative learning with peers. Skills learned in these ways include swimming, cooking, house-building, and archery. (See also chapter 5.)

For the Ashéninka, all learning takes place against the backdrop of the spiritual life. For the Ashéninka, many of life's mysteries have spiritual explanations, and they cite beliefs about witchcraft as explanations for why children must avoid other children. This avoidance strengthens the social bond between parent and child. As individuals participating in a group belief system, Ashéninkas enhance technical skills by using the magical *ivenki* plant. Simultaneously, in all teaching and learning, history, traditional stories, moment-to-moment needs and motives, and designated educational activities sit dependently within the Ashéninka systems of religious beliefs. (See chapter 6.)

The comprehensive character of socialization

No single theory of socialization adequately describes the breadth of processes and agents of socialization of the Ashéninka. The individualistic philosophy of socialization describes the agency of the individual in creating society, but it fails to take adequate account of the social interaction needed for children to become members of their culture. The sociologistic philosophy of socialization describes the hold that culture has on individuals between generations, but it fails to account for the variation between individuals. Soviet activity theory describes the psychological processes whereby external social activity becomes internalized by the child in socialization, but it does not explain the out-of-awareness learning of much everyday knowledge. Wentworth's simplified definition of socialization, which is based on activity theory and tries as well to avoid the weaknesses of individualism and sociologism, states: "Socialization is the activity that confronts and lends structure to the entry of nonmembers into an already existing world or sector of the world" (Wentworth 1980:85). This definition lays out socialization as activity that facilitates a novice becoming a member of the next generation's world, but it does not account for the learning of knowledge despite "inactivity" (that which is learned but is not the focus of instruction).

Elick, who lived among the Ashéninka for several years as a missionary and researcher, suggests a sociocognitive theory of how the Ashéninka view learning. He states that the Ashéninka perceive three distinct kinds of knowledge.

> There is that which is innate, "folded up", as it were, within the newly born individual. As the child grows and develops physically this innate "knowing" will unfold slowly, providing the knowledge needed to permit him to interact intelligently with his physical and social environment. Thus a boy's body and soul both recognize when he has reached adulthood. His voice changes (physical evidence), and his generalized sexuality becomes specifically goal-oriented ("spiritual" evidence). While our terms "intelligence" and "maturation" may come the closest to describing this innate quality, I have the distinct impression the [Campa] do not perceive it as merely a potentiality for acquiring knowledge, but rather as a congenital, "primitive" knowledge itself which will slowly unfold into consciousness as the child grows....The second kind of knowledge is "that which is taught" by someone, usually an older person, to another. This is shared experience, knowledge that is deliberately passed from one person to another. It is knowledge of quite a different kind from the former, though the two function together to make the "complete" person. A third kind of knowledge is that which men acquire from spirit mentors. (Elick 1970:228–229)

Elick interprets this view as the Ashéninka's own theory of learning: body-knowledge learned by maturation, social-knowledge shared between individuals, and spirit-knowledge received from spirit-mentors. Elements from other socialization theories are present here, but the separateness of body, mind, and spirit knowledge limits what is learned to specific domains, instead of integrating all knowledge into the whole of Ashéninka individual development.

These theories, perspectives, and definitions all describe parts of socialization but none is comprehensive. To better approximate a description of socialization, one should avoid dividing what is learned among mind, body, activity, and culture, preferring to include these in a general description, as suggested by Lave.

> The point is not so much that arrangements of knowledge in the head correspond in a complicated way to the social world outside the head, but that they are socially organized in such a fashion as to be indivisible. "Cognition" observed in everyday practice is distributed—stretched over, not divided among—mind, body, activity and culturally organized settings (which include other actors). (Lave 1988:1)

The preceding chapters described socialization contexts and processes separately, but these should be seen as related to the whole cognitive development of the individual. Ashéninkas are born into an ecological, cultural, religious, and historical context that limits what can be learned, and influences the value of learning particular skills or knowledge. The motivation and activity of socialization occur within these contexts—the contexts being a part of socialization.

Regarding the historical and ecological contexts, in the Ucayali region, families are isolated, have little contact with Spanish speakers, have access to abundant wildlife, and have few opportunities to work for money. Families in the Perené region, on the other hand, often live in villages integrated with mestizo families, have intense contact with Spanish speakers, have little access to wild game, and have many opportunities to earn money. Skills such as speaking Spanish and hunting with a bow have very different values in these two regions.

Regarding the cultural context, the Ashéninka are born with physical characteristics that signal their heritage and most grow up learning Ashéninka speech and body language. Social characteristics that make the Ashéninka distinct from others include their reserve and impeccable honesty. These physical and social characteristics hinder their "fitting in" in several outside situations, reinforcing Ashéninka ethnic separateness. Ashéninka traditional stories reinforce several Ashéninka-specific values and beliefs about spirits, magic, and justice. These guide both adults' and children's social interactions and provide part of the motivation for learning to avoid physical danger and embarrassment. Distinctive Ashéninka physical attributes, cultural practices, contact history, and personal history vary between individuals, just as the socialization experiences of each varies, though many experiences are similar and appear to be more "Ashéninka" than "other".

Agency in socialization cannot be consistently described for the Ashéninka case. Though ecology, culture, religion, and history somewhat constrain socialization, these do not determine individual activity. Neither can agency be characterized as either the teacher or the learner, though some skills tend to have a dominant organizer of the learning activity. In some learning situations, the child initiates learning, as when a boy practices with a bow or a girl cooks with her small pots. In other situations, an adult takes the lead in teaching a skill like spinning cotton. A mother may teach her daughter even though the child lacks motivation to learn. Agency in the learning of skills is variable enough to question its legitimacy as a significant factor of socialization. One boy begins making arrows on his own, but another is taught first by his father. Common to both situations is the need for a boy to learn arrow making as a survival skill at the appropriate age. To learn to make arrows is more linked to needs and the age of the child than it is to the agency of either the child, an adult, or society.

Not everything is learned consciously. As mentioned earlier, the Ashéninka learn culturally distinctive speech and body language. Though the contents of these are culturally defined, verbal and nonverbal systems of symbols are acquired across cultures through learning that takes place primarily out of awareness. Social roles and teaching styles depend on more conscious approaches to instruction. Interviewees often said that they teach their children as they themselves were taught through informal Ashéninka traditional pedagogy constrained by culturally defined practices. Adults typically use the same motivational strategies, illustrative stories, and apprenticeship practices to teach their own children as their parents used to teach them. Though adults of other cultural groups may demonstrate skills and give strategic criticism similar to Ashéninka practice, the Ashéninka have a unique intersubjectivity between adult and child that is situated primarily, though not exclusively, in the unique relationship between the Ashéninka and the spirit world and between adult and child (usually isolated from child-child interactions, except for school).

The persistent character of socialization

A tension between traditional and modern ways often accompanies rapid social change. In the Ashéninka case, increasing contact with Spanish speakers and dependence on the market economy force choices regarding socialization for adults and children. Parents must decide if they will speak only Spanish to their infants to give them an advantage in school, if they will dress the child in traditional clothing, and what traditional skills to teach the child. Children must decide if they want to play the "school-game", how much of the teacher's culture to adopt, and what their vision is of the person they want to be when older.

The problem of socializing the young in a changing society is a largely unaddressed issue. When adults prepare their children for change, they must acknowledge that their own learning becomes obsolete and is unacceptable for new conditions. This is evident in the Ashéninka case when people tell how their parents wanted them to go to school so they would be "a new person, not ignorant". When adults do not admit change and its inevitability into their ways of teaching, their children may reject their elders' ways as impractical. This is seen as women continue to teach all young girls to spin cotton, though most girls reject learning how to weave.

Often adults do not or cannot directly address change or its sources, and children must look to their experienced peers for help, as when children must help each other with school assignments or tell each other how to act in the presence of Spanish speakers. But, if prohibitions keep children from socializing with each other, and from being teachers or models, then sources of learning beyond parents greatly diminish. With increasing contact between cultures, Ashéninka young people face numerous sources of confusion about what and how they are to learn. These issues touch on the problem of transfer in learning that leads to contradictory adult goals: adults want schools for their children but they do not want many of the changes they bring.

When commenting about Ashéninka young women who left the area to work as maids in urban homes, one man told what he thought of people who appear to forget their cultural heritage.

M: These girls are trying to be like the people outside, not wanting to admit they are Ashéninka. They don't really forget the Ashéninka language but try to deny that they are Ashéninka. From my point of view, they are the enemy. I don't like it! If I live ten or twenty years in Lima, I will return to my house and continue to be an Ashéninka. I will speak the Ashéninka language and do everything that is Ashéninka. I will eat like an Ashéninka and live like an Ashéninka. I don't need to act like something else. That is disgusting. (T.87.21.ROB)

This speaker holds this opinion though he has been married to a mestizo woman for fifteen years. He expresses the typical Ashéninka feeling that someone born of Ashéninka parents and socialized as an Ashéninka should always identify as an Ashéninka, though he may marry an outsider and work part-time (as this man does) in a nontraditional profession.

Modern Peruvian and traditional Ashéninka culture are both learned by the Ashéninka (in some regions more than others) and practiced in different domains. In the traditional daytime schedule, for example, an adolescent boy accompanies his father to the *chacra* or on a hunt. In a modern daytime schedule, however, the boy's daylight hours are allocated to the school and play. Two fathers tell of this kind of change.

M: The boys here don't hunt much because they have school and play a lot. They hunt more during vacations. (T.88.01.SAM)

M: My sons don't really go hunting with me very much because they are always in school. I go alone a lot. It's not like when I was their age. (T.88.05.ARM)

Boys often spend their weekends and vacation days following the traditional pattern of accompanying their father. Schooling and changing ways are becoming more accepted as the norm in many villages.

Parents generally see the loss of hunting time and decreased hunting competence as a necessary cost of having their children attend school. Women also note the dramatic increase in the number of girls who do not learn to weave because they spend most of their day in school.

M: Some women know how to weave, but I see that none of the young girls know how to even spin cotton.
R: Why?
M: Because now they use store-bought material and thread to sew their *cushmas*; they have forgotten. Before, they spun and wove and exchanged these for knives, machetes, or anything else they needed. They traded. If someone wanted an ax, they traded a *cushma* for it. If they wanted a machete, they traded a *cushma* or a bag for it. (T.87.02.ALB)

Just as the adoption of metal tools produced irreversible changes for the Ashéninka, the reallocation of hours they spent in hunting and weaving to going to school is changing Ashéninka society. Women produce fewer woven goods for exchange, and men are less effective at providing a nutritious diet for the family. The school teacher often assigns seating in such a way that siblings are separated into different grades and study groups, forcing nontraditional interactions between children. Though parents tell of a fear that their child may be bewitched by another child, for the most part they tolerate their children's interaction with others in school.

One culture being superior or more legitimate than another is not the issue for Ashéninka children and adults. More important are the motives they have in sending their children to school in the first place.

> Each community's valued skills constitute the local goals of development. Societal practices that support children's development are tied to the values and skills considered important. In the final analysis, it is not possible to determine

whether the goals or practices of one society are more adaptive than those of another, as judgments of adaptation cannot be separated from values. For mid-class American children, the skills of schooling may relate closely to the skills required for participation in many aspects of adult life. (Rogoff 1990:12)

The school teacher presents a culture—Peruvian—that is very different from Ashéninka culture. Children are assigned seats, different standards of personal hygiene are enforced, the schedule is regimented, and different conversational styles are preferred. Children adapt to the "school culture" with varying success, some quickly and effectively while others slowly and painfully.

The importance of understanding the variations in what children are expected to learn in different cultures is linked to the assumptions of this book that thinking and learning are functional efforts by individuals to solve specific problems of importance in their culture, and that developmental courses vary in their goals rather than having a universal endpoint to which all should aspire. Thus in understanding cognitive development, it is essential to take into account the particular problems that children are attempting to solve and their importance in the culture. (Rogoff 1990:116)

As with learning traditional Ashéninka culture, learning elements of a new culture is situated in its own complex blend of history, beliefs, motives, practices, and persons. Each individual child goes to school with a unique blend of goals, family support, temperament, and prior knowledge as he or she participates in the work of schooling.

To speak of agency in the learning of a new culture is as difficult to describe as is the case for the learning of traditional culture. The Peruvian Ministry of Education and the school teacher have a structured curriculum to present to the child. Though the teacher does his job and the child learns, we cannot say that success or failure can be credited to one or the other without looking at the broad context within which learning occurs.

It is impossible to avoid judgments of good and bad courses of development if one is attempting to influence another group. But if the aim is to *understand* development, it is essential not to impose assumptions about the goals of development of one group on individuals from another. Interpreting the activity of people without regard for their goals renders the observations meaningless. (Rogoff 1990:117)

Socialization to modern Peruvian culture is not limited only to learning school-taught skills. The teacher may want children to become less reserved; parents may want their children to speak Spanish; and children may want to decrease the social stigma of being "primitive". Agency in the socialization to modern culture is similar to learning a new skill, being broadly situated in contexts, goals, and actions.

The changes experienced by individuals vary by degree. Traditional Ashéninka socialization experienced changes from the seventeenth century forward, but not to the degree experienced by Ashéninka children in areas of intense contact. As intensifying contact and schooling continue to spread to other Ashéninka regions, the pace of social and economic change will increase. We cannot assume that Ashéninka reaction to change will be the same as it has been in those places where it has already occurred. The experience of change is different for children today in areas of contact from what it was thirty years ago. Socialization contexts and processes are so broad that the experience in one region may be different from another, though some of the experience will be similar because some share a context of learning in the culture.

We can expect to find much that differs from the Ashéninka case in the study of socialization and change in other cultural groups. Even if many parallels exist between the contexts of the Ashéninka and others, groups may put different weights on different goals and motivations. Socialization is more than just the transfer of culture from one generation to the next, or the young's assimilation of traditional or modern ways. Rather, it is the work of the child and others to find a comfortable fit between the child and the world. If socialization is viewed from this perspective, finding no change is as significant as finding it.

> Another related implication is that learning is never simply a process of transfer or assimilation: learning, transformation, and change are always implicated in one another, and the status quo needs as much explanation as change. (Lave and Wenger 1990:8)

The multi-situated, comprehensive, and persistent character of socialization applies to the conceptions of the transfer of school-taught knowledge. Lave criticizes theories of learning transfer that begin with what is taught in the school.

> In the conceptual schema of cognitive psychology, cognitive transfer (or its absence) is held responsible for continuity (or discontinuity) of activity across situations. This genre of research speaks only in hypothetical voice about what

cognitive activities outside school might be like, relying on the concept of transfer to provide a plausible account of relations between schooling, the workplace, and the everyday lives of jpfs [just plain folks]. Learning transfer is assumed to be the central mechanism of bringing school-taught knowledge to bear in life after school. (Lave 1988:23)

In the Ashéninka case, a consistent understanding exists between adults and children regarding motivations for and activities of instruction. The need to learn a skill is evident to the child and what is learned is often put to use immediately. In the school, Ashéninka children have more difficulty learning the material, often repeating the early grades several years. Often the children are unclear about the applicability of learning something that is presented in a manner foreign to that used in their homes.

Ashéninka success in school is more dependent on the situation in which the child finds himself than on the structure of the school or the nature of the material presented. A child attends school because certain historical events place the school and child in proximity and the parents respond by sending the child to school. Parents' motivations for sending their children to school may vary, but children also react to the school in terms of anticipated need, social acceptance, and identity formation. To know the material taught in the school may be secondary to the child going through the school experience. As a member of the school community, the child may accept the role of learner and practice the skills taught to "fit in" the school society, which is his "community-of-practice" during certain hours of the day.

The person has been correspondingly transformed into a practitioner, a newcomer becoming an oldtimer, whose changing knowledge, skill, and discourse are part of developing identity—in short, a member of community-of-practice. This idea of identity/membership is strongly tied to a conception of motivation. If the person is both member of a community and agent of activity, the concept of the person closely links meaning and action in the world. (Lave and Wenger 1990:34)

Skills learned in the school that are later used outside typically result from the individual's having a nontraditional responsibility such as village treasurer or paramedic. Reading, writing, and math are infrequently used outside school, but knowing these skills qualifies individuals to attempt tasks that use these skills. The performance of skills is likely to be somewhat modified for the purposes of specific tasks.

> The central idea is that "the same" activity in different situations derives structuring from, and provides structuring resources for, other activities. This view specifically opposes assumptions either that activities and settings are isolated and unrelated, or that some forms of knowledge are universally insertable into any situation. Different situations, and indeed different occasions subjectively experienced as "the same," are instead viewed here as *transformations* of structuring resources given a realized form through their mutually constitutive articulation, weighted in different proportions from place to place and time to time. (Lave 1988:122)

It is not only skills that are transferred across contexts. Parallels can be drawn between Ashéninka traditional socialization and school socialization. Ashéninka norms of conduct such as reserve, honesty, humility, caution, and skillfulness are transferable to the school situation, though these may be expressed differently in the society of school from in the home. These in turn help shape the school experience for the child, classmates, and teacher. Socialization is persistent in the sense that it can adapt to change and it can occur in multiple settings: be it an isolated traditional Ashéninka family, a modern village, or a school or church—the child's goals are to be accepted and to prosper.

Conclusion

The voices in this study told of Ashéninkas interacting with their world to be socialized into it. The stories were often similar, because the Ashéninka share a common history and culture, but the stories also varied, because contact history and individual goals often differed. Ashéninka socialization, like socialization in all cultures, is situated across several contexts and much of the spiritual, individual, and group values persist between generations, even in times of drastic change. It is impossible and inappropriate to predict those patterns of socialization that will persist as the pace and unpredictability of change for the Ashéninka pick up. However, the fundamental values of humility, cultural integrity, and spiritual dependence will, no doubt, continue to figure prominently as the backdrop against which the agents, occasions, and motives of socialization work.

Appendix

Methodology

Ethnographers participate in people's daily lives for extended periods of time, engaging to the extent possible in daily activities, watching what happens, listening to what is said, and asking occasional questions as unobtrusively as possible to supplement fieldnotes. The hypotheses and questions for study emerge as the study proceeds in the setting selected for observation, and analytic categories are generated in the field. Techniques used in ethnography include interviewing, observing, collecting life histories, studying written documents relative to the history of the group, and recording contemporary and traditional stories.

The goal for the ethnographer is to make cultural inferences from what people say, the ways they act, and the artifacts they use. Ethnographers normally have a central focus around which they center their attention. In my research, the central concern that emerged was the socialization of young children.

Participation in Ashéninka daily life

Village living

In my fourteen years of Ashéninka and Asháninka study, I have been seen in different roles. My first contact with the Ashéninka was in the summer of 1970, as an undergraduate visitor, accompanying a member of SIL

International (SIL) on a school supervision trip in the lower Perené region. I was the traveling companion of someone trusted by the Asháninka. Everyone treated me graciously, and I was introduced to the Asháninka characteristics of generosity with food, respect for another's privacy, and boisterous laughter whenever something amusing happened.

In 1974, I returned to the Ashéninka as a literacy specialist and member of SIL. That year, accompanied by my wife, I supervised the extension of an airstrip in the Pajonal area. The men and older boys impressed me with their strength. Everyone chewed coca leaves during the workday—men and women, adults and adolescents—to give them strength and to extend the time between meals.

Two years later, my wife, infant daughter, and I flew by small plane to a village on the Sheshea, a tributary of the Alto Ucayali River. SIL had assigned us to learn the Ashéninka language and culture. At the time, the only location accessible by plane in the Ucayali region was a village with a Seventh-Day Adventist (SDA) church and private school. The SDA missionaries endorsed our locating there and made the logistical arrangements, including the loan of a house.

The Ashéninka were somewhat confused about the purpose of our stay, being unsure regarding our possible affiliation with the SDA mission. We did nothing in the church other than occasionally attend. We asked only for water and help with the washing of clothes, which we paid for at a rate recommended by the Ashéninka lay preacher. We frequently went from house to house, practicing the little of the Ashéninka language we knew. We provided entertainment for our neighbors, who laughed at our stumbling over difficult phrases and at the antics of our eleven-month-old daughter. We also provided some medical assistance to those in the village by treating intestinal parasites, minor burns, cuts, fevers, and infant vomiting and diarrhea. We exchanged the necessary medicines for cash, food, or handiwork. That visit showed us the strictness of the SDA behavioral code and the degree of Ashéninka dependency on the river patrons. We also discovered that different family groups segregate to different sides of the village and that the generation over sixty years old at the time had immigrated from either the Pichis, Pajonal, or Tambo regions during the rubber boom.

The next year, we decided to look for another study site to live among Ashéninkas less influenced by the SDA religion. I surveyed the Yuruá River near the border with Brazil, discovering that they, too, immigrated from the Pichis, Tambo, and Pajonal regions during the rubber boom, the Yuruá now being only sparsely populated. These mobile Ashéninkas keep a home base on the Peru side of the border but go to Brazil or across the watershed divide to the Sheshea for work or to play soccer. I next surveyed the Cohengua, a tributary of the Alto Ucayali, accompanied by Ashéninkas from a village beside the Ucayali River. I found a location where the headman had hopes that a school would some day be established. He and his relatives were willing to host us and help me build a house and airstrip. The airstrip attracted several families. Those on good terms with the headman settled along the airstrip and others settled about one kilometer away. We continued to study the language and culture, as well as give measles, polio, and DPT vaccinations and treat minor illnesses.

Our increasing language fluency made us less of a novelty. At the request of the headman, we began to teach basic reading and math skills on our porch. Later, we brought in a language assistant from a village with a school to help us learn the language. We taught him how to teach from the school texts we prepared, and he soon replaced us in the teaching role. The Ashéninka teacher stayed after we left, teaching adults and children. The villagers built a thatched schoolhouse and more families moved to the area. A year later, the Ministry of Education officially established the school and appointed our ex-assistant as the government-salaried teacher.

Over the next few years, I lived for periods of two months with my family in a village in the Pajonal region and another village in the Pichis region. Between village stays, I made survey trips to the Perené, Apurucayali, and Pachitea regions. All extended village stays had the same components—I was accompanied by my wife and children, we studied the language, we participated in the daily activities of our hosts as much as possible, and we provided medical services if they were not otherwise available.

With notebook and tape recorder always at hand, I was known to everyone as particularly interested in the Ashéninka language. When asked why I wanted to learn the language, my reply was that I planned to write books in their language. We never stayed in one village for more than a total of four months because we wanted to reduce the possibility of dependency, as well as stay clear of village politics, and we wanted to get a better overview of the Ashéninka.

We participated in the daily lives of our hosts whenever opportunities presented themselves. I went hunting, fishing, worked in gardens, and accompanied men on visits to neighbors. My wife visited with Ashéninka women while the infants played. We also went to parties and participated in village-wide sporting events.

We always lived in a small house with a thatch roof that was either made to our specifications (open porch and walled bedroom) or was loaned to us for the time of our stay. We avoided economic relations with others as much as was practical, trying not to be a source of material goods. The Ashéninka saw us as big people who were somewhat entertaining, nondemanding, and with an acute interest in the Ashéninka language and culture. Our porch usually had someone on it who wanted to talk with us, play with our children, look through magazines, or listen to themselves on the tape recorder.

Education development program

In 1980, my involvement with the Ashéninka changed its emphasis. The Peruvian Ministry of Education had recently signed a ten-year contract with SIL, and funds became available for me to do a five-year education development project. This began five years of writing textbooks in the Ashéninka and Asháninka languages, publishing a three-volume compilation of traditional stories, getting to know and consulting with Ashéninka political leaders about education concerns, and training more than 100 teachers for bilingual schools. This period expanded my overview of the Ashéninka and those around them as I traveled extensively, visiting more than thirty Ashéninka villages.

Observation

Systematic study of Ashéninka culture included taking notes. From 1970–1985, the observations were of a general nature. In trips to the Ashéninka in 1987 and 1988, I focused most of my observations on the settings, agents, goals, and processes of teaching and learning. I noted naturally-occurring activities of adults and children that suggested a learning activity or use of a learned skill or value. I logged these in written field notes, took photographs, and collected the tools used for the skills.

Documents

Documentary evidence of Ashéninka family life is found in the journals and research findings of missionaries and anthropologists who lived among the Ashéninka and learned the Ashéninka language (Bodley 1970, Elick 1970, J. G. 1868, Stahl 1932, Stull 1951). Other documents chronicle the historic events of the region (Biedma and Tibesar 1981, Ortiz 1978). Travelers and explorers recorded many impressions of the Ashéninka (Baker 1983, Foster 1924, Sabate 1877, Sandeman 1939, Sinclair 1895). Transcriptions of traditional and contemporary stories tell of family relations and express the values shared by the Ashéninka (Anderson 1985; 1986a; 1986b, Fernández 1986). Data from these sources corroborate many observations and testimonies of interviewees and help describe the context in which learning activities occur.

Traditional stories

From the beginning of my study of the Ashéninka language and culture, I asked almost everyone I met to tell stories to the tape recorder. For nearly two years, I recorded few stories because people said they did not know any stories; they told stories only in an abbreviated form; or they mixed more Spanish words into the stories than I expected. These kinds of stories were particularly prevalent in the Ucayali and Pajonal regions where I had supposed the best storytellers lived. The groups of the Ucayali were extremely isolated and those of the Pajonal had little outside contact; thus, I expected them to produce the most traditional stories. These conditions of isolation seem, however, to have reduced the audience for the stories, so only the most basic stories were told, and those only to children. I recorded stories of a trip upstream, the jaguar, the origin of the Caucasian, and the bear who kidnapped a woman. I had heard that in other regions they told stories of God living on earth, the moon as a man, the great flood, and demonic beings. I tried to get people to tell me these stories, but without success.

I was dissatisfied with the quality of my oral literature compilation until I traveled to the Pichis and Apurucayali areas. On a survey trip on the Apurucayali, I found a man who filled more than two cassettes with stories, doubling the number of different stories in my compilation.

A year later, 1979, I attended my first general assembly of the leaders of villages in the Pichis region. I was introduced to the assembly, where I explained my work. The next evening, I heard laughter coming from a side of the plaza. There I found a man telling stories—his listeners unable to contain their laughter. I asked if I could record his stories and he consented. When he finished, I asked if any others would like to tell stories. Two others volunteered, so I recorded their stories also. These were busy days, and I was unable to talk with the storytellers beyond our recording sessions.

Back at my office in Pucallpa, I asked a language assistant if he knew the name of the most talented storyteller. He told me he knew a storyteller who was well-known for his ability to tell stories. A few days later, I planned a trip to his village to ask if he could come to Pucallpa to work with me while we awaited the birth of our second child. He agreed and accompanied me back to Pucallpa.

I soon found that the storyteller was a connoisseur of traditional culture. We started by making a list of Ashéninka animal and plant names. We followed a semi-structured format, looking at the picture of a similar plant or animal in a book and trying to remember the names of others. The list was fairly complete, almost too complete: I have since discovered that he coined many descriptive names that were unrecognizable to others. After plants and animals, I asked for the names of supernatural beings, stars, planets, mythical beings, and any other category I could think of. These long lists not only gave us a good start on a dictionary (Payne 1980), but they also helped the storyteller remember folktales.

For the next few days, the storyteller told me enough stories to fill twenty-three hours of audio cassettes. I started by asking him to tell me the stories he knew, but when he could not remember others, we began to go through the list of names. For example, when we got to the jaguar, he told more than a dozen stories about jaguars. When we got to the monkey section, he could remember origin stories: of times when many different kinds of monkeys were people. Sometimes, a theme or motif would appear, like lakes rising quickly to drag people away. In such cases, I asked for other stories with the same theme.

Ashéninka storytelling sessions would ideally take place at night, in the storyteller's home, with an animated audience, and—for the researcher's purposes—with an unobtrusive video camera present. Actually, the storytelling sessions were done during the day, in a small study room, with only one other Ashéninka and me as the audience, and to an audio cassette recorder. Much of the narrative is lost because of the absence of a video recorder, since the storyteller used facial expressions and hand movements, and manipulated objects in the office to help tell his stories. The presence of another Ashéninka helped to keep the stories going. Ashéninka storytelling is partly interactive, with the audience laughing at the funny parts, asking questions, and giving other feedback to prompt the storyteller to do his best at telling the story.

Two people worked on processing the recordings after the storyteller finished. An Ashéninka who was a fluent speaker of Spanish and wrote correct Spanish did the initial translation of the texts into Spanish. These were useful to get a general sense of the content, since I was unable to read Ashéninka narratives at the time. I later discovered that the translator wrote a flowery form of Spanish that hid the simple beauty of the narratives, making necessary new translations a few years later. Another assistant transcribed the tapes, a task that took many months. I had him make as exact a transcription as possible, preserving the onomatopoetic words and all repetitions. However, because we had used a tape recorder that sometimes gave only fitful performance, some errors exist in the initial transcriptions.

Some stories—about ten per cent—contained events and themes that my assistants considered perverse sexual activity. They agreed to do an initial transcription of the material but did not want to do further editing. Though they listened to such stories in the company of other men at parties, they thought them inappropriate for publication. They did not object to working on other stories that spoke of normal sexual relations and bloody violence or contained scatological humor. The objectionable stories were left in their initial form, while I began working through the other ninety per cent. From these data, I studied the language's morphology, lexicon, syntactic, and narrative structures.

Processing of the stories was time-consuming. The handwritten stories were typed into a word processor, printed, and edited to correct misspelled words, to delete overly repetitive phrases and onomatopoetic sequences, and to conform to written punctuation conventions developed as we worked. We had to decide where a sentence began, where a paragraph began, where to put in a comma, and how to represent the onomatopoetic words. Since the stories would have Spanish translations, we followed Spanish punctuation conventions whenever possible.

Ashéninka artists made drawings to illustrate many stories. I contracted five different artists to read or listen to the stories and then draw their interpretation.

After the stories were edited to publication standards, we translated them again into Spanish, keying them into a word processor and doing edits until they were suitable for publication. To date, three volumes of stories have been published (Anderson 1985, 1986a, 1986b). Other stories are in fieldnote form. Though not exactly in the form told on the tapes, the stories preserve the themes, actions, conversations, and basic structure of the originals. The English translations included in this study are from the Ashéninka originals, deleting repetitive phrases and some irrelevant asides or details.

Interviews

Interview procedures

The primary method of data collection was semi-structured and unstructured interviews. I did these in the summers of 1987 and 1988. The focus of questioning in 1987 centered around issues of language, ethnicity, and socialization. The interviews of 1988 probed deeper into socialization and change. Questions were developed in the field and modified over time. Most interviews were in the home of those interviewed, so they could easily refer to objects, places, and people.

I interviewed some subjects in Spanish, but most were interviewed in the Ashéninka language with the help of a bilingual interpreter. I used two primary interpreters, one the first year and another the second. They helped me phrase questions in a way easily understood by those interviewed and added an Ashéninka insider as part of the audience addressed.

Most of the interviews were recorded on a small cassette recorder. Questions typically sampled settings, activities, and processes associated with learning activities.

Life histories

I asked most interviewees to tell their autobiography to help put the data in context. Life circumstances, such as being raised by non-Ashéninkas, not having a mother or father, or the length of time in school helped to interpret other responses.

I interviewed both men and women between the ages of twenty and eighty. Some were nonliterate and others had years of post-secondary schooling. Some were monolingual with little contact with other cultures, and others were bilingual in Spanish with extensive contact with mestizos. Those interviewed had varied economic experiences. All toil in subsistence agriculture and earn money as contract laborers, as professional employees of the government, or as maids in urban homes. Those interviewed come from various geographic and ecological settings, some having restricted access to land and others having access to extensive tracts of land. Though all were interviewed in the Perené and Pichis regions, many came from the Ucayali or Pajonal regions.

Most Ashéninkas interviewed have identified themselves as followers of the Seventh-Day Adventist (SDA) church and few have identified with the Catholic church. Some are sophisticated followers of the SDA faith, others are nominal followers, and many have become disaffected with the faith because of the strictness of the moral code. World view, values, and attitudes toward outsiders and outside institutions are somewhat influenced by their involvement with the SDA faith. I probed to find indications of worldview and values. I asked about knowledge of magical plants, use of medicinal plants, coca chewing, experience with the SDA faith, sorcery, and the values of honesty and respect for elders.

Interview topics

Our minds are selective in what is recalled. We often forget our most embarrassing moments but vividly recall a near-death experience (Labov 1972). To take advantage of this selectivity, I asked people to recall many different learning activities. For one person, learning to spin cotton was uneventful, but it was very eventful for another. I asked what was learned from a parent or other adult and what they had, in turn, taught to their children. I probed for differences between how one was taught and how the same person taught another.

Of the learning activities recalled, I probed to discover the processes of the activity, asking for details about the setting, participants, tools used, ages of the child during different stages of learning, order in which sub-skills were learned, and what was said by the participants. I asked for explanations of why something was taught. This line of questioning often showed motivation for learning and expectations of those involved.

The questions were not sharply defined, allowing the interviewees to give information that might otherwise be omitted. Questions were in three main areas, with probes to expand the data and to fill the gaps in the initial responses. With most questions, I probed about the effect of the experiences (embarrassment, anger, shame, sadness, etc.).

1. Main question: Tell me about your life.

   Supplemental probes:

   > Ancestry
   > Where lived
   > Economic experiences with non-Ashéninkas (type of labor, exploitation, land conflicts)
   > Religion (church, shamanism, sorcery)
   > School experiences
   > Participation in rituals (hunter's diet, use of magical plants)
   > Language used in different contexts (Spanish or Ashéninka)
   > Cultural attitudes
   > Ethnic pride and stigma

2. Main question: What were you taught by your parents or grandparents?

3. Main question: How did you and your children learn to hunt, make arrows, work in the *chacra*, cook, spin cotton, weave cloth, weave mats, become shamans, build houses, build canoes, chew coca?

Supplemental probes:

Setting
Age of the child
Who involved, procedures
What was said
Why important
Problems and resolution
How practiced
Acceptable level of competence at different ages

Interview transcriptions

Interview data were recorded on a small cassette recorder of less than professional quality. Responses to all questions were either in Spanish or in the Ashéninka language, with a subsequent translation into Spanish.

I transcribed the tapes myself, but I soon found exact transcriptions to be tedious, especially when I gave long probing questions that yielded little response. Some responses repeated those previously given or said something completely irrelevant to the question or the study. To speed up the processing of data, I began to summarize the questions and give free translations into English. Sometimes I did not include minor probes in the transcriptions, though the responses to the probes are included. For example, when I asked a woman how her mother taught her to spin cotton, I did not include some probes in my transcriptions, such as, "How old were you? What did you say? What did she say? How did you feel?" These probes only helped complete the narrative response to the original question. I included the probes in the transcriptions when they changed the nature of the original question. For example, when I asked, "Did your parents speak to you in Spanish when you were a child?", a probe like, "In what contexts did they speak to you only in Ashéninka?" yielded a response that did not flow with the first question.

Field research

First trip

My first field trip, specifically designed to fill in the gaps from earlier work, was in August 1987. The trip was exploratory in nature; I was interested in culture change and Ashéninka traditional educational processes, but I was unsure of the best location in which to do the field research or the specific questions to ask. Once I decided on a general itinerary, I sent word of my planned arrival to a friend who later became my interpreter and boatman. I flew by small plane from Pucallpa to Puerto Bermúdez and stayed a couple nights in a hotel. My first activity was to greet different government employees and merchants in the town whom I had befriended over the years, informing them of the purpose of my visit and exchanging personal news. Throughout the afternoon and the next day, I saw many Ashéninka friends to whom I spoke and asked for interviews.

In the evening, I began to interview Ashéninkas I had encountered that afternoon. I purposely tried to keep the interviews to under an hour because I wanted to interview many people and make the interviews seem casual to those being interviewed. This worked well, with the interviews varying from twenty minutes to two hours in length, and varying with individual style of response and the age of the interviewees—younger ones had less to say than older ones.

My initial set of questions were the following:

Tell me about your life.
In what contexts do you speak Spanish?
What are your uses of literacy?
Why did your parents send or not send you to school?
Why are some people proud of their culture and others not?
What did your parents teach you when you were a child?
How did your parents teach you each of these things?
How do you teach these things to your children?

As I interviewed, I probed around the responses, seeking expansion and depth of response. Sometimes the question was not fully understood and I needed to rephrase it. The responses eventually followed patterns, with responses from different respondents being very similar. My probes also started to follow a pattern, with some probes becoming new questions.

I interviewed almost anyone in Puerto Bermúdez who was available, but I was especially interested in interviewing those who were directly involved in the history of the region: older political leaders, teachers, and lay preachers. I also wanted to interview those people who were skillful storytellers, thinking they could better articulate their experiences and opinions. I found many of these people in Puerto Bermúdez and listed those along the Nazareteki River whom I might find to interview.

When we finished in Puerto Bermúdez, my traveling companion and I went by motorized canoe up the Pichis and Nazareteki rivers, stopping at the houses of old friends and acquaintances. If the person was at home and was agreeable to an interview, we stayed until it was finished. If the person was not at home, we left word that we would like to talk to him the next day, giving an approximate hour of our arrival.

The trip and interviews were opportunistic in many respects. We made many unscheduled stops on our trip because an old friend was there whose presence we had not expected. Sometimes strangers whom I did not know were anxious to volunteer their responses to my questions because the topics interested them. I often found topics to explore more deeply after hearing a personal history. For example, when one teacher told me that his wife was Amuesha, I explored how they used his language, his wife's language, and Spanish in different contexts, especially in the village where he taught. When one woman said she had been taken as a slave, I tried to learn more.

All persons were willing to be interviewed without direct payment. I was well-known because of my work for the previous ten years in the valley. For many, the educational development project I administered either got them a job, gave them free training, got a job or training for a close relative, or helped get a government-sponsored school for their village. Others were employed by me earlier to help write textbooks, to narrate a collection of traditional stories, or to help me in linguistic analysis. These expected some kind of compensation, like getting a radio repaired in Puerto Bermúdez, a meal and hotel room for the night, or truck passage paid to La Merced while accompanying me. I paid my interpreter for his time and use of the canoe and motor.

When my scheduled time in the Pichis region was over, I traveled by road from Puerto Bermúdez to La Merced, the overland transportation hub for the Perené region. In La Merced, I greeted education and other government officials, merchants, and those working in the office of the regional Ashéninka legal defense organization. I told of my studies, my research, and exchanged information about family.

In the Perené region, I took a slightly different tack in my questioning. Since few traditional skills like weaving and making arrows are practiced, and the Ashéninka have had intense contact with mestizos for more than two generations, I planned to ask mostly about ethnicity and language issues.

Though I lived in La Merced and San Ramón for almost two years, far fewer Ashéninkas of the region know me than do those in the Pichis and Ucayali regions. My primary contacts in the Perené were the families of those taught in bilingual teacher-training courses, the families of teachers, and regional Ashéninka political leaders. I varied from this pattern only once, when I had the opportunity to interview a retired teacher who came from the Puno region of the Andes with Frederick Stahl to establish a Seventh-Day Adventist school for the Ashéninka. In this case, I only asked about the history of the school and of his personal experiences as a teacher to the Ashéninka, probing to get his perspective on why he thought some Ashéninkas were opposed to schooling and why others were enthusiastic supporters.

In the Pichis region, almost all those interviewed were men. I wanted to interview at least as many women as men in the Perené region. This was possible because most of the teacher candidates I taught from the Perené were women, and many of them had sisters or mothers who were more willing to be interviewed than those of the Pichis. I wanted to interview the women because men in the Pichis region emphatically told me that women who go off to work as maids often reject the Ashéninka culture, something men are unlikely to do.

I asked older people about the skills they were taught by their parents. I also asked them how they became speakers of Spanish and why their parents sent them to school. I probed to see if they felt any stigma or pride attached to the Ashéninka language and culture, and if they had difficulties in school. I asked young adults about mixed marriages, the advantages and disadvantages of being Ashéninka and showing it, and their ideas on what would eventually happen to the Ashéninka language and culture.

Ashéninkas work in their fields for most of the day, so I scheduled my trips to travel mostly in daylight hours, arriving just before dusk. Because of my relationship with those I visited and my showing hospitality to those who visited us years before in La Merced, I was always fed well and given good sleeping accommodations. After catching up on family news and delivering some letters from my wife and from people in the Pichis region who knew I was going to the Perené, I explained about my studies, the purpose of my research, and the kind of questions I intended to ask. After dinner, we sat as a group and I asked my questions, the room lit by kerosene lamps and a record kept by a small cassette recorder.

Those I questioned were relaxed, enthusiastic in their answers, and entertained by each other's responses. Often, everyone broke out in laughter. These were generally questions that no one had asked before, but topics for which they had strong feelings. Everyone knew I was a strong supporter of bilingual education, literature in the Ashéninka language, and culture. I assumed they would express similar opinions, but I was asking for their justification for such feelings.

Second trip

I made a follow-up trip to the Ashéninka in August 1988, clearer on the focus of my questions and the gaps to be filled. The trip to the Perené gave historical perspective to Ashéninka culture trends, but I did not find as many families continuing in traditional activities as in other regions. By this time, my research interest had narrowed to the socialization of Ashéninka children, but the trip was again exploratory because I anticipated refining my questions and observations in a third trip (which I was unable to make). I traveled by small plane from Pucallpa to Puerto Bermúdez, expecting to find the same traveling companion and interpreter who accompanied me the previous year. My original plan was to go with him to the villages with bilingual schools to the east of the Nazareteki River. I chose that site because I trained the bilingual teachers in those villages, and the Ashéninkas there were said to follow a traditional lifestyle, as well as the fact that most people there are monolingual speakers of the Ashéninka language. I planned to ask questions similar to those asked the previous year, but focus more on how their parents taught them traditional skills and how they were teaching these skills to their children. I also planned to observe the bilingual schools, to compare the instructional styles of the teachers, classroom management of the different schools, and the parental enthusiasm for the school, teacher, and style of instruction.

My plans changed. I sent the letter telling of my plans to my interpreter a month in advance, but it did not arrive until two weeks after my arrival at Puerto Bermúdez. The brother-in-law of my interpreter told me that he had just gone home and would not return for ten days, when he would be on duty in the Puerto Bermúdez clinic as a paramedic. I searched Puerto Bermúdez for another suitable companion but found none that had the time to accompany me on such a rigorous journey that included long hikes with my personal and research gear. As I searched, I greeted old friends and informed the education and other government officials of my visit, itinerary, and purpose. As I went, I noticed that the town appeared to be unusually vacant for the week following Peruvian Independence Day.

In the late afternoon, I encountered a former linguistic assistant whom I had missed visiting the previous year. He told me that the town was largely deserted because the government had pulled out the police force because of threats from insurgents in the Pozuzo area many days' travel away. Many prominent merchants in the town left on extended vacations. In the evening, I asked trusted friends if I or those I visited were in any danger, and they unanimously replied that the risk was small. At that point, I decided to change my travel plans only slightly. My linguistic assistant invited me to visit his village, reminding me of the poor state of the village school, which lacked study materials for the children. He suggested that if I were to spend my entire time in his village, a fitting gesture would be to give the children sufficient study materials for the second semester. That evening, my new companion went on a shopping spree and bought notebooks, pencils, pens, sharpeners, rulers, marking pens, chalk, and pencil erasers for the thirty children in the primary school and ten children in the kindergarten.

The village lacked a headman, though it had an elected leader. A Seventh-Day Adventist school was founded there in the late 1950s, which taught the relatives of a headman who has since died. His four daughters and their families lived there also. These women, now in their 60s and 70s, have many of their children and their families living in the village, bringing the total population to about ninety persons. Everyone is related by blood or marriage to the four sisters, with only one family being the exception.

I was surprised to find the range of origins of the spouses of the descendants of the first headman. All four of the sisters have remarried recently to younger men from the Pajonal and Perené regions and a mestizo man who lives the Ashéninka lifestyle, though he speaks no indigenous language. The sons and daughters of the four sisters have spouses from upstream, downstream, the Pajonal, and the Perené. The only family not related to the four sisters came from the isolated hills of the western boundary of the Ucayali region. They came to the village accompanying a son of one sister after a trading expedition.

My host-interpreter was the elected village leader. The afternoon I arrived, he called a general meeting for all the men and women of the village. I explained the purpose of my visit, asked for their help, and explained my gift to the village school. The response was positive, so I set up a tentative schedule to visit each household and interview all adults.

I first asked the questions of my interpreter and his wife. I asked for brief personal histories and how they learned specific skills. The year before, I had asked about the procedures for doing a specific skill, like making an arrow. On this trip, however, I asked more about interactions between parent and child and the effect on children of these interactions. These questions were sometimes difficult to explain, so I used both Spanish and Ashéninka.

My interpreter was a capable speaker of Spanish, having completed university entrance requirements before deciding to remain in the jungle. He was also a very capable mother-tongue speaker of the Ashéninka language, living in a village where the Ashéninka language is valued. I tried to state the questions in the Ashéninka language, but I also asked the questions in Spanish, phrasing them in a way that is easy to translate into Ashéninka. My interpreter then rephrased the questions in Ashéninka, careful to rephrase them again if not understood in the initial form. I understood most of the replies, but the recording quality was not good enough for me to make an Ashéninka transcription. I tried to hire this interpreter to do the Ashéninka transcriptions, but neither of us had the time to devote to the project.

Some of those interviewed preferred to respond in Spanish, while others preferred to respond in Ashéninka. The quality of the responses appears to vary little between languages. When someone responded in Spanish, I often asked them to say the Ashéninka words they used in a learning interaction.

My interviewees were taken by surprise by my questions. No one had ever asked questions like, "How did you learn to weave?" Then I probed by asking something like, "What happened when you made a mistake while weaving?" I followed by asking, "How did you feel when your mother hit (or laughed at) you for making a mistake?" These final two probes were developed after a couple interviews showed that everyone has vivid memories of making mistakes and of the interactions and feelings that followed those mistakes.

I went to each house, sometimes accompanied by my interpreter and sometimes alone, if I thought Spanish was a strong language for the interviewee. Arriving at a house, we usually found someone home, accompanied by at least one child. We interviewed either the man or woman of the house as a child called the spouse in from the *chacra*. When we arrived at a house, we always found someone involved in some activity, such as cooking, spinning, weaving, making a basket, or repairing a roof. This was usually the opening topic of conversation. By being in the home, I could ask to see both adult and child-sized tools used for different activities. Sometimes an adult showed how they help their child to learn a particular skill, like how to hold the bow or how to pull on the cotton while spinning. In the home, I saw the written materials around the house, such as a Seventh-Day Adventist poster, a shelf of magazines and books, or the children's notebooks from school. When I asked how old a person was when taught a skill or when a significant event happened, the interviewee could point to a child or grandchild standing nearby to suggest an approximate age. When visiting one home, I observed and asked about a twelve-year-old boy with Down's syndrome. I had little knowledge of this, but in the home, I saw the boy interact with his parents and siblings.

Less than half the homes were in the village proper. The other half were scattered on the other side of the stream, five to ten minutes walk apart. I usually visited a home when school was not in session. As I arrived at a house, I could see the children doing various activities: homework in their notebooks, helping the father in the *chacra*, bringing firewood, going hunting or fishing, helping the mother make manioc beer, preparing manioc for dinner, spinning cotton, or entertaining an infant sibling or cousin.

My interpreter and I spent a few hours mapping the village and making a list of everyone and noting how they were related. This was the best way to get an inventory of the children of school age and to list them with the correct household. This activity revealed that my interpreter's brother had two wives and many children. It also showed the high degree to which siblings from one family marry siblings from another family.

Though I did not intend to include school observation data in this study, I spent many hours inside and outside the school building during my free time, watching and listening to the class and occasionally tape recording and taking photographs. I observed the behavior of the students, who appeared to be much like other elementary classes I have seen. Except for their clothing, the first-graders would appear at home in most schools. I kept notes of the daily schedule, the time the teacher spent on each activity, and the time the teacher spent with each ability group in this one-room school. I observed the daily schedule over many days, noting the emphasis on different subjects, the time devoted to different subjects, and the teacher's interaction with the children during recess.

I always informed people whenever I used the tape recorder. No one objected to its use, but I had some difficulty with others who wanted to listen to what someone else had said. I only played back recordings in the presence of the person interviewed. One elderly man was on my porch for hours as his granddaughter and her friend listened to his recordings.

I brought a 35 mm. camera to take color slides and black and white prints. I also brought a Polaroid camera and sufficient film to take a picture of every family interviewed and every child in the school. My first picture was a Polaroid of the entire village at the general assembly, which I posted to the outside the school. Whenever I went to a home to interview, my first picture was a Polaroid of the family that I gave to them. I took individual pictures of each child after my first day at the school, not taking 35 mm. pictures until later. I hoped that this would solve the problem of people promising to send back pictures but never getting around to it. I discovered this to be an effective way of thanking people for letting me take their picture with the 35 mm. camera, a fair exchange from the Ashéninka point of view.

At the end of my stay, I did a final interview with the teacher, totally private, in which he gave me an evaluation of each child, from both academic and behavioral perspectives. His evaluations correlated with observations I had made in the class, especially of the children who were not dressed well or who appeared to have little interest in school. He often gave explanations for the ability of the child relating to the home life of the child, with generally positive evaluations for children from the homes of the educated, church-going parents and negative evaluations for children from the homes of nonliterate parents who are not interested in the church.

Shortcomings in the data

Standard Ashéninka question format

I could not ask questions easily because English and Ashéninka questioning styles differ. In Ashéninka, I can ask who, what, where, why, and how, but these questions normally have a tag at the end that suggests an answer. For example, "Who taught you to spin cotton?" is properly asked, "Who taught you to spin cotton, your mother?" A reply typically is something like, "Yes, my mother" or "No, my grandmother taught me." Also, the Ashéninka language does not have the conjunction "or", which makes ridiculous a question like, "Were you ashamed or defiant when they laughed at you?" One must ask either one question or the other; two separate questions in succession without an intervening answer is poor style and is probably misunderstood.

By asking questions according to good Ashéninka style, I might be accused of leading the interviewee, putting words in his mouth. My interpreters often asked questions using a tag, usually the response he gave or the response given in the previous interview. Fortunately, the responses to the questions were often in long narrative form, with the original question sometimes getting lost in the detail of the response. For short responses, I probed until satisfied that enough detail was given to consider the response to be reliable.

Interviewee self-report

The data for this study relied heavily on the self-report of interviewees. This kind of data needs to be considered cautiously because the interviewee's self-report is often influenced by cultural and situational contexts. For example, when a woman said that she and her sisters never fought as children, it is possible that (1) they really did not fight, (2) they fought but she might think that I consider fighting to be bad and not want me to lower my opinion of her, or (3) they fought, but the Ashéninka norm discourages fighting, so she is really reporting the Ashéninka ideal.

To overcome the weakness of self-report, I asked the same questions of many people to see if patterns emerged in the data, especially from those who appeared to be more relaxed during the interview. I tended to avoid or cut short those interviews in which the interviewee gave only minimal, ideal responses and could not give more detailed responses when answering my probes. I put more trust in the responses that were unexpected or which included much detail. The self-report data must not be generalized to represent all Ashéninkas but, combined with emergent patterns, documentary evidence, and observations, it contributed much to the insights of this study.

Language limitations

Ethnography is typically done in the language of those being observed as the observer participates in the social group (Heath 1982). I was unable to do all my research using the Ashéninka language. From 1977–1981, I studied the language and practiced it in village settings, but I never became as fully fluent as in Spanish. I did learn enough, however, to carry on normal conversations in context, to understand almost any written text, and to get the gist of conversations I observed. During the research, I successfully spoke Ashéninka in interactions with the children, initial greetings, and chitchat, but I depended on Spanish to express myself in interview situations.

When I used an interpreter, I understood the questions as he rephrased them in Ashéninka. If one varied greatly from my intent, I withdrew the question and rephrased it. I understood the responses, unless those interviewed used many topic-specific words beyond my vocabulary. This deficiency affected my ability to express myself efficiently, but I believe the data suffered little from this limitation. The responses to the questions produced many lengthy and detailed responses.

Lack of observation opportunities

When doing ethnography, observation is prolonged and repetitive in natural contexts (Spindler 1982). Ideally, I would observe the Ashéninka doing the activities described in the interviews, but because Ashéninka learning is opportunistic and they value privacy, my intrusions were impossible. Ashéninka children are continually learning and it is difficult to separate a learning situation from a practice or utility situation. For example, a mother and daughter often spin cotton together, and the mother occasionally gives some instruction to the daughter, but only when there is reason to do so. When a boy goes into the forest with his father, the father teaches and the child learns as the opportunities arise. Even if I was to accompany the pair into the forest, I lack the knowledge shared by the two.

The Ashéninka are one of the more reserved groups of the Amazon basin (Brown 1974). They show a strong respect for the privacy of others. They do not watch another person eat, do not touch the property of another unless invited, and always speak respectfully to the elders. I approached my research with the attitude that I should not offend the Ashéninka by word or action. I tried to show restraint in my initial contacts, not taking pictures unless enthusiastic permission was granted. I did not spy on people as they worked and I did not handle their property before asking permission. Neither did I ask questions that might offend. This reticence no doubt affected the data because I might have asked more probing questions about family relations, sorcery, violence, religion, and the school teacher had I been willing to disregard these Ashéninka values. Despite my hesitation, many of my questions were answered without my asking them.

Interviewees limited

My data might have been strengthened if I had had a more random sample. However, close relationships and trust take time for the Ashéninka. Hvalkof (1986) says that in the Pajonal area, the people are hostile, even to their own. Many who wrote of the Ashéninka in the nineteenth century called them the "fierce Campas" (Sabate 1877). These hostile feelings to outsiders might have something to do with the *Pishtaco* story of the Amazon, which everyone has heard.

> Some years ago a bizarre rumor spread throughout the Amazon basin, a tale still believed in many tribes. It is said the white men come to the selva with their gifts in order to capture Indians, take them to secret places, and render them into oil which is used to power airplanes, motor boats and autos. So fueled, these craft return, bearing more gifts, seeking more Indians. (Baker 1983:11)

> The Campas have also taken over the wide-spread *pish(i)tako* belief of the Peruvian Highlands. According to the Campa form of this belief, there are diabolical Caucasians in the towns who kill Campas to extract the grease from their bodies for use in automobiles and airplanes. The Campas, indeed, cast a suspicious eye on all Caucasians. For the Campas, there is something demonic about Caucasians: they are powerful,

yet not benevolent, they are wealthy, yet not generous; are they human, are they mortal? (Weiss 1972:200)

In my travels through the Perené and Pichis regions, I noticed the suspicious glances of Ashéninka and mestizo strangers who were near me on the bus or trail. Though these attitudes can be overcome, I chose to work with those who already knew me. Also, the relationship of trust I had with interviewees provided a relaxed atmosphere during the interview. Given the nature of the questions and responses, I believe that a random sample would not have yielded significantly more insightful responses. Moreover, randomization of transient jungle dwellers and seasonal regional market dwellers would have been fraught with uncertainties.

Inability to return to the field site in the near future

This study focuses on issues that could be explored more in future trips to the field site. Ideally, I would have gone back and probed deeper about the issues or interviewed a broader sample of people. This was not possible because the Perené, Pichis, Ucayali, and Pajonal areas were all included in the Peruvian security zones because of the Sendero Luminoso and Tupac Amaru insurgency activity in the area. The Ashéninka appeared to be neutral regarding the insurgency, but my presence might have jeopardized myself or those I interviewed. My years of work with the Ashéninka, the abundance of research done by others in the area, the large compilation of traditional stories, and my two productive trips to the field site provided me with adequate, though perhaps not fully sufficient or always ideal, data for this study.

Glossary

aaa	a papagayo bird call
ajai	exclamation
aguaje	a palm tree
ametyo	kind of spider
añuje	agouti
ashipa	a plant
boquichico	kind of fish
carachama(s)	a kind of fish
chaaa	jaguar sound
chaak, thopak	vomiting sound
chacra	garden
chamairo	a vine which is chewed with coca leaves
chek	sound of arrow hitting target
chemiririri	sound of thorns scraping something
chicha	fermented corn drink
cushma	robe, clothing
daledale	an edible root
eee	a greeting
ef	sound made climbing a hill
hiriki	a kind of bean
iii	sound of giggling
ijiii, jai, jai	sound made to say food tastes good
ishire	soul

ivenki	a kind of magical plant
jaaam	sound of a jaguar
jiii	an exclamation
jmmm	sound of thorns scraping something
jopo	a kind of tree
kajaa	coughing sound
kaviari	insane, deranged
kentanentantsivenki	a drink to ease pain
kipatsi	earth
koiii	swallowing sound
kontarek	sound of splitting something
kori	sound of gulping down something
lupuna	a kind of tree
manta	a shawl used by women to carry a baby or things on the back
manthari	sound of stick scraping the ground
matsi	witch
matsivenki	magical plant to protect from witchcraft
menki	sound of moving something from side to side
metzitziti	ideophone for heaviness
monje	kind of bird
mook	sound of vomiting
oretsi	a big grasshopper
oye	water boa
paco	kind of fish
palmiche	kind of palm
pamaki	kind of tree
papagayo	a kind of parrot
paujil	kind of bird
peta	sound of birds flying away
petapeta(jaaa)	sound a chicken makes
peyari	evil spirit
piche	chewing sound
pifayo	a kind of palm fruit
pikoka	a kind of leaf
pinitsi	magical plant
pituca	an edible root
pok	sound of jaguar eating
pona	a kind of palm tree
sabalo	kind of fish
sachapapa	an edible root

sapok	sound of bird flying
sakiri	sound of painting
satak	sound of shooting arrows
shaari	sound of shucking corn
shepik	sound of grabbing
sheripiari	tobacco drinker
sheripiyari	tobacco drinker
sherok	sound made placing one on a bed
shiii	sound of swallows
shimiro	tree with a fragrant bark
shiretsi	malevolent ghost
shoi	sound made securing a lock
shoiritzi	kind of bird
sopirek	sound of something popping out
tak	sound of shooting arrows
takik	sound made descending from tree
tampishi	a vine
tankorek	sound made rising to a standing position
tek	sound of something running
tho	sound of spitting blood
thonkitziro	a kind of tree
tilo	magical plant
tok, mooo	sound of water overflowing
tonkorek	sound of one rising to a standing position
trompo	an arrow with a large blunt end
tsiririri	something bleeding
tyak	sound of chopping
tzirek	sound of rock falling
unchala	kind of bird

References

Adam, Lucien and Charles Leclerc. 1890. Arte de la lengua de los indios Antis o Campas: Un vocabulario metódico i una introducción comparativa. Paris: J. Maisonneuve.

Amich, José. 1870. Noticias históricas de las misiones de fieles e infieles del colegio de propaganda fide de Santa Rosa de Ocopa. Barcelona: Imprenta de Magriñá y Subirana.

Anderson, Ronald J. 1985. Cuentos folklóricos de los ashéninka, Tomo I. Yarinacocha, Peru: Instituto Lingüístico de Verano.

Anderson, Ronald J. 1986a. Cuentos folklóricos de los ashéninka, Tomo II. Yarinacocha, Peru: Instituto Lingüístico de Verano.

Anderson, Ronald J. 1986b. Cuentos folklóricos de los ashéninka, Tomo III. Yarinacocha, Peru: Instituto Lingüístico de Verano.

Baker, Will. 1983. Backward: An essay on Indians, time, and photography. Berkeley: North Atlantic Books.

Barclay, Frederica. 1985. El nacimiento de una region. La colonia del Perené y su impacto sobre la región de Selva Central. Amazonía Indígena, 5(10):3–10.

Benavides, Margarita. 1986. La usurpación del dios tecnológico y la articulación temprana en la Selva Central Peruana: Misioneros, herramientas y mesianismo. Amazonía Indígena, 6(12):30–35.

Biedma, Manuel and Antonio Tibesar. 1981. La conquista franciscana del Alto Ucayali. Lima, Peru: Editorial Milla Batres.

Bodley, John H. 1970. Campa socio-economic adaptation. Abstracts International 31. (University Microfilms: 71:10,695).

Bodley, John H. 1972a. A transformative movement among the Campa of eastern Peru. Anthropos 67:220–228.

Bodley, John H. 1972b. Tribal survival in the Amazon: The Campa case. Copenhagen: International Work Group for Indigenous Affairs.

Brown, Ann L. and Roberta A. Ferrara. 1985. Diagnosing zones of proximal development. In J. V. Wertsch (ed.), Culture, communication, and cognition: Vygotskian perspectives, 273–305. Cambridge: Cambridge University Press.

Brown, Mario. 1974. Cosmovisión de los ashánincas (campas). In J. M. Mercier and G. Villenueve (eds.), Amazonía: Liberación o esclavitud? Lima, Peru: Ediciones Paulinas.

Buenaventura L. de Uriarte, Mons. 1982. La montaña del Peru. Lima, Peru: Gráfica 30.

Casanto Shingari, Raul. 1986. 25 años de experiencia organizativa en la sociedad asháninka del Perené. In J. Gasche and J. M. Arroyo (eds.), Balances amazónicos: Enfoques antropológicos, 225–237. Lima, Peru: Editorial Venus.

Chirif, Alberto. 1981. La última frontera campa. Shupihui 6(17):25–43.

Cole, Michael and Peg Griffin, eds. 1987. Contextual factors in education: Improving science and mathematics education for minorities and women. Madison: University of Wisconsin.

Constitución Política del Perú: Año 1979. 1979. Lima, Peru: Libraría Atlas.

Craig, Allan. 1972. Franciscan exploration in the central montaña of Peru. Actas y memorias del XXXIX Congreso Internacional de Americanistas 4:127–144. Lima, Peru: Instituto de Estudios Peruanos.

Elick, John W. 1970. An ethnography of the Pichis Valley Campa of eastern Peru. Dissertation Abstracts International 31. University Microfilms 70:14, 275.

Fernández, Eduardo. 1986. Para que nuestra historia no se pierda: Testimonios de los asháninca y nomatsiguenga sobre la colonización de la región Satipo-Pangoa. Lima, Peru: Centro de Investigación y Promoción Amazónica.

Foster, Harry L. 1924. The adventures of a tropical tramp. New York: Dodd, Mead and Company.

Hammersley, Martyn and Paul Atkinson. 1983. Ethnography: Principles in practice. London: Tavistock.

Heath, Shirley B. 1982. Ethnography in education: Defining the essentials. In P. Gilmore and A. A. Glatthorn (eds.), Children in and out of school: Ethnography and education, 33–55. Washington, D.C.: Center for Applied Linguistics.

Heath, Shirley Brice. 1989. The learner as cultural member. In R. Schiefelbusch and M. Rice (eds.), The teachability of language, 333–350. Baltimore: P. H. Brookes.

Heath, Shirley Brice and Richard Laprade. 1982. Castilian colonization and indigenous languages: The cases of Quechua and Aymara. In R. L. Cooper (ed.), Language spread: Studies in diffusion in social change, 118–147. Bloomington, Ind.: Indiana University Press.

Hvalkof, Soren. 1986. El drama actual del Gran Pajonal. Primera parte: Recursos, historia, población y producción asháninka. Amazonía Indígena 6(12):22–30.

Izaguirre, Bernardino. 1923–29. Historia de las misiones franciscanas y narración de los progresos de la geografía en el oriente del Perú. Lima, Peru: Talleres Tipográficos de la Penitenciaría.

J. G. [Juan Gastelu]. 1868. Los campas: Descripción de los usos y costumbres de la tribu que habita las rejiones del Apurímac. Lima, Peru: Imprenta del Estado.

Kessler, J. B. A. 1967. A study of protestant missions and churches in Peru and Chile: With special reference to the problems of division, nationalism and native ministry. Goes, The Netherlands: Oosterbaan and Le Cointre.

Kindberg, Willard. n.d. Campa folklore. Yarinacocha, Peru: Centro Amazónico de Lenguas Autóctonas Peruanas.

Labov, William. 1972. Some principles of linguistic methodology. Language in Society 1:97–120.

Lave, Jean. 1988. Cognition in practice: Mind, mathematics and culture in everyday life. New York: Cambridge University Press.

Lave, Jean and Etlenne Wenger. 1990. Situated learning: Legitimate peripheral participation. Report IRL90–0013. Palo Alto, Calif.: Institute for Research on Learning.

Lehnertz, Jay. 1972. Juan Santos: Primitive rebel on the campa frontier (1742–1752). In XXXIX Congreso Internacional de Americanistas; Historia, etnohistoria y etnología de la selva sudamericana 4:111–125. Lima, Peru: Instituto de Estudios Peruanos.

Miles, Matthew B. and A. Michael Huberman. 1984. Qualitative data analysis: A sourcebook of new methods. Beverley Hills, Calif.: Sage.

Ortiz, P. D. 1978. El Perené: Reseña histórica de una importante región de la selva peruana. Lima, Peru: Imprenta Editorial San Antonio.

Payne, David L. 1980. Diccionario ashéninca-castellano. Yarinacocha, Peru: Instituto Lingüístico de Verano.

Rael, Juan B. 1977. Cuentos españoles de Colorado y Nuevo México I. Santa Fe: Museum of New Mexico Press.

Rogoff, Barbara. 1990. Apprenticeship in thinking: Cognitive development in social context. New York: Oxford University Press.

Rogoff, Barbara and William Gardner. 1984. Adult guidance of cognitive development. In Barbara Rogoff and Jean Lave (eds.), Everyday cognition: Its development in social context, 95–116. Cambridge, Mass.: Harvard University Press.

Sabate, Luis. 1877. Viaje de los padres misioneros del convento del Cuzco a las tribus salvaje de los campas, piros, cunibos y sipibos en el año de 1874. Lima, Peru: La Sociedad.

Sandeman, Christopher. 1939. A forgotten river: A book of Peruvian travel and botanical notes. London: Oxford University Press.

Sinclair, Arthur. 1895. In tropical lands: Recent travels to the sources of the Amazon, the West Indian Islands, and Ceylon. Aberdeen, England: D. Wyllie and Son.

Spindler, George D. 1974. The transmission of culture. In George D. Spindler (ed.), Education and cultural process: Toward an anthropology of education, 279–310. New York: Holt, Rinehart and Winston.

Spindler, George, ed. 1982. Doing the ethnography of schooling: Educational anthropology in action. New York: Holt, Rinehart and Winston.

Spradley. 1979. The ethnographic interview. New York: Holt, Rinehart and Winston.

Steward, Julian H. and Alfred Metraux. 1963. Tribes of the Peruvian and Ecuadorian montaña. In Julian H. Steward (ed.), Handbook of South American Indians 3:535–551. New York: Cooper Square Publishers.

Stahl, Ferdinand. 1932. In the Amazon jungles. Mountain View, Calif.: Pacific Press.

Stull, Ruth. 1951. Sand and stars: Missionary adventure on the jungle trail. New York: Fleming H. Revell.

Tibesar, Antonio S. 1952. San Antonio de Eneno. Primitive Man 25:23–39.

Torre López, Fernando. 1978. Notas etnográficas sobre el grupo anti o campa. Folklore Americano 25:43–71.

Varese, Stefano. 1968. Las minorías étnicas de la montaña peruana: Esquema para una antropología de urgencia. Lima, Peru: Universidad Nacional Mayor de San Marcos.

Varese, Stefano. 1973. La sal de los cerros: Una aproximación al mundo campa. Lima, Peru: Retablo de Papel.

Vygotsky, Lev S. 1978. Mind in society: The development of higher psychological processes. Michael Cole, V. John-Steiner, S. Scribner, and E. Souberman, (eds.). Cambridge, Mass.: Harvard University Press.

Weiss, Gerald. 1969. The cosmology of the Campa Indians of eastern Peru. Dissertation Abstracts International 30. University Microfilms 69–18,132.

Weiss, Gerald. 1972. Campa cosmology. In Historia, etnohistoria y etnología de la selva sudamericana 4:189–206. XXXIX Congreso Internacional de Americanistas. Lima, Peru: Instituto de Estudios Peruanos.

Weiss, Gerald. 1975. Campa cosmology: The world of a forest tribe in South America. In Anthropological papers of the American Museum of Natural History 52(5):217–588. New York: The American Museum of Natural History.

Wentworth, William M. 1980. Context and understanding: An inquiry into socialization theory. New York: Elsevier.

Wertsch, James V. and C. Addison Stone. 1978. Microgenesis as a tool for developmental analysis. Quarterly Newsletter of the Laboratory of Comparative Human Development 1(1):8–10.

Wertsch, James V. and C. Addison Stone. 1985. The concept of internalization in Vygotsky's account of the genesis of higher mental functions. In James V. Wertsch (ed.), Culture, communication, and cognition: Vygotskian perspectives, 162–179. Cambridge: Cambridge University Press.

SIL International
Publications in Sociolinguistics

Recent Publications

For further information or a full listing of SIL publications contact:

International Academic Bookstore
SIL International
7500 W. Camp Wisdom Road
Dallas, TX 75236-5699

Voice: 972-708-7404
Fax: 972-708-7363
Email: academic.books@sil.org
Internet: http://www.sil.org

www.ingramcontent.com/pod-product-compliance
Lightning Source LLC
Chambersburg PA
CBHW071852270326
41929CB00013B/2200